MARK
GOSPEL OF ACTION

Personal and Community Responses

Edited by

JOHN VINCENT

First published in Great Britain in 2006

Society for Promoting Christian Knowledge
36 Causton Street
London SW1P 4ST

British Library Cataloguing-in-Publication Data
A catalogue record for this book is available from the British Library

ISBN-13: 978–0–281–05831–0
ISBN-10: 0–281–05831–8

1 3 5 7 9 10 8 6 4 2

Typeset by Graphicraft Ltd., Hong Kong
Printed in Great Britain by Ashford Colour Press

Contents

Foreword

Is it possible to bridge the 'ugly ditch'? The ugly ditch (the phrase was coined by G. E. Lessing) began to be dug in the eighteenth century when biblical criticism drew attention to vast cultural and other differences between the world of the Bible and the world of modern Europe. As biblical criticism developed in the nineteenth and twentieth centuries the ugly ditch got deeper and wider. How was it possible for what went on in the totally different world of the Bible to have any meaning or relevance for today's world? For many practitioners of biblical scholarship this was considered to be an illegitimate question. The task of biblical scholars was to study the past; to investigate the history and religion of ancient Israel and the beginnings of Christianity as these things had actually happened. The results obtained provided raw material that could be used by theologians, but whether or how biblical texts had any meaning for today was not the business of biblical scholarship. Generations of theological students training for ordination suffered under this regime and were given little help to face the task of bridging the ugly ditch as they entered the pulpit and were expected to expound the Bible to their congregations.

The idea that biblical scholarship was a value-free enterprise concerned primarily to investigate the past was challenged in the 1920s by scholars such as Karl Barth and Rudolf Bultmann, but it was in the 1970s that liberation theologians and feminist biblical scholars began to clamour for the right to approach the Bible from different angles and to insist that it had meanings for their situations. The essays contained in the present volume draw on many of the insights that have been gained from liberation and feminist approaches to the Bible, and they also make use of what has come to be known as *Wirkungsgeschichte*, a term difficult to translate adequately into English, but which has to do with taking account of the ways in which biblical texts have been used in Christian practice, action, preaching, theology, art and music since New Testament times.

The main purpose of this Foreword, however, is to draw attention to something that is implicit in a number of the essays, and to place it in the context of some recent work on cultural memory and on biblical texts as interpreted experience. The concern of the present book is not the *meaning* of Mark for today, but the *use* of Mark, and several of the contributors describe the way in which Mark's Gospel has affected their lives by calling them to practical discipleship. This links with recent publications by the Egyptologist Jan Assmann on cultural memory,[1] and Jörg Lauster on the interpretative implications of religious experience.[2]

Traditional biblical scholarship has been guilty of a strange oversight. While it has poured much effort into seeking to retrieve the events that are described or implied in the biblical narratives, it has failed to understand what those narratives signified for the communities that compiled them. Assmann argues that traditional societies compiled history-like narratives for the purpose of communication – communication with hearers/readers of the time of compilation, and communication with hearers/readers who would live later. Lauster applies this idea to the biblical narratives, arguing that the communities that produced them were trying to communicate their belief that reality should be understood in terms of particular religious experiences and commitments. As applied to Mark's Gospel the following points can be made.

Mark's Gospel is not intended primarily to be a *source of information* about the life and teaching of Jesus. The community that produced Mark's Gospel was a community of *disciples* of Jesus. Its members had been moved by the preaching and worship centred on Jesus to interpret reality in terms of Jesus' mission and significance, and to adopt a way of life that in some regards was radically different from that of the rest of society and which carried the danger of persecution and martyrdom. The main purpose of Mark's Gospel was communication – communication to present and future members of the community with a view to calling hearers/readers into a discipleship that would make sense of reality and of experience.

Viewed from this angle, it can be argued that it was a mistake in the first place to dig the ugly ditch that separated the world of the Bible from its modern investigators. They assumed that a value-free and objective reconstruction of biblical times and events was their main task, and while this was not an illegitimate or impossible enterprise, it had the effect of diverting attention from the biblical texts as witnesses to interpreted and lived experience, intended to challenge hearers/readers to consider their own commitments and understandings of reality. So deeply has the 'ugly ditch' idea become embedded in modern uses of the Bible that even some of the liberation and feminist approaches have assumed that fundamental to their task was the reconstruction of past situations and their analysis in terms of present problems.

The discipleship provoked by the gospel witness has taken many forms in the course of Christian history. These have included martyrdom, monasticism, the solitary living of hermits and the radical alternative lifestyles of Quakers and others, as well as attempts to make discipleship a feature of church institutions that were reluctant to take seriously the message and implications of Jesus. The essays in the present volume come from writers whose general perspective is that of contemporary Britain, and of a world characterized by poverty, injustice and various types of discrimination. What challenges to discipleship in such situations does Mark's Gospel provoke? What types of discipleship does it produce? How do particular incidents and narratives in Mark provide resources for coping with the demands of discipleship?

These are questions that are explored in the contributions that this volume contains.

John W. Rogerson
Biblical Studies Department
University of Sheffield

Notes

1 Jan Assmann, *Das Kulturelle Gedächtnis: Schrift, Erinnerung und Politische Identität in Frühen Hochkulturen* (Munich: C. H. Beck, 1992); *Religion und Kulturelles Gedächtnis* (Munich: C. H. Beck, 2000).
2 Jörg Lauster, *Religion als Lebensbedeutung: Theologische Hermeneutik Heute* (Darmstadt: Wissenschaftliche Buchgesellschaft, 2005).

Preface

This volume has its origin in the Institute for Socio-Biblical Studies, which John Rogerson convenes at the Urban Theology Unit in Sheffield. For three July meetings, in 2003, 2004 and 2005, a group of us, organized more or less by myself, met together to work at a project which we originally defined thus:

> The purpose of the volume is to assemble a selection of pieces on Mark's Gospel, written from a variety of different contemporary contexts, focusing on the ways that Mark's Gospel, or specific passages or elements in it, are seen 'at work', or as being 'used'. The emphasis is upon specific people, situations, communities and projects, within which there is an intentional or implied use of Marcan material or themes.

I wish to acknowledge my indebtedness to John Rogerson for his unfailing support, and to all the contributors for their willingness to engage in the process of listening to and reading each other, offering criticisms and suggestions, and discovering and pressing on with the new requirements of a new agenda. We lost several potential contributors along the way, as the experience or the expectation of practice is not yet (!) the prime concern of biblical interpreters.

I further acknowledge our debt to Ruth McCurry of SPCK for affirming our endeavour and sharpening up the final version, and to my colleagues in the Urban Theology Unit for their solidarity, and especially Judith Simms, who typed up many versions of it!

The July Institute continues its meetings, bringing together contemporary socio-biblical responses, both to Mark's Gospel and to other Scriptures. I would be delighted to send details to anyone interested.

John J. Vincent
Urban Theology Unit
210 Abbeyfield Road
Sheffield S4 7AY

Contributors

David Blatherwick worked for three years as a solicitor's articled clerk, before being accepted as a candidate for the Methodist ministry. He trained at Wesley House, Cambridge, spent a year at Göttingen University, and was assistant tutor at Wesley College, Headingley, for two years. He has subsequently served the Methodist Church in a number of inner-city and suburban circuits, and the then British Council of Churches as Ecumenical Officer for England. David's interest in Mark's Gospel is reflected in 'The Markan Silhouette?', *New Testament Studies* 17 (1970–71), pp. 184–92. Other published work includes *This Stab of Fire* (Epworth, 1971) and *Adventures in Unity* (British Council of Churches, 1975). He has recently completed a study, 'The Storm-Stilling: Mark 4.35—5.1', awaiting publication.

Christopher Burdon is Principal of the Northern Ordination Course and Honorary Lecturer of the University of Leeds, after 18 years in parish ministry. Mark's Gospel as the key to Christian faith and community was expressed in his *Stumbling on God: Faith and Vision in Mark's Gospel* (SPCK, 1990). He has also published articles on Mark in *Theology*, and in the *Journal for the Study of the New Testament*. His doctoral study on the reception history of the book of Revelation, building on his concerns with politics and poetry, was published as *The Apocalypse in England* (Macmillan, 1997). Chris currently teaches biblical studies for two other ministerial formation courses in addition to the NOC.

Mary Cotes is a Baptist minister and grew up in London. After teaching French for a number of years, Mary trained for the ordained ministry at Northern Baptist College, reading theology at Manchester University. She remained in Manchester to pursue doctoral studies in Mark under the supervision of first Barnabas Lindars and then Christopher Tuckett. Having served in a Baptist pastorate in central Exeter, Mary then worked in an ecumenical one in South Wales, where she was a regular contributor to religious programming on BBC Radio Wales and lectured in theology at Glamorgan University. Since 2003, Mary has worked in Milton Keynes as Ecumenical Moderator of the Mission Partnership of the Milton Keynes Churches' Council.

John Fenton is the son of a Liverpool vicar, and went to school and university at Oxford. After ordination in 1944, he worked as a curate near Wigan in Lancashire, and then on the staff of Lincoln Theological College (1947–54). He was vicar of Wentworth, in the Sheffield Diocese (1954–58),

Principal of Lichfield Theological College (1958–65) and St Chad's College, Durham (1965–78), and a canon of Christ Church, Oxford (1978–91). He retired in 1991, and now lives in Oxford. At Lincoln, Lichfield, Durham and Oxford, John taught Mark to students. He also wrote three books on Mark, the latest being *More About Mark* (SPCK, 1999). He sees Mark, after centuries of neglect, as the most appropriate Gospel for the Church in its present state.

Leslie J. Francis is Director of Welsh National Centre for Religious Education and Professor of Practical Theology at University of Wales, Bangor. He was first attracted to Mark's Gospel by meeting Austin Farrer and by reading his *A Study in St. Mark*. He developed the SIFT method of preaching, which applies the psychological functions identified by Jung: Sensing, Intuition, Feeling and Thinking. Three books (co-authored with Peter Atkins) employ this method through the gospel readings of the three-year cycle of the Revised Common Lectionary. He employs the method weekly in Llanedwen church, Anglesey, and offers courses in personality and preaching at St Deiniol's Library, Hawarden, and in other locations.

Geoffrey Harris is Senior Tutor for Biblical Studies at the East Midlands Ministry Training Course, based at the University of Nottingham, in the School of Education. He lives in Lincoln, where up to 2002 he was also a part-time Methodist circuit minister. He has taught Mark at St John's, Nottingham, and elsewhere. He has recently written a book called *Mission in the Gospels* (Epworth Press, 2004), with a chapter devoted to Mark. The book considers how the early Christians tried to reflect and act on their own understanding of Jesus' mission, and how that could affect our mission today.

Christine E. Joynes is Associate Director of the Centre for Reception History of the Bible at the University of Oxford. She has taught undergraduate and postgraduate courses on Mark's Gospel at Oxford Brookes University and the University of Oxford, and one of her current research interests is the reception history of Mark. By exploring the use and influence of this Gospel she hopes to highlight different ways of interpreting the text. She is presently writing the Blackwell Bible Commentary, *Mark's Gospel through the Centuries*, and other recent publications on Mark include *The Reception History of Mark's Gospel* (Oxford: Farmington Institute, 2005) and 'The Returned Elijah? John the Baptist's Angelic Identity in the Gospel of Mark', *Scottish Journal of Theology* 58 (2005), pp. 1–13.

Susan Miller teaches New Testament Studies at the University of Glasgow, and is a member of the Contextual Bible Study Development Group. She first became interested in the Gospel of Mark during a course taught by Joel Marcus, the author of the *Anchor Bible Commentary: Mark 1—8* (New York: Doubleday, 2000). Her interest in feminist interpretation encouraged her to research the role of women in Mark's Gospel, and her thesis *Women in Mark's*

Gospel has been recently published (London: T&T Clark International, 2004). For the past ten years, Susan has been a member of the Iona Community. She is interested in reading the Bible in relation to issues of social justice, and she has taught courses on the Gospel of Mark and on the Bible and social justice.

Ched Myers is a biblical interpreter and community group training officer with Bartimaeus Co-operative Ministries, based in Pasadena, California. His classic study on Mark, *Binding the Strong Man: A Political Reading of Mark's Story of Jesus* (Orbis Books, 1988), was followed by *Who Will Roll Away the Stone? Discipleship Queries for First World Christians* (Orbis Books, 1994) and *Say to This Mountain: Mark's Story of Discipleship* (Orbis Books, 1996). His most recent publication is *The Biblical Vision of Sabbath Economics*, published by the Church of the Saviour in Washington in 2001.

Andrew Parker, an ordained minister of the Church of Scotland, has spent his life as a grass-roots activist, earning his living as a manual worker. He worked first in France till his expulsion in 1973 (for political activity unbecoming in a foreigner), then in Castlemilk, Glasgow, and finally in London's East End. He is a community activist and biblical interpreter, living in London. His life as a Christian disciple has been determined by his sense of being called to follow Jesus to the margins of society. His publications include a series of cartoon volumes, *Political Parables* (1980) and *Painfully Clear: The Parables of Jesus* (Sheffield Academic Press, 1996).

John Riches is currently an Honorary Research Professor at Glasgow University, Editor of *Expository Times* and a member of the West of Scotland Contextual Bible Study Group. With his wife, he runs a One World shop, and is an Episcopalian priest. He is attracted to Mark by its vivid and dramatic narrative sense, and the subtlety of its account of Jesus' dialogues with those he encounters. 'It's a work which disturbs and encourages its readers to reach out for the new and the life-giving, as we discover in our CBS groups.' Presently John is working on a reception-historical commentary on Galatians. His last book was *Mark and Matthew: Conflicting Mythologies* (Edinburgh: T&T Clark, 2000).

Christopher Rowland is the Dean Ireland Professor of Holy Scripture in the University of Oxford. His works on the Gospels include *Christian Origins* (rev. edn, 2002). He is the co-editor with John Vincent of the series, British Liberation Theology (Sheffield: Urban Theology Unit, 1995–), and with Andrew Bradstock of *Radical Christian Writings: A Reader* (Oxford: Blackwell, 2002). He is co-editor or the Blackwell Bible Commentaries series on reception history, and with Judith Kovacs wrote the Series Commentary *Revelation* (2004). He has a particular interest in methods of grass-roots readings of Scripture.

John Vincent, a Methodist minister, lectures part time at the Urban Theology Unit, where he is Director Emeritus, and at Sheffield University Biblical Studies Department and Birmingham University Theology Department, where he is an Honorary Lecturer and Doctoral Supervisor. Books on Mark are his Basel dissertation, *Disciple and Lord: The Historical and Theological Significance of Discipleship in Mark* (Academy Press, 1976), *Mark at Work* (with John D. Davies, BRF, 1986) and *Radical Jesus* (Marshall Pickering, 1986; 2nd edn, Ashram Press, 2004). His most recent publications are a 'Radical Alpha Course', *Journey: Explorations into Discipleship* (Ashram Press, 2001–04), a booklet *Radical Christianity* (Ashram Press, 2005) and *Outworkings: Gospel Practice and Interpretation* (Urban Theology Unit, 2005).

Ian Wallis has been Rector of Houghton-le-Spring, in the Durham Diocese, since 1995, before which he was Chaplain and Director of Studies in Theology at Sidney Sussex College, Cambridge (1992–95). The Human One's summons to discipleship in Mark has motivated, inspired and characterized Ian's own spiritual journey and practice of faith. His work on Mark includes 'Your Faith Has Saved You: A Redaction-Critical Analysis of the Synoptic Logion' (MLitt thesis, Cambridge University, 1987), *The Faith of Jesus Christ in Early Christian Traditions* (Cambridge University Press, 1995 and 2005), *Holy Saturday Faith: Rediscovering the Legacy of Jesus* (London: SPCK, 2000) and 'Before the Big Bang: Echoes of Jesus in the Faith of his Followers', *Theology* 106 (2003), pp. 12–19.

Part 1

NEW WAYS INTO THE GOSPEL

1

What have we here?

CHRISTOPHER ROWLAND

Throughout this collection there is an implicit recognition of the importance of the Gospel of Mark for modern Christians. The fortunes of this text have changed dramatically over the last two hundred years. From being in the shadow of the Gospel of Matthew it has emerged to become a major witness to the original move to a written gospel and in the last thirty years it has stimulated a range of studies that have seen in this text a major contribution to political theology, particularly from a liberationist point of view. One thinks here not only of the major study by Ched Myers, but also earlier studies by Fernando Belo and Michel Clévenot, as well as the writing that John Vincent has done over the years.

The link of Mark with liberation theology, however, is a mixed blessing for the reception of this text. The reception of liberation theology into European theology, in particular biblical theology, has been lukewarm. In an editorial in *Theology* in 1990, Leslie Houlden welcomed the work of liberation theologians, but thought that they were not served well by what he called their 'Northern imitators'. Leslie is among those who have sounded a gently sceptical note. He has mounted a defence of conventional biblical study. To him liberation exegesis seemed to hark back to the banished voice of yesteryear in its apparent concern to promote a new form of biblical theology. The exegesis of the basic ecclesial communities seemed to him 'little more than the discernment of scriptural analogies to present situations and concerns', which 'is essentially the procedure of every devout Bible study group in Christendom'. He wondered whether they had capitulated too much to the spirit of the age and expressed, the view that 'the Bible has other jobs to do than dance to our late twentieth century favourite tunes'.

In one form or another this is an issue that recurs as a theme within the discussion of the relationship of the Bible and the world, especially since modernity. In the academy, there has been over the years a concerted attempt to keep faith matters out of the discussion. Typical of this are the words of John Ashton, which perfectly describe the scholarly consensus.

> . . . the old distinction between meaning and meaning for must be upheld.
> Feminists and liberationists, and any whose programme is based on or prompted

by current ethical concerns – whether or not these have a direct biblical input – may be perfectly entitled to seek for further inspiration and encouragement in the bible itself. They will have their own agenda and will usually, no doubt, focus their attention upon texts they think likely to yield some dividends, by way of inspiration or argument, to the cause they are eager to promote. But in so doing they should not pretend that they are attempting to *understand* the biblical text. Provided that they declare their interest openly, having already decided what they wish to find in the text (resembling the majority of Christian readers in the pre-critical era), then they may go their own way without fear of being disturbed by any of the findings of traditional exegesis. The two tracks may be parallel but they will never converge.[1]

Ashton suggests that exegesis involves two steps: understanding and interpretation. I agree with this but think that the order must be reversed: interpretation, finding meaning in texts (with all that this involves in terms of 'reading in' via illustrative parallels or the insight of experience) is always going to be an experimental affair which will run the risk of misunderstanding in the quest for understanding. That experiment can hardly ever be an abstract activity devoid of influence from outer concerns feeding into the interpretation of the text. The twin track approach may be neat and tidy but it masks the extent to which in 'traditional exegesis' contemporary issues motivate the agenda.[2] What is more, understanding of a text may in some circumstances be enhanced by the process of application (put simply, how you live or act conditions the way in which you understand). If our interpretation depends on understanding, we shall find ourselves too quickly before the bar of the experts, who understand or offer interpretation until we acquire those reading skills that alone can make understanding possible.

The prioritization of this kind of detached exegesis, which is such a hallmark of academic reading of the Bible, arguably loses some of the power of this remarkable text and its effects. The ways in which this is missed by the modern academy is in part a feature of the Pontifical Biblical Commission's document on the interpretation of the Bible. In that document we find a recognition of the importance of an 'actualizing' of the Scripture (to use the term suggested in the Pontifical Biblical Commission's document of 1993),[3] in which understanding of the text comes in the process of living the texts. That seems to be one of the points that Lash wishes to make in suggesting the understanding of the Scriptures is incomplete without attention to the performance of them. An understanding of biblical texts may be particularly vouchsafed to those who have an affinity with what that text is saying on the basis of the obedience of faith. Those seeking to engage with the address, promise, commission, praise, pardon and liberation of Scripture may best understand the biblical texts.

I have often found myself coming back to those words that Barth wrote at the start of his commentary on Romans, in which he reproached the historical critics for their preoccupation with the 'pastness' of the text and pleaded instead for a wrestling with the text in one's own time and place. He expressed this memorably as 'wrestling with the text, so the walls which separate the twentieth century from the first century become transparent, and the actual meaning is thereby disclosed'.[4] This is true exegesis. In contrast, Barth was right to state the following:

> Judged by what seems to me to be the principle of true exegesis, I entirely fail to see why parallels drawn from the ancient world should be of more value for our understanding of the epistle than the situation in which we ourselves actually are and to which we can therefore bear witness.

What in effect Barth does in Romans is an excellent example of the exegetical task as actualization (that is, the reading of texts in the light of new circumstances), which seeks to listen to the text and respond in the context in which it is read. For Barth, the divide between meaning and meaning for is pulled down in the process. Barth's does represent a sincere attempt to discover what the text has to say, which is certainly pervaded with theological learning, but without the inhibitions of the norms of historical exegesis. Now, it may be the case that later in his theological career Barth lost sight of this highly contextual exegesis. Tim Gorringe has, however, reminded us that this approach may have continued to inspire Barth, and the lack of explicit contextual hermeneutic in his theology should not disguise the extent to which this may have been going on.[5]

Writing about the Bible is often either lofty and pious, with due deference to Christian doctrine, or coolly detached and cerebral, cut off from the everyday struggles of faith and the practice of faith communities. We either relegate it to ancient history, deciding it has nothing to say to us, being irrelevant to a modern world where very different demands are made of people, or we read it through the lens of a Christian tradition, which can give us the answers to questions about our sexuality, our lifestyle and our beliefs before we engage with the Bible itself. But there are ways nonetheless of wrestling with the biblical text, with the commitment of discipleship, without ending up as a conservative evangelical. This is what is typical of many liberationist readings – engaging with the texts in the context of commitment and action, not with the detached eye of the academic historian for whom these texts differ very little from many other texts from antiquity.

What I am articulating is a reaction not only to a robust traditionalism, whether in evangelicalism or in Roman Catholicism, in using the Bible as a non-negotiable guide, but also to a liberal, academic engagement, which distances readers and makes it difficult for the Bible to 'speak' to them. I am as concerned as any that the integration of the biblical texts and life is crucial; yet, as important, is the way in which one engages with those texts. In this respect the liberationist perspective is light years away from much conservative thinking. John Vincent, in his essay, rightly points us to the 'the correspond-ence of relationships' model of Clodovis Boff.

Clodovis Boff describes an approach to the Bible where there is an oscil-lation between the Bible in its context and the readers in their present context. The contemporary situation throws up opportunities to interpret experience and conduct through the lens of Scripture, and, most impor-tantly, vice versa, to discern the meaning of Scripture through the lens of experience. Scriptural texts, read analogically, thereby illuminate everyday life. In this action and commitment are the necessary contexts of discerning God in the midst of human existence.

Such an analogical approach (if that is the most appropriate way of describing it) not only describes how New Testament writers related texts, tradition and action, but also closely parallels the hermeneutical insight into an aspect of Latin American liberationist hermeneutics, as set out by Clodovis Boff.[6] Boff's 'correspondence of relationships' method sees the Bible read through the lens of the experience of the present, thereby enabling it to become a key to understanding what the scriptural text bears witness to – the life and struggles of ancestors in the faith. This in turn may enable one to view the present situation in a new light as a result of the cor-respondences that might exist between text and life. Two things are impor-tant about Boff's model. First, this is not only about thought, but also about action; it is about the lived lives of people seeking to embody the way of God in faithful struggle for justice. Second, this method does not presuppose the application of a set of principles of a theological programme or pattern to modern situations:

> We need not, then, look for formulas to 'copy' or techniques to 'apply' from scripture. What scripture will offer us are rather something like orientations, models, types, directives, principles, inspirations – elements permitting us to acquire, on our own initiative, a 'hermeneutic competency', and thus the capa-city to judge – on our own initiative, in our own right – 'according to the mind of Christ', or 'according to the Spirit', the new unpredictable situations with which we are continually confronted. The Christian writings offer us not a *what*, but a *how* – a manner, a style, a spirit.[7]

'Not a *what* but a *how* – a manner, a style, a spirit.' What Boff wrote about the interpretation of the Bible applies just as much to the way in which Christians approach the whole of living. Mere application of principle or resort to the past can never do justice to the particularity of one's context.

In much of the interpretation going on in the texts in this book, we are not dealing with the kind of analytical exegesis that is typical of modern academic writing, in which the intention of the author and attention to the precise meaning of words and phrases predominate. Instead, we see rather oblique relationship with the Scriptures, in which the words become the catalyst for discernment of the divine way in the present. It is, as some recent Brazilian popular educational material puts it, 'enabling one to look at the world with new eyes'. The wisdom of experience is as much the vehicle of the Holy Spirit. What counts is not so much what the text meant to Isaiah, Jesus or Paul, but what import these words may have in the circumstances of the present.

The claim to be able to understand the Scriptures without recourse to learned divines is a repeated theme throughout this collection. It is one which is deeply rooted in the Christian tradition, going back to the words of Jesus in Matthew 11.25. Patterns of biblical exegesis which have emerged in parts of Latin America over the last twenty years offer a more recent example of the way in which the practical faith of the non-professional reader can be resourced by a mode of reading of the Scriptures which does not need (even if it was often supported by) sympathetic intellectuals.[8]

The perspective on Scripture surveyed in this book has a long pedigree in Christian theology. According to liberation theology, understanding comes through action; theology is the 'second act'. Scripture then acts as confirmation of that intuitive knowledge of God. The radicals in Christianity have stressed the presence of God in the persons of the poor and also God's activity in history. But it is not just the radicals. Perhaps the most influential theoretician of biblical interpretation is Tyconius. As a recent commentator on Tyconius has pointed out, Tyconius linked the Bible with his contemporary world in a way anticipatory of liberationist hermeneutics, and in contrast to the distancing of the Bible from current events which is typical of writers like Augustine. Tyconius believed that biblical models were intimately linked with the events of the present and that the words of the Bible directly addressed Christians in the present.[9] He was a Donatist, a member of a church criticized by Augustine. Yet Tyconius' theology and biblical interpretative principles were adopted by Augustine. In *The City of God*, Augustine's view of the Church as a site of evil rather than a place of light, and the world as a place of darkness, owed much to Tyconius. More explicitly, in *De Doctrina Christiana* Augustine acknowledges his debt to Tyconius' methods of biblical interpretation. These are complex points, but what is important for our present concern is the way in which he emphasizes the importance of Scripture in all its variety having a present application to the life of the Church. He would have agreed very much with Paul's words in 1 Corinthians 10.6: 'these things occurred as examples for *us*', a sentence repeated again a few verses later (1 Cor. 10.11). The 'actualizing' of biblical texts means going beyond the preoccupation with 'what it meant back then', to the essential text as it comes to life in the midst of the community reading and seeking that continuity of experience and action with the communities whose stories are reflected in the Scriptures. Tyconius describes this as a kind of typology in which the biblical story, attentively read, can offer a framework for contemporary life.

His church, with its tradition of persecution and harassment, looked to martyr stories, especially the martyr stories in the Bible, such as the death of Jesus. These are not just things that happened 'back then', but are models, catalysts for life. They are not prescriptions, but intellectual and ethical stimuli, and means of encouragement.

Notes

1 J. Ashton, *Studying John* (Oxford: Clarendon Press, 1994), p. 206f. This contrast between understanding and application is paralleled (though coming from a very different philosophical starting point) in Nick Wolterstorff's distinction between 'authorial discourse interpretation' and 'performance interpretation' in his 1993 Wilde Lectures, *Divine Discourse: Philosophical Reflections on the Claim that God Speaks* (Cambridge: Cambridge University Press, 1995).
2 This is one of the points made by Nicholas Lash in his essay 'What Might Martyrdom Mean?' in his collection *Theology on the Way to Emmaus* (London: SCM Press, 1986).
3 J. L. Houlden, *The Interpretation of the Bible in the Church* (London: SCM Press, 1995).
4 K. Barth, *The Epistle to the Romans*, English translation (Oxford: Clarendon Press, 1933), p. 11.
5 T. Gorringe, *Karl Barth: Against Hegemony* (Oxford: Oxford University Press, 1999).
6 This discussion is found in C. Boff, *Theology and Praxis: Epistemological Foundations* (New York: Orbis Books, 1987), ch. 2. It is found also in R. S. Sugirtharajah (ed.), *Voices from the Margins: Interpreting the Bible in the Third World* (London: SPCK, 1991), pp. 9–35, on which this discussion depends.
7 Sugirtharajah (ed.), *Voices from the Margins*, p. 30.
8 See Gerald West, *The Academy of the Poor* (Sheffield: Sheffield Academic Press, 1999).
9 See M. A. Tilley, *The Bible in Christian North Africa: The Donatist World* (Minneapolis: Fortress Press, 1997), p. 116.

2

How we got here

JOHN VINCENT

The studies in this volume come from contemporary Christian disciples 'living with' the records of Jesus as contained in the first Gospel, the Gospel of Mark.

Authors write from their own experience. Their lives, or parts of them, have been influenced by what they perceive to be elements in Mark's stories, which they have picked up and interpreted, or even lived by, in some specific parts of their own lives.

At the Urban Theology Unit in Sheffield in 2003, 2004 and 2005, when we shared our plans and pieces for this volume, we provoked each other to become more specific about the actual particulars of the way or ways in which some element or elements in Mark had become activated in our own practice as disciples, ministers and scholars. At one meeting, someone exclaimed, 'It's not just ways in which we use Mark's Gospel. It's ways that Mark's Gospel uses us.' Or, as another member commented, 'It's ways whereby "the Spirit takes of the things of Jesus, and shows them to the disciples", as John 16.14 has it.'

While each author writes from his or her own experience, he or she also writes within a common world of interpretation of the Gospels in the twenty years between 1985 and 2005. Each of us became aware of the possibility and legitimacy of 'personal readings' and 'community readings' by a variety of routes.

Certainly, the beginnings of this recent return to personal and political readings of the gospel relate significantly to the advent of liberation theology in the late 1960s. Liberation theology has 'as its hermeneutics or specific reading or interpretation . . . an examination of the whole of scripture from the viewpoint of the oppressed'. This picks out 'not only important but relevant themes':

> God the Father of life and advocate of the oppressed
> liberation from the house of bondage
> the prophecy of a new world
> the kingdom given to the poor
> the church as total sharing.[1]

Liberation exegetes see this as a fundamental rediscovery of what is truly significant in the Bible, especially in the Gospels. Equally, they see it as a

9

reclaiming by ordinary people of what had become the preserve of professionals, though the professionals had often 'missed it':

> We, exegetes or interpreters, priests or pastoral workers, who were always the
> owners of the Bible and of knowledge about the Bible – we are not capable
> of having the same vision, the same joy, gratitude, wonder, novelty, and com-
> mitment that the people bring to the Bible.[2]

In Britain, there has been a mixed reception for liberation theology, and various reasons may be given for this.[3] The perspective of the less privileged is
now recognized, at least in some quarters, and the Bible is seen as a key to
understanding not only spiritual issues, but even more deeply personal, social,
cultural and political issues. Consequently, many see liberation exegesis as having a vital role to play in Britain:

> In fact, liberation exegesis is as appropriate to a First World as to a Third World
> context. It is a method which sets out to awaken the exegete to the context
> of his or her reading of the Bible, and this by definition applies to all con-
> texts and not simply to the ones within which the theology of liberation ini-
> tially emerged.[4]

Liberation understandings of the Bible and the gospel naturally proceed from
individuals or groups who come to a sense that they are being oppressed in
one way or another. Thus, the Bible proves to be a significant element in the
liberation of specific groups of Christians.

Feminist writers have concentrated almost equally on the Bible as the record
of unredeemed oppressive patriarchy and on the value of individual stories
of courageous liberated women within that record.[5] Black Christians have
seen biblical models for oppressive practice and have found 'empowering texts'
and much 'Bible-based practice' in Black churches, though not in many white
ones.[6] Again, the current debates concerning sexuality have produced many
instances in which a personal and political style of empowerment and liberation is traced to liberative reading of scriptural traditions otherwise co-opted
by establishment or repressive ecclesiastical interpretations.[7]

Disciples in non-western countries, especially, developed many new
Reader Responses to Mark, seeing it in the light of their own experiences
of colonial and post-colonial realities, and tracing in the Marcan record elements of similar experiences. R. S. Sugirtharajah surveys readings that he
describes as dissident, resistant, heritagist, nationalist, liberationist and dissentent,
as well as colonial and post-colonial.[8]

Groups who identified with the biblical groups of the oppressed led
others to engage with their situations. Once the perspective of liberationist
interpretation took root, it became clear that all biblical passages and all contemporary interpreters equally needed to be seen in the light of their social,
economic, cultural and political contexts.

Hence, the present volume may be seen as a contemporary British, white, middle-class, main-line churches', academically aware reading of, or 'take on', Mark. It legitimizes itself alongside the growing library of similarly contextual and group-based bodies of current interpretation. Indeed, one may express surprise that British gospel scholars have not done this before, but shelter beneath the umbrella of a model that is dominated by western literary theory, which its proponents assume fits any context and is both impartial and based on studies that are historically verifiable. In fact, British studies are everywhere else seen as influenced by our current cultural, social, political and psychological interests. So that here we perhaps only do intentionally and consciously some of the things that our colleagues elsewhere often do without intending to!

We then might achieve a situation where we could discuss the relative appropriateness of our cultural contexts as against those of other interpreters with different contexts, orientations and interests. That necessitates a debate between contemporary contexts, which we are in no shape at present to undertake. But if context is so important in both biblical understanding and biblical interpretation, then a debate between contexts is inevitable and proper.

These are interpretative opportunities that are available to anyone, wherever they live, whatever they do, and however they describe themselves. They are opportunities that will certainly be influenced by the age, race, sex, nationality, profession, education and relative wealth of the interpreter. Obviously, the 'social location' of disciples is a decisive element in their perception. Indeed, it becomes important that we use the same critiques for ourselves and our current situation about what, where, when, why, how and with whom, that we learn from historical criticism have to be used for biblical texts and stories.

Naturally there are also, within these contexts, questions that individual disciples ask. They are not the questions that biblical students or even biblical scholars necessarily ask. But they are arguably the questions that the first hearers of the stories asked. So the question arose, 'How can I live my life in my context by learning how disciples in the Bible lived their lives in their contexts?'

Thus, everyone gets in with their stories.

The question becomes important for an individual reader, a group of readers, or a congregation, 'How can I get the same kind of critique going for myself, my group, or my congregation, as I use for a biblical story?' This is often asked negatively: 'We live in such totally different worlds, how can we, with our lives and problems, in the situations we are in, with the decisions we face, possibly get any help from these far-off biblical stories?'

Clearly, there is never going to be a 'correspondence' in a strict or literal way. There is not even a 'correspondence of terms', because our terms, the words we use, the worlds we live in, are so different. But, as Clodovis Boff, who discusses this problem, claims, we could have a 'correspondence of relationships', which seeks 'to re-effectuate the biblical act, the act that gave birth to the Bible itself as a text'.[9] We need not a repetition of the text, but a repetition of the kind of action that created the text – 'creative fidelity' to the actions of Jesus, in the case of a Gospel.

'Creative fidelity' does not mean naive repetition, but it does mean getting the feel of what became good news in New Testament times, and seeking similar kinds of things today. It could mean asking questions like:

> If certain people told these stories
> to shore up attitudes, beliefs, ways of life and expectations
> which were extraordinary and God-inspired then,
> in the old times,
> What kind of attitudes, beliefs, ways of life and expectations
> of people today
> might feel identified with the biblical ones
> and thus might feel incorporated
> in the divine mysteries contained there?[10]

This question begins with the gospel experiences visible in the New Testament and asks what kind of experiences are like them today.

The personal hearings, like the social/location hearings, inevitably cast back into the Gospel itself. Are there elements within the hearings and actings-out of our own contemporary disciples which betoken similar elements which can be predicated to the first hearers, or to the first communities, or to the writer, Mark, or even beyond that to the first storytellers, to the first disciples and to the one who called them?

The question we then take back to the text is thus the opposite one from the previous quotation. It begins with our questions today, and looks then at the questions of the people in gospel times:

> If this or that piece of the story,
> or this or that character within it,
> or this or that conflict, or interest,
>   or policy, or strategy discernible within it,
> is found to be life-giving, or significant,
>   or indicative,
> by us, our people, now,
> then what might this say about the people almost
>   visible in and through Mark's Gospel –
>   the first hearers,
>   the first gospel-creating communities,
>   the first oral storytellers,
>   the writer, Mark,
>   the first disciples,
>   the caller of disciples, Jesus,
> and their conflicts, interests, policies and strategies?

These are the questions addressed in the approaches of 'outworkings' and of 'gospel practice criticism'.

In this sense, there is an interesting 'take' on the traditional concerns of the historical–critical method. These concerns had been precisely to seek out the original hearers and communities (through audience criticism), the original writers (through redaction criticism), the original reasons for the stories' shape (through form criticism), and the possible original history behind the stories of Jesus, disciples and others (through historical criticism).

Historical criticism traditionally claimed to work the other way round. It claimed to work to uncover the original history behind the present stories (historical criticism) by examining the elements that are present because of the shape of individual pieces or pericopes (form criticism), or of specific writers (redaction criticism) or of specific communities (audience criticism). But gospel study at present is seeing these two motivations – back towards history, and forwards from history – as problematic; it is seeing them as inescapably parts of how people live and work with the text, rather than necessarily foolproof routes to history. To try to trace the history of how people in the past engaged with the text is the task attempted by present-day reception criticism. To encourage us in our own lives to make our own history with the text is the task attempted by practice criticism.

This brief survey hopefully explains how we got to where we are today. Over the past twenty years or so, there have been particular methodological pointers, some of them by our essayists. They have sought to produce models and methods for 'getting from this to that' – from Gospel to today, from today to Gospel. There are significant differences between their approaches, some of which naturally derive from their contexts, some from the perspectives of the writers. The methods are an invitation to the smorgasbord of ways of 'using' the Gospel today.

Notes

1 Leonardo Boff and Clodovis Boff, *Introducing Liberation Theology* (London: Burns and Oates, 1987), p. 32.

2 Carlos Mesters, *Defenseless Flower: A New Reading of the Bible* (Maryknoll, NY: Orbis Books, 1989), p. 18.

3 Cf. John Vincent, 'Liberation Theology in Britain, 1970–1995' in *Liberation Theology UK*, ed. Chris Rowland and John Vincent (Sheffield: Urban Theology Unit, 1995), pp. 15–39.

4 Christopher Rowland and Mark Corner, *Liberating Exegesis: The Challenge of Liberation Theology to Biblical Studies* (Louisville, KY: Westminster John Knox Press; London: SPCK, 1989), p. 53.

5 For a summary, see Rosemary Radford Ruether, *Women and Redemption: A Theological History* (London: SCM Press, 1998), pp. 209–40, 273–81.

6 Cf. Joe Aldred and Garnet Parris, 'The Bible and the Black Church' in *Bible and Practice*, ed. Chris Rowland and John Vincent (Sheffield: Urban Theology Unit, 2001), pp. 52–65.

7 Cf. Deryn Guest, *When Deborah met Jael: Lesbian Biblical Hermeneutics* (London: SCM Press, 2005).

8 R. S. Sugirtharajah, *Post-colonial Criticism and Biblical Interpretation* (Oxford: Oxford University Press, 2002), pp. 43–73. In general, cf. *Reading from this Place: Social Location and Biblical Interpretation*, ed. Fernando F. Segovia and Mary Ann Tolbert, Vol. 1: *In the United States*; Vol. 2: *In Global Perspective* (Minneapolis: Fortress Press, 1995). On the relation of contextual Bible studies to contextual theologies, cf. John Vincent, 'Developing Contextual Theologies' in I. K. Duffield, C. Jones and J. Vincent, *Crucibles: Creating Theology at UTU* (Sheffield: Urban Theology Unit, 2000), pp. 23–32.

9 Clodovis Boff, *Theology and Praxis: Epistemological Foundations* (Maryknoll, NY: Orbis Books, 1987), p. 296, n. 26.

10 John Vincent, *Hope from the City* (Peterborough: Epworth Press, 2000), p. 37.

3

Some methods and models

1
Movements with texts

This paper was contributed by Norman Gottwald in teaching sessions in Sheffield and New York for the New York Theological Seminary British Doctor of Ministry programme, 1980–88. Part of the aim of this programme, continued by Sheffield (1991–2001) and Birmingham (2003–, as a PhD in Ministry) Universities, is to develop a mutual learning between contemporary situations and stories and biblical situations and stories, in order to develop a Project for Ministry. The initial parts of the process are described thus by the present programme director, Ian K. Duffield:

> The first step in the process is the formation of a small group of people who work together, the 'Site Team', in the DMin jargon. They begin by analysing their current ministerial situation in all sorts of ways.[1] This draws upon practical experience, statistical data, historical records, and observation. In particular, the group is asked to ascertain the key *joys* and *sorrows* of both their congregation and the community in which they are set – whether it be a small neighbourhood, a housing estate, market town, city centre, or region. From this 'Situation Analysis' of their particular context, they are invited to engage in a mutual exploration of some biblical passages that appear to have some particular relevance or resonance to their faith community in its background setting. The search is for 'suggestive stories' and 'evocative parallels' which will in some measure correlate with their own experience and struggle, for an 'imaginative identification', as John Vincent calls it,[2] between ourselves, our contexts and our possible actions, and biblical ones.[3]

Norman Gottwald's paper was originally entitled, 'From Here to There and Back: On Using the Bible in DMin Projects and Other Contemporary Projects'.

Movements with texts
Norman Gottwald

All hermeneutical appropriations of Scripture have three movements:

- First, the move from my situation to the text.
- Second, the movement within the text (exegesis proper).
- Third, the move from the text's movement back to my situation.

The move from my situation to the text

Why do I choose this text, theme or socio-religious situation instead of others? Have I adequately considered other options? Have I made sufficient use of biblical reference works to canvass these opinions? Have I considered what appeals to Scripture are made by theological/ethical works that treat 'my situation' most relevantly? Should I use already 'tried and true' texts, or venture into fresh textual resources, thematic possibilities and socio-religious contexts? Am I prepared to abandon a false or abortive start when the text or theme or biblical period do not speak to the problem that I first thought they did?

My situation

'My' emphasizes that I am the participant-observer-interpreter of a situation. The 'situation' necessarily involves others and will disclose its social structural character on analysis. The situation may first present itself as a practical or a theoretical issue of theology or ecclesiology. I may need to stretch myself to locate how that 'church' or 'faith' situation is imbedded in and affected by a wider cultural and social structural situation. Also, 'my situation' is immediate, possibly even urgent. I may only recently have become fully aware of it as a problem or possibility. But the situation was there, usually before I entered it or became entirely aware of it. So I must examine the *history* of the immediate situation and its *connections* to other realities.

The text

For convenience, 'text' means any biblical subject matter: single or multiple text, word studies, themes or motifs, socio-religious situations in biblical times, etc. It also implies that it is necessary to press the written text back into *somebody's experience* in a situation that was problematic, promising, threatening for the speaker-writer and for *some community*. Text is not mere disembodied word, but a speaking from out of someone's situation which *may* have one or another analogy with the interpreter's situation.

The movement within the text

'Movement' here has a double sense, closely related in terms of exegetical practice. First, there is the movement of the text's own internal life, both as a literary composition of a certain genre and as an expression of a response to a situation. This movement will connect and contrast in varying ways with earlier/later and similar/dissimilar texts. Second, there is the movement that I as an exegete must go through in order to penetrate the text's distinctive movement. Exegesis provides for a number of 'fixes' or 'checks' on the text. Often called 'exegetical steps', their exact sequence is less important than that they all receive consideration as of relevance to an understanding of the text.

Exegesis

'Exegesis' is always in danger of being 'behind the times', both behind the crying questions from real life situations and behind the latest developments in biblical studies. Nowadays, this means that many standard biblical reference works will not be attuned to the language/symbolism and socio-economic/political issues that rise out of real life and that new methodologies are addressing in Scripture. I will need to concentrate on a search for these up-to-date studies so that my exegesis will fully tap the biblical situations as they are now viewed – and just as I have striven to understand my own situation in terms of the latest analytic resources.

The move back to my situation

If I have made a well-grounded initial move into biblical texts, and *if* I have fully entered their own movement by means of shrewd and revealing exegetical moves of my own, *then* my return from Scripture to my own situation should flow naturally. The 'naturalness' of my return does not imply or prejudge what I will bring back with me, or that my 'cargo' on return is what I had expected when I began my biblical journey. I must be especially cautious not to fall into old habits of neglecting the form and substance of the biblical materials in favour of 'inspirational' or 'idealizing/moralizing' points, or even 'allegorical' hopping from text to text – all of which say less of my spiritual acumen than of my lack of imagination and intellectual laziness.

In short, I must *'bring back' the whole text in its situation to my situation in its wholeness*. The potential 'application' of Scripture to my situation may be less direct or of a very different sort than I had expected. In actuality, new questions may be posed which force me into another 'biblical trip' and another way of looking at my situation.

2
Programme for study

The method of *Mark at Work* resulted from several years of work together in the period 1975–79 at the Urban Theology Unit, led by Alan T. Dale (author of *Winding Quest* and *New World*) together with John D. Davies and John J. Vincent. The method developed encourages people to use references to Mark's Gospel as related to their own journeys of discipleship. As they proceed in their discipleship, people find themselves confronted with an issue, a challenge, an opportunity or an invitation which makes them feel that they are being confronted by something which calls to mind a similar situation or phenomenon in the gospel story. 'Snap', they cry – 'I have an experience or an event or an issue which is "like" one in the Gospel.'

So, Mark and Mark's Gospel are still 'at work'. Mark with his stories and happenings is 'alive and well' in the contemporary world. Mark's dynamic stories of conflict, oppression, tragedy, humanity, healing, liberation, community and human wholeness are sparking off and being sparked off by similar stories today. From this initial 'snap', a whole process of discoveries ('studies') and future possibilities ('spin-offs') emerges.

The piece printed here is based on John D. Davies and John J. Vincent, *Mark at Work* (London: Bible Reading Fellowship, 1986), pp. 14–18, 'Programme for Studying a Passage'. The method has been widely republished and used in many places. In more elaborated form, it is used in John Davies, *Only Say the Word* (Norwich: Canterbury Press, 2002), pp. 29–38.

Programme for study
John Davies and John Vincent

At its simplest, any Bible study has to involve three elements:

- imagining
- thinking
- deciding.

Also, it inevitably involves looking back on the past; so we could describe it as a kind of loop movement (see Figure 1).

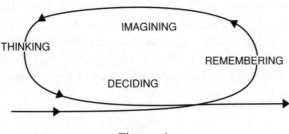

Figure 1

We study the Bible to help us to sort out plans and priorities. This sort of aim – whether in Bible study or in anything else – involves a similar kind of loop as we look at the past and plan for the future (Figure 2).

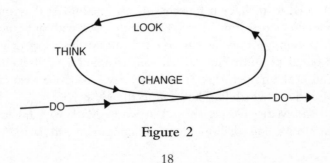

Figure 2

We take this kind of pattern and apply it to the study of a story in the Gospel. First, we use our imagination to see connections between the situation in the Gospel and our own situation (snaps); then we think objectively about the meaning of the text (studies); then we move towards the future and discover the decisions which are suggested for our future work, in the light of our study (spin-offs) (Figure 3).

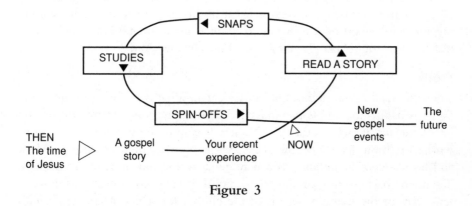

Figure 3

Whatever the type of passage, the study should in principle have the following ingredients.

Starting where we are

On the diagram, we are at the point marked 'NOW'. We are the people we are, at the point in time which is *now*, at the position which is *here*. We are on a line of experience. Behind us is our own immediate past; also behind us is the history of the whole Christian movement. Our task is to go on making that history, to be people through whom God continues to make gospel actions. But, at this point marked 'NOW', we take time off from our task in order to go back to our sources and check our priorities. We move off the line of experience, so as to reflect on our own immediate experience and on the experience of the first members of our movement. So we pick up our copy of the Gospel.

Reading a story

Start with a story, with one of the episodes in the gospel narrative. Before you get into technicalities, be *yourself*. What catches your interest in the story? What 'clicks' with you, with your experience or imagination? With whom do you identify? And why? This is about *you*. At this point, you can't be wrong – even if you are technically misunderstanding the text. Before worrying about misunderstandings, claim the story as *yours*. Catch the story from your own point of view. Tell it to someone else, with your particular slant.

Snaps

By a 'snap' we mean the first impression, the snapshot. Snap – the two similar cards. Snap – the connector of two electric cables. Snaps make connections between us, as we are, and the story. Snaps work in our *imaginations*.

For example, you might take Mark 2.1–12, the first 'big' story in Mark's Gospel. You might identify with one or other of the characters in the story. 'I feel like Jesus – always being interrupted'; 'I think I'm a scribe, always picking holes in other people'; 'I know what it's like to be flat on my back waiting for help' – said by a miner who recalled being trapped in a rock-fall; 'I feel like the roof – people just knock holes in me'. And so on.

Studies

Then we need to start a more objective search. What is going on in the story? What is happening to people and why? This is the point where you need a bit of *specialist knowledge,* for this is where it is quite possible to get the story wrong or (more likely) to fail to see points which would be clear to Mark and his readers. For instance, you may need to find out more about the Old Testament background, or the social, political and economic conditions of Jesus' day, or the living problems of the church for which Mark wrote. This is where you may have to get your books out, to consult your minister, to adjourn your meeting until next time and delegate one of your members to do some research for you.

But the 'studies' phase is not necessarily bookwork. Build on the 'identifications' you have already made. If you are doing this with others, divide your group into little teams around the characters that interest you.

To continue our example of Mark 2.1–12, these teams could be Jesus, the bearers, the crowd, the patient, the scribes. In each team, ask 'What is happening to us? What are our goals and our problems?' – and the 'we' is not you as a group of readers or church members, but you in the role of Jesus, the bearers, etc. Don't say, 'I think the scribes have problem X' but 'I am a scribe and as such I have problem X'. Then let each team send a couple of delegates to the team that is causing their problems and face them with it; or let each team send to the team to which they are causing problems and ask, 'What is the problem that I am causing you?' Then the issues in this complex story can be faced in pairs of roles. For instance, the paralysed man, by his presence, causes problems to the crowd or congregation, for whom he is an interruption. The crowd or congregation is a problem to the bearers. The bearers present a problem to Jesus. Jesus is a problem to the scribes. The scribes are a problem to the paralysed man. What is motivating these groups of people? How do they express their needs and attitudes? What are their responses?

Very many stories of Mark are stories of conflict between various interest groups. Each of these interest groups has some legitimacy, but Christ's presence tends to polarize these interests into faith and anti-faith.

Go for the roles, not for individual character analysis. Mark does not ask us to go in for deep psychological speculation. Individual characters belong uniquely to their own context. People in their roles are transferable; we can find them in our own context. So, for instance, when we read that Jesus was 'indignant' about the condition of a leper (Mark 1.40–45 – this is the best translation of the original words), we don't speculate about what was so specially wrong with this particular leper. We ask, 'Who is the leper for us, in our society today? Who is fulfilling the role of "leper"? What does a Jesus-following church do in order to carry on Jesus' work towards such people?' If we do this honestly, we may well find that we see more clearly why Jesus was 'indignant'.

In our 'studies' phase, we are seeing two things at once. We are seeing an action or saying of Jesus, and we are seeing something of the impact or effect the story made on the gospel-writer Mark. We see that it is a story which he and his community remembered and treasured and valued so much that it got written down. Only a tiny fraction of the things that Jesus said and did were so significant to the Christian community. So it's useful to ask what was so special about the particular story we are studying. How did it help Mark's community to face up to their problems? So, Mark is, in a sense, another character represented on the printed page you are reading. If your group breaks into little teams to get into the role of the different characters of the story, don't forget to include Mark. Let a team try to think out why Mark found the story worth remembering and recording for his church. This will help you to discover meaning in the story for your contemporary situation.

Spin-offs

Then we turn back from our 'studies' and get into the direction of our *present life*. What are the '*spin-offs*'? What are the mandates, implications, applications? What effect is this Bible study going to have on your church's programme? Does it support you, criticize you, offer you new suggestions for action? Does it help you to cope with the effects of your gospel programme? Does it direct you towards gospel activity in your neighbourhood?

At this point, no one from outside your situation can tell you what is right for you. The most that anyone else can do is to tell you stories of how the gospel material has worked out elsewhere.

This moment of change of direction is, in many ways, the most important moment of the whole Bible study. Your seriousness at this point will make all the difference; it will show whether you are interested in merely having a pleasant discussion, or whether you are really doing business with the policies of Jesus. You may well find that there are all sorts of pressures, conscious and sub-conscious, to delay or omit this shift of direction. It is a change of mood and a change of skill. You have to move, perhaps with some pain, from the intellectual pursuits of 'there and then' into decision-making for the 'here and now' – and you may well find that you run into real-life conflicts of interest. So don't leave this change of direction until too late in your meeting. You must change from being a story-reader to being a story-maker.

Before there can be a story to tell, it has to be acted out; and that new action is your task. You go on to work out, in action, the roles that you have been examining.

1 You and your church are part of the needy world that Christ heals and nourishes. In what ways are you needing Christ's healing for your paralysis, your leprosy, your demon-possession, your hunger?

2 You and your church are part of the disciple community which Christ teaches, and which so often misunderstands and obstructs. Where and how are you failing to co-operate with him and to learn from him? What has he been teaching you in the last year or two?

3 You and your church are part of the rejoicing crowd which has an eye and a song for the signs of God's love in the world. What is God doing in your bit of the world, and how are you celebrating it?

4 Above all, you are the Body of Christ himself; through you, God wishes to continue the gospel events once typically acted out by Jesus of Nazareth. What is God trying to do for his world through your particular group or church?

3
Practical exegesis

All of the interpretations in this collection are contextual; all are community-related; and all are both political and personal. All texts get used for many practical purposes:

> Whether we like it or not texts are sites of struggle. In their production they betray the ideological conflict of their day, and in the history of their use they have served very different ends. They can enable change but may just as easily be co-opted in the service of a dominant ideology. Biblical texts in particular are tied up in a particular set of human struggles because of their authoritative status, and the careful exposition of their use is a necessary part of the interpretive enterprise.[4]

Practical exegesis seeks to bring discipline to the way that texts get 'co-opted' for other people's agendas – and our own.

The piece by Christopher Rowland is a fruit of his colleagueship with John Vincent and others through the annual July Institute for British Liberation Theology at the Urban Theology Unit (UTU) in Sheffield, and the biannual Consultation on Liberating Theologies, now at Wistaston Hall near Crewe. The theme at one Institute at UTU was 'Bible and Practice', and this led to a publication of the same title in 2001.

The piece below by Christopher Rowland is adapted from a longer report on 'Practical Exegesis in Context', by Christopher Rowland, Bridget Rees and Ruth Weston in *Bible and Practice*, ed. Christopher Rowland and John Vincent (Sheffield: Urban Theology Unit, 2001), pp. 10–26, at pp. 22–6.

Practical exegesis
Christopher Rowland

With the rise of a more participative exegesis there are important questions to be raised about the role of the expert. Despite the demands that are put on me to tell people what the text means, I try to resist offering a neat solution, not least because I firmly believe that there is every possibility that those who participate in the Bible study will have insights open to them which will be every bit as profound as anything that I can offer, and frequently more so. The primary task is to enable that to happen. I look for ways in which participants in biblical interpretation can utilize or appropriate my expertise as a professor of Holy Scripture as well as the mutual support, insight and constraints of reading together in community. It is not at all clear how to employ a professional exegete. Frequently there is either a demand for the expert to pronounce or to expound on a subject and for him or her to function as problem-solver rather than facilitator.

A parallel situation is described by Gerald West[5] in an account of his work with grassroots Bible study in South Africa. He describes the careful and subtle way in which he as an academic was part of the process of biblical interpretation. The primary thing he got people to do was to attend to the detail of the text and to check a tendency to wander from it. He describes his role as a facilitator as an enabler of forms of criticism which would, if asked, require him to provide resources on the kind of situation, community and society which produced the text. The familiar resources of modern academic biblical study were not used as a 'way in' to the text, however. Rather, the Bible study started with the life interests of the participants. The task of biblical scholars is not to do the reading for ordinary readers, nor simply to accept uncritically their readings. Rather, it is to read the Bible, as he puts it, *with* ordinary readers. In so doing one has to be as aware as one can be of one's own interests, and discern and engage with the power relations implicit in the reading process. Andrew Curtis's research in inner-city Sydney has also demonstrated the way in which untrained readers can use and contribute to biblical interpretation from their experience.[6]

There is a continuing need to provide those basic tools which are needed to 'allow the faculties to act'. Ancient Jewish and Christian interpreters contented themselves with offering exegetical guidelines as a way of enabling interpretation of the Scripture to take place rather than doing the job for people, which most commentaries tend to do, suggesting to the reader how to go about making the connections and using the text as a gateway to God's way for themselves. Nevertheless, as scholars like Erasmus and Tyndale realized, there is a constant need to enable biblical literacy by providing the tools necessary for the exploration to take place:

- assessment of the various manuscripts of the Bible;
- translation;
- the provision of the circumstances in which text and experience can be explored, the testing of those explorations in the light of the gospel;
- careful consideration which helps challenge lazy, self-indulgent or superficial reflection;
- the different understandings and misunderstandings down the centuries which can inform and guide contemporary readings;
- the use of historical imagination to aid understanding and reflection on the text.

We should pause over the use of the phrase 'careful reflection' in this context. Exegesis in the contemporary world has come to mean the close reading of the text. Nevertheless, the analytical and critical may not be the best way of understanding the Bible. This point is well made by the following quotation:

> There are two ways of reading. The first is when one reads and puts oneself and one's mind in control of the text, trying to subject its meaning to one's own understanding and then comparing it with the understanding of others.
>
> The second is when one reads putting the text on a level above oneself, trying to bring one's mind into submission to its meaning, and even setting up the text as judge over oneself, counting it as a higher criterion.
>
> The first way is suitable for any book in the world, whether it be a world of science or of literature. The second is indispensable in reading the Bible.
>
> The first way gives humans mastery over the world, which is their natural role. The second gives God mastery as the all-wise and all-powerful creator.
>
> But if we confuse the roles of these two methods, we stand to lose from them both. For if we read science and literature as we should the Gospel, we grow small in stature, our academic ability diminishes and our dignity among the rest of creation dwindles.
>
> And if we read the Bible as we should science, we understand and feel God to be small, the divine being appears limited and His awesomeness fades. Thus we acquire a false sense of our own superiority over divine things, and this is the very same forbidden thing that Adam committed in the beginning.[7]

Down the centuries there have been two poles of exegesis: letter and spirit. Close reading of the text can be so preoccupied with the letter of the text that its call to repentance, its offer of hope, can be missed. If we concentrated on close reading only, we would risk missing the importance that Paul (among others) places on the spirit which gives life rather than the letter which kills. Fear of the 'spiritual exegesis' of the radicals since the Reformation should not diminish the central role it must play in the exegesis of Scripture. When I read the Gospels in the contemporary academy I am surrounded by a plethora of interpretative approaches, but I approach the text as a problem. Scripture is treated as a problem which the 'enlightened' interpreter can solve. The emphasis in criticism is on analysis and not enough on silence, contemplation and imagination. If I read the Bible, say, as part of the Ignatian Exercises, I put myself in a very different relationship to the text: of hearer, of subject, even of suppliant. The attitude of mind is very different. The challenge, in this case, is to oneself in the first instance rather than to the Scriptures.

Of course, modern readers, however much they are committed to the 'receptionist' approach, will find themselves at times perplexed and resistant to Scripture. They will engage in analysis and explanation, puzzling over the way it overlaps, or not, as the case may be, with their contemporary experience of life. The kind of attitude I have in mind is that which Coleridge wrote about in his words: 'in the Bible there is more that finds me than I have experienced in all other books put together'. Coleridge feared those who elevated the Bible and its details as much as those who dissected the text of Scripture and thereby killed its spirit. The bibliolaters and the textual analysts have this in common: they do not allow themselves to be in that passive mode, to allow the Bible to (to quote William Blake's words) 'rouze the faculties to act'.

Now that will not always work. Many times we shall find ourselves in the position of not engaging with the text.

Many people have said to me when I have told them that I am interested in the Apocalypse that they find the book barbarous and off-putting and that it should not form part of a Christian canon. There are two responses. First of all, what is it about us in our time and place that we cannot engage with the book? Have we a view of Christianity that is so safe and cosy that we cannot see the way in which the gospel, with all its stories and metaphors, holds up a mirror to our world and reflects a picture of injustice and disorder where we only see comfort and order? But, second, is God calling us to a task of obedient receptivity in which we learn to find images and stories which capture what the Spirit says to the churches much as John found himself using images which doubtless were part of the mental furniture of his day? That was what Blake was doing in his illuminated books. The mistake would be to suppose that that task is finished and that all we have to do is interpret what is past. What we need to do is to go on finding, or better allowing ourselves to be receptive to God showing us, ever-new ways of communicating the challenge and comfort of the gospel.

4
Reception history

Reception history is the bringing together of the variety of ways in which, down the centuries, texts have been 'received' and 'used'.

A key figure in recent developments is Ulrich Luz, of Switzerland. Luz wants to plot the understanding of texts not in terms of ideas, conclusions, literary comparisons or analyses, but rather in terms of what he calls the *Wirkungen* of a text – the text's results, operations, outcomes, results, effects.[8] He sees every reader being in a succession of readers through history, who each bring their own interests and demands:

> When real readers fill in the hollow form of a text, they bring with them their own selves, their person, their biography, their religion, their experiences, their analysis of society. Whoever, thus burdened, fills up a text's empty form, will also harass and twist it (*strapazieren und verbiegen*) as far as they can.[9]

Luz compares this with the South American Severino Croatto who speaks of 'entering into the text with presuppositions as to its meaning'. This demands that we clarify our own situation – 'whence I come, and who I have become through history'. It demands that I hold to my horizon, which will also help to clarify where others have come from and who they have become through history. Thus, the study of workings-history reminds us 'to stand by our own particularity, and not to interpret biblical texts as vaguely "neutral", but rather to see them as part of what we are as Christians today'.

Reception history[10]
Christine E. Joynes

The various methods for reading Mark in this part of our volume take as their starting-point the assumption that the gospel should be recognized as relevant in our present context. The reader is therefore encouraged to bring to the text questions such as 'How do I respond to this biblical passage?' or 'How does Mark's Gospel impact upon my current (twenty-first-century) situation?' However, focusing only upon the present runs the risk of over-looking the important contribution that the past has made to our contemporary situation. Some further reflection on the relationship between past and present readings of Mark can therefore enrich our discussion. Reception history provides a useful tool for this task.[11]

Reception history is a method of reading the Bible that bridges the gap between past and present by highlighting the different ways in which the Bible has been interpreted throughout history.[12] It seeks to investigate the impact of biblical texts across the centuries, because it 'is based on the premise that how people have interpreted, and been influenced by, a sacred text like the Bible is often as interesting and important as what the text originally meant'.[13]

Identifying Mark's reception history is complicated by the Gospel's synoptic nature, since the tendency of interpreters has been to harmonize the Gospels and give preference to the fuller accounts of Matthew, Luke and John.[14]

Nevertheless, alongside these harmonizations, there remains a rich variety of extant material that is specifically designated as Marcan, ranging from Pseudo-Jerome's commentary on Mark to Osvaldo Golijov's *La Pasión según San Marcos*. As the following overview aims to demonstrate, such interpretations contribute to our understanding of Mark's Gospel today.

Defining the present through the past

By investigating the use and influence of Mark's Gospel in the past, the interpreter becomes aware of continuities and divergences in the streams of tradition that have surfaced between the time when a biblical text such as Mark was written and our own contemporary context. Moreover, this investigation is highly significant, for, as Gadamer pointed out, our own consciousness has been formed by the content of this temporal gap.[15] Similarly, Prickett observes:

> Our twenty-first-century Bible is the product not merely of the Gospel writers' reflections on the life of Jesus and their interpretations of the Hebrew Bible. It has been enriched by Augustine, by Anselm, Dante, Shakespeare, Donne, Herbert, Milton, Lowth, Coleridge, Kierkegaard, Browning, Maurice, Hopkins, Arnold, Eliot, Barth, Lewis, Auerbach, Auden, and a host of other critics, theologians, philosophers, novelists and poets – a few of whom we have read and can identify, but also a multitude of others whose contributions have been invisibly filtered down to us. It is not so much a case of, 'if we can see further, it is because we stand on the shoulders of giants'. We *do* stand on the shoulders of giants: we *should* be able to see further – the direction in which we look is, however, up to us.[16]

So we find that the polyphony of history is an integral feature of the Bible. Reception history reminds us that we are not impartial observers operating in an ahistoric space. By investigating the impact of past interpretations, we come to understand our own contemporary situation much more clearly and discover who we are. Through reception history, we are therefore better equipped to clarify the pre-assumptions which as interpreters we bring to Mark's Gospel, and to recognize our own situatedness in a particular time and place. As Nicholls comments:

> Understanding involves the interpreter as a person and so involves the context of that person in culture and tradition. This is not just some weary assertion that we can never be free of our own prejudices and limits, it is a positive celebration of our own human identity, our human finitude, as the arena in which we seek (and potentially find) understanding.[17]

Enlarging the horizons of biblical interpreters

A further contribution of reception history is to prompt us to rethink who we categorize as biblical interpreters. As Prickett's quotation highlights, historical instances of the Bible's use encompass interpretations from a wide range of contexts and media, incorporating readings outside the academy, from both Church and culture. For example, reception history frequently demonstrates how individuals and communities have been affected by Mark's Gospel and have sought to embody it in their lives. This is a distinctive feature of reception history, broadening the horizon of material traditionally classed as 'biblical interpretation'. Artists, writers and composers are also included as biblical interpreters alongside the academic and the religious believer. We are thereby reminded that understanding a biblical text occurs not simply through elucidation of its statements but by engaging all the senses and involving the whole human being.[18]

This widening of the boundary of biblical interpretation opens our eyes to the horizons of others. Reception history prompts us to examine Catholic, Protestant, Anabaptist, and feminist readings of the same text and leads us to understand more of how the Bible has shaped these various identities. Engaging with the past is therefore not simply a matter of self-understanding, but also of understanding others through the rich variety of biblical interpretations that have emerged. Through this experience our own horizons are enlarged.

Engaging with the multivalent text

A brief foray into the reception history of Mark produces an array of interpretations and highlights the dynamic nature of the Bible: it is not a static text with a single meaning. This is illustrated below in my essay 'John the Baptist's death: irrelevant legend or political challenge?' We find the Bible speaking to new people in different situations and being interpreted in fresh ways. Biblical interpretation is therefore a journey of perpetual discovery. Thus Ford notes:

> The biblical text itself is a new communicative performance which embraces fresh elements but still can only act as an indicator of the full richness to which it testifies. This very *undetermination of the text* opens the way for generation after generation of interpretation in many modes, from commentary and liturgy to drama, ethics and systematic theology.[19]

We can celebrate the plurality of past interpretations as testimony to the dynamic nature of the biblical text; at the same time we are also confronted with the ambiguity of the Bible. The reception history of Mark reveals fascinating ways in which gaps in the text have been filled by different interpreters. The motives, actions and consequences of features that are implicit or unspecified in the biblical text are elaborated in a vast number of directions. This variety of possible readings of Mark alerts us to competing interpretations and challenges us also to adjudicate between them. Examining how to arbitrate between such competing interpretations would require a separate essay; nevertheless, it is noteworthy that reception history makes a significant contribution to this broader issue of interpretation.

Conclusion

This short overview has attempted to illustrate some of the ways in which reception history enriches our interpretation of Mark today. By engaging with interpretations from across the centuries we find:

> The ugly ditch between past and present [is] transformed into a highly diverse landscape with ups and downs, unexpected views and a wealth of wonderful and sometimes strange flowers. The interpreter of today is in one very specific place in this landscape.[20]

Through an appreciation of the use, influence and impact of Mark in the past, we become aware of the specificity and particularity of our own readings. As a result of broadening the category of biblical interpretation, reception history also leads us to encounter the gospel in unfamiliar places, thereby enlarging our vision. The assortment of interpretations uncovered by reception history points us to the dynamic, and also ambiguous, nature of the Marcan text. The past therefore shapes and transforms our interpretation of Mark's Gospel in the present, and through reception history we become aware of the rich interpretative potential of the Gospel.

5
Practice interpretation

What practice criticism adds to reception criticism is the insight – or the argument – that people do not hear stories or tell stories simply because of their own opinions or beliefs about them or their commitment to the community which holds them dear. They primarily value and tell stories because they have some present interest in the stories, which derives from their present lives of discipleship and community living. Practice criticism seeks to add the actual practices of discipleship and community activity to the elements that determined why certain stories were valued, the shape that those stories were given, and the slants that certain words, phrases and references could acquire because of the interests, activities or functions that characterized the disciple's and the community's life.

The basic argument of gospel practice criticism or interpretation is simple enough: if the Gospel describes 'the acts of Jesus' or 'Jesus' projects', then our interest is with consequent 'acts' and 'projects', which continue to reflect or are based on the primary acts and projects.

Every such act takes place in a specific social, cultural, ethnic, class location, so that whenever it takes place, its happening makes some people 'interested parties'. Such sectional or economic or group interests are in the text's stories, which themselves describe divine or divinely motivated divisive or conflictual activities or acts. The 'imitation' of God or Jesus is thus transformed from the areas of motive, spirituality and inwardness, with which Christians and churches are so much at home today, into the areas of intentional practice, contrary embodiment, prophetic entrepreneurship and alternative community creation, which are in fact (it seems to me) the contemporary equivalents of the divine practice(s) revealed in Scripture, certainly so far as secular, analytical or phenomenological analysis is concerned.

> Practice is the way the scriptural tradition is carried on in history, because Practice was the way in which it originated. A story or a passage of scripture functions as an interpretative and provocative medium between action and action, between practice and practice. The text is the essential 'mediator' or 'medium of transference' from the action behind the biblical passage, over into the action awaiting the contemporary disciples acting in faith.[21]

A particular area in which this use of gospel passages for ministry and mission discernment and planning has been developed is that of urban mission and urban theology.[22]

The piece developed here is the fourth in a series on 'Outworkings' in the *Expository Times*, all of which are now published in *Outworkings: Gospel Practice and Interpretation* (Sheffield: Urban Theology Unit, 2005), pp. 33–6.

Practice interpretation
John Vincent

Gospel practice criticism seeks to develop insights into the ways in which the originating practice of God, Jesus, disciples or Christian community recorded in Scripture provoke, inspire or support corresponding or identified practice in a reader's community and discipleship, in early church times, historically and today.

As John Riches says, the aim is 'the embodiment of these texts in the lives and actions of their readers, the continuing body of Jesus' disciples', so that they 're-appropriate the story in terms which correspond to their own contexts'. The gospel stories 'require imaginative elaboration, and in that process they come to life and are realized in many different ways in different reading groups and communities'.[23]

One crucial point is at what stage theological reflection is appropriate. I think that liberation theology's four stages of See–Judge–Act–Reflect is the correct one – that is, that seeing a contemporary need, judging it to be a gospel issue, and acting in relation to it, all come before reflection – indeed, are all part of the process on which the reflection takes place. What I call 'theological practice' *precedes* theological reflection, I think.[24]

Another crucial point is how biblical studies as a whole takes on board not only the long history of the 'reception' of stories, but even more how proper account can be taken of the present-day 'reception' being practised by disciples today. As Christopher Rowland has said:

> It is not that the 'action-reflection' model is invariably going to offer the right meaning of a text, but it does at least lay on us an obligation to take such insight with as much seriousness as we might the effusions of one who is recognised as an expert in exegesis. The implication of the liberationist perspective is that academic endeavour might not, in some instances at least, offer us the best or most appropriate understanding of a text, and that one who is engaged in working out the meaning of the text for today might often capture the spirit of the text better.[25]

We need to go on experimenting with these crucial issues. Meantime, the work of 'Bible practitioners' in the contemporary world goes on, and the resulting insights need to be shared and carried forward. Let me share a recent experience of it – an example of contemporary practice criticism, in which we began to refine a methodology for it.

In October 2004 I worked with Ched Myers at a three-day consultation with 60 community workers and ministers in Lawrence, Massachusetts, on the theme 'Working with the gospel in the inner city'. Ched lectured on 'Aspects of the inner city: community organising from the periphery', with sessions on 'biblical and social analysis', 'The social architecture of insulation', 'Local parish as capacity builder', and 'Social reconstruction'.[26] I lectured on 'Working in the inner city with Mark's Gospel', with sessions on 'Beginning from the bottom (Mark 1)', 'Getting it going on the street (Mark 2)', 'Gospel praxis community (Mark 3)' and 'Everything we ever needed to know (Mark 4)'.[27]

The conclusion of some of the participants was: as Ched tells the stories of the strategies, people, motivations and politics of community development among deprived people in contemporary cities, we hear the stories of Jesus and his disciples in the Gospel of Mark; as John tells the stories of the strategies, people, motivations and politics of Jesus and his disciples in the Gospel of Mark, we hear the stories of community development in contemporary cities.

Our work together led to my conclusion that we are developing the beginnings of a new methodology, though we lack any systematization of it as yet. There are four elements:

1 *Situation analysis of the passage.*[28] Here we study the *context*, the location, the situation, the place the story occupies as a secular phenomenon. This is the view *around* the reality. The decisive question is: what is all around the story that determines its position in geographical, ethnographic, political, economic and cultural locations?

2 *Practice analysis of the passage.*[29] Here, we seek to discover and reactivate the *happening*, the event, the incidents described and provoked by it. This is the

view *within* the reality. The decisive question is, 'With what other stories of people doing things, which get told as significant, does this story provoke comparison?'

3 *Endogenous analysis of the passage.*[30] Here, we feel after the *content*, the core, the pith, what comes up from inside, which indicates the nature and motivation of the happening. This is the view *deeper into* the reality. The decisive question is: what arises from within it which bespeaks the inner spirituality, ethos, intentionality, commitment, style?

4 *Political analysis of the passage.*[31] Here, we move into analysis of the *politics*, the strategy, the historical purpose, that the passage indicates. This is the view *out from* the reality. We want to know what predictable or plannable political and organizational strategies are indicated.

The four elements of analysis are then taken to our own contemporary situations, where we ask of them similar questions.

1 Situation analysis. *Where* is this story at home? *What contexts* are like it? Who today feels especially at home in this biblical situation?
2 Practice analysis. *With what* is this story at home? *What practice* is like it? Who today has practice or happenings like these particular scriptural ones?
3 Endogenous analysis. *With whom* is this story at home? *What people* are like it? Who today has similar 'fire within' to the people in the biblical action?
4 Political analysis. *What movement* is this story like? *What policies* does it empower? What movement today would be coherent with the biblical strategy?

All this is tentative, and needs supplementing from the experiences of others. Contributions from fellow labourers are most welcome.[32]

6
Stories to live by

All the models and methods we have considered put an emphasis on three factors, both at the scriptural end and at the contemporary end. First, what was the context then, and what is our context now? Second, what was the purpose of the writer then, and what is ours now? Third, what did people actually do then, and what might we actually do now, faced with these stories and texts?

Ched Myers' piece shows how these are not mere theoretical questions. He begs us to get three things clear. First, all these strategies are part of a proper attempt to claim back the stories for people, for disciples, for practitioners, for the non-privileged. Second, it all means that we have to welcome the fact that we must settle for talking about the text's meaning for specific people, including ourselves, rather than having a definitive reading. Third, it all comes down in the end to what we do with the stories in our lives.

Our volume is, after all, only and sufficiently the record of what some contemporary readers/hearers/disciples have done or have tried to do, impelled by Mark's records. The writers knew about the historical and literary 'problems' with the text, but in the end said, 'Yes, this is something I can go with.' And that is, of course, the invitation of our volume to the reader – what is there in Mark that you can 'go with'? What are the stories you can live by?

Ched Myers' piece is a shortened version of an article, 'Stories to Live by', published in *Sojourners* (March/April 2000), pp. 32–5, 51.

Stories to live by
Ched Myers

Can we reach hearts and minds within and outside of the Church with the biblical good news that is older and deeper and wiser than presidential press releases or commercial hucksting? I suggest three ways we might re-engage the Bible for the next generation. First, we will have to recover it as a 'people's book' through practices of populist literacy. Second, Christians will have to improve our willingness and ability to discuss differing readings of Scripture. Finally, we must more faithfully embody our interpretations in order to make the Word flesh in our world.

Over the last three decades, base communities around the developing world have re-animated ordinary people to understand and apply the stories of Scripture. This movement, however, has not 'trickled up' significantly to the developed world. Perhaps this is because of our socialization into the culture of being spectators in our highly technological society. Our over-reliance on experts, whether they are plumbers or politicians, has rendered us passive. Our feelings of alienation or inadequacy towards the Bible is perhaps due less to clericalism – though that continues to be a problem in many Christian traditions – than to the modernist influence of academic culture.

The guild of professional biblical scholarship feels increasingly less accountability to living communities of faith or a responsibility to translate their finding to the 'laity'. Their complex linguistic, historical and literary methodologies confound regular church folk, convincing many that they are not equipped to study the Bible on their own. Others simply reject biblical criticism altogether and retrench in simplistic – if highly formulaic – popular Bible study formats, blissfully ignorant of 'hermeneutical problems'.

Throughout the ages this 'people's book' keeps getting expropriated by the expert scribal classes. Jesus himself complained bitterly of this betrayal (Mark 2.25; 7.9; 12.24, 35). It is true that the biblical stories originate in times and cultures far removed from our own, and that we need to take thoughtful care in our handling of these texts. It is also true, however, that we all have a certain 'narrative competence' that enables us to interpret stories in meaningful ways, using the power of imagination, experience and analogy – no matter what our level of education.

If we are to err, let it be on the side of trusting our people with these stories, because the Bible was written for and about ordinary people, especially the poor. A strategy of 'populist re-enfranchisement' must, of course, encourage disciplines of study and reflection that will nurture biblical literacy. The popular education techniques pioneered by Paulo Freire are crucial here: starting with what we know, drawing from our experience of the world, questioning and being questioned by texts we are studying.

For example, we can start with cultural texts from our world – a newspaper, a cartoon, an advertisement – in order to practise interpreting symbols, implied messages, or the retelling of older stories. Ordinary people are in fact very sophisticated in their ability to decipher the hieroglyphics of modern media discourses. Such exercises will create positive momentum that can carry over when we turn to cultural narratives that are not as familiar to us, as is the case with the Bible.

With a little encouragement, we can learn to pay attention to form as well as content in biblical literature, to genre, to plot, character and setting. We can become mindful of context, including the relations of social power and whose voice is being heard, both in the biblical text and in our world as readers.

Everyone can do this – and everyone's input in important. Bible study is a community venture. Like any other discipline, it takes practice, devotion and commitment. We need to learn – and relearn – our way around the whole of the biblical narrative, especially the Old Testament. And we need to keep the process fun, interactive and in constant relationship to our concrete situation. In populist Bible study we may get things wrong, but we nevertheless have the right – and duty – to struggle with these texts.

How can differences be discussed? A given interpretation must necessarily be argued with care (from the Latin *arguere*, to make clear); after all, important issues are at stake. But we also need the discipline of conversation (from the Middle English *conversen*, meaning to associate with; also from the Latin *conversus*, meaning to turn around). Conversation holds within it the possibility of mutual conversion. This requires that partners commit themselves to two disciplines.

First, each positional group must be willing to articulate and to examine honestly the interests and values that underlie its reading of Scripture. The reality of 'interpretive interests' is recognized in Scripture itself: 'A lawyer stood up to test Jesus. "Teacher, what must I do to inherit eternal life?" Jesus answered him, "In the Law, what is written? How do you read it?"' (Luke 10.26).

Jesus' counter-question seeks to investigate not only the text, but the community of interpretation as well. In this case, the lawyer cites the text (though

Luke 10.27 is already a conflation of Deuteronomy 6.5 and Leviticus 19.18), but it is his reading of that text that is at issue – namely his agnosticism on the matter of who constitutes a 'neighbour' (10.29).

No matter how passionate our viewpoint may be, we should always remain open to others, because Scripture itself is multifaceted and further reflection or different perspectives may yield a more compelling reading. After all, our contexts as readers change through time and space. The biblical tradition was itself in formation for a millennium and has engendered a rich and diverse interpretive legacy for another two millennia. One need only study the history of the interpretation of any biblical passage down through the centuries to see how contingent our readings are.

The Church has not been particularly well served by the long and necessarily combative hermeneutic tradition (embraced both by authoritarian conservatives and liberal academics) that assumes a text has only one 'correct' reading. Fortunately, postmodernism has exposed the fallacy of claims to either doctrinal or historical–critical objectivity. Women, ethnic communities and churches of the poor have offered readings that not only reveal facets of Scripture that white male academics and clerics could never see, but that also unmask the hidden interpretive interests of those professional classes!

Questing after (or insisting upon) the 'one true reading' is neither the only nor the best way to honour the authority of Scripture. Indeed it may concede too much power to the interpreter. We Christians might do better to rediscover a more Jewish approach. The rabbinic tradition, broadly speaking, has seemed more comfortable with the notion that only a multiplicity of approaches can do justice to the marvellously deep and wide spectrum of meaning(s) in the sacred texts. This both preserves the text as the centre of the community and allows us to offer our various interpretive efforts to the body for discernment. This perspective is ritualized by Jews on the feast of Simchat Torah, when the scrolls are taken by synagogue elders into the middle of the congregation and held lovingly while everyone dances in celebration around them. It always brings me to tears.

Embracing pluralism does not preclude critical engagement with other interpretive positions. There are matters of integrity and justice at stake, and not all readings are benign or respectful. After all, Scripture acknowledges that even the devil can cite Scripture (Luke 4.9–12). It is the responsibility of scriptural communities to guard against our natural tendency to use texts to justify ourselves. As Dietrich Bonhoeffer put it, Christians need to learn to read Scripture 'over against ourselves' rather than simply 'for ourselves'.

Thus we must allow Scripture to question, as well as to support, the positions we take. 'Is this not the reason you are wrong, that you know neither the scriptures nor the power of God?' (Mark 12.24). Jesus' sharp query is addressed to all of us, challenging us to move beyond rigid interpretative positions and toward creative self-examination.

The best way to persuade others of our reading of Scripture, of course, is not by telling it, but by showing it. True biblical interpretation is about convictions, not abstract opinions. 'Opinions are the stuff of debate and discussion', writes James McClendon. 'They may require thought, but they require no commitment. Convictions, on the other hand, are less readily expressed but more tenaciously held . . . They are our persuasions, the beliefs we embody with some reason, guiding all our thought, shaping our lives.'

This means our conversations about Scripture should focus on our actual practices and what we are willing to live by, and steer away from theoretical imperatives or what people in general ought to do. A classic statement of this 'epistemology of embodiment' is found in the Lucan exchange between Jesus and the lawyer referred to earlier. Twice the scribe gives Jesus the 'right' theory (Luke 10.27, 37a); twice Jesus responds with an invitation to practise: 'You have answered correctly; do this and you will live' (10.28); 'Go and do likewise' (10.37b).

Postmodern America hardly needs more shrill opinions – we have popular talk radio for that. The Bible invites us to join Jesus in making the Word become flesh (John 1.1ff.), exegeting the text with our lives. 'No one has ever seen God; the Son . . . has made him known [Greek *exegesato*]', says John 1.18. 'Unless Christian communities are committed to embodying their scriptural interpretation,' write Stephen Fowl and Gregory Jones, 'the Bible loses its character as scripture.' How does one argue that Jesus meant what he said about love of enemies, or the last being first, or the way of the cross, except by trying to experiment with such truth with our own lives?

'Their evil is mighty', concludes Silko's elder, 'but it can't stand up to our stories.' This native wisdom is good theology for Christians. But only if we know our stories, listen to one another in our quest to understand what they require of us, and embody them in the world.

Notes

1 See John Vincent, *Situation Analysis* (Sheffield: Urban Theology Unit, 1973), rev. Christine Dodd (1991), Ian K. Duffield (1998).
2 John Vincent, 'Imaginative Identification', *Epworth Review* 23.3 (September 1996), pp. 14–20.
3 Ian K. Duffield, 'From Bible to Ministry Projects' in *Bible and Practice*, ed. Chris Rowland and John Vincent (Sheffield: Urban Theology Unit, 2001), pp. 66–76, pp. 66–7.
4 Christopher Rowland, 'In this Place' in *Reading from this Place*, ed. Fernando F. Segovia and Mary Ann Tolbert (Minneapolis, Fortress Press, 1995), Vol. 2, pp. 168–80, p. 172.
5 Gerald West, *The Academy of the Poor: Towards a Dialogical Reading of the Bible* (Sheffield: Sheffield Academic Press, 1999).

6 Andrew Curtis, 'Re-Reading the Gospel of Luke Today: From a First Century Urban Writing Site to a Twentieth Century Urban Reading Site', Open University dissertation, 1998.

7 Words of Abba Matta El-Meskeen, founder of the Monastery of St Macarius, Wadi El-Natrun, Egypt and printed in their monthly journal *St Mark*, November 1981.

8 Ulrich Luz, *Matthew in History: Interpretation, Influence, Effects* (Minneapolis: Fortress Press, 1994), p. 3.

9 Ulrich Luz, 'Kann die Bibel heute noch Grundlage für die Kirche sein?', *New Testament Studies* 44.1 (July 1998), pp. 317–39, p. 330 (my translation).

10 An extended version of this essay can be found in *The Reception History of Mark's Gospel* (Oxford: The Farmington Institute, 2005).

11 See further the new Blackwell Bible Commentary series, edited by John Sawyer, David Gunn, Christopher Rowland and Judith Kovacs, with its focus on reception history.

12 For a helpful discussion of the difference between 'reception history' and 'history of interpretation', see Mary Callaway, 'What's the Use of Reception History?', at <www.bbibcomm.net/news/latest.html> (accessed 27 February 2005). On the issue of how to define reception history, see also Rachel Nicholls, 'Is *Wirkungsgeschichte* (or Reception History) a kind of intellectual *Parkour* (or Freerunning)?' at <www.bbibcomm.net/news/latest.html> (accessed 20 November 2005).

13 Judith Kovacs and Christopher Rowland, *Revelation: The Apocalypse of Jesus Christ* (Oxford: Blackwell, 2004), p. xi. There is not space here for a detailed discussion of the relationship between historical criticism and reception history, but it is worth noting that though they are contrasting methodologies they are not necessarily mutually exclusive.

14 For further discussion of the difficulties for the reception history of Mark raised by its synoptic relationship, see my Farmington paper, *The Reception History of Mark's Gospel*.

15 See further, Hans Georg Gadamer, *Truth and Method* (London: Sheed & Ward, 1975).

16 Stephen Prickett, 'Polyphonic Carrolling: Heteroglossia, Pluralism and Editing the Bible', in Alastair G. Hunter and Philip R. Davies (eds.), *Sense and Sensitivity: Essays on Reading the Bible in Memory of Robert Carroll* (Sheffield: Sheffield Academic Press, 2002), p. 349.

17 Nicholls, '*Wirkungsgeschichte*', p. 8.

18 Cf. Ulrich Luz, *Matthew 1—7: A Commentary*, trans. Wilhelm C. Linss (Minneapolis: Augsburg, 1989), p. 98.

19 David Ford, 'Dramatic Theology: York, Lambeth and Cambridge' in Jeremy Begbie (ed.), *Sounding the Depths: Theology through the Arts* (London: SCM Press, 2002), p. 75. My italics.

20 Ulrich Luz, *Studies in Matthew* (Grand Rapids: Eerdmans, 2005), p. 353.

21 John Vincent, *Outworkings: Gospel Practice and Interpretation* (Sheffield: Urban Theology Unit, 2005), p. 3.

22 Cf. John Vincent, 'An Urban Hearing for the Gospel' in C. Rowland and J. Vincent (eds.), *Gospel from the City* (Sheffield: Urban Theology Unit, 1997), pp. 105–16; John Vincent, *Hope from the City* (London: Epworth Press, 2000),

pp. 158–68; Andrew Davey in *Urban Christianity and Global Order* (London: SPCK, 2001), pp. 66–86; Andrew Davey, Michael Northcott, Ian K. Duffield, Stuart Jordan and John Vincent, 'Reflections and Discernments' in *Faithfulness in the City*, ed. J. Vincent (Hawarden: Monad Press, 2003), pp. 229–306; Laurie Green, *Urban Ministry and the Kingdom of God* (London: SPCK, 2003), pp. 81–95; Tim Stratford (ed.), *Worship, Window of the Urban Church* (London: SPCK, 2006); John Vincent, *Theology from the City* (London: Epworth Press, forthcoming).

23 John Riches, 'Introduction to John J Vincent's "Outworkings" ', *Expository Times* 116.5 (February 2005), pp. 153–54.

24 Cf. John Vincent, 'Theological Practice', *Theology* (September 2004), pp. 343–50.

25 Christopher Rowland *et al.*, 'Practical Exegesis in Context' in *Bible and Practice*, pp. 10–26, p. 12.

26 Cf. Ched Myers' earlier work, *Who Will Roll Away the Stone? Discipleship Queries for First World Christians* (Maryknoll, NY: Orbis Books, 1994).

27 J. D. Davies and J. J. Vincent, *Mark at Work* (Bible Reading Fellowship, 1986), pp. 21–38, 47–53, has some work on Mark 1—4. For Mark 2, see now my article, 'Outworkings: Disciple Practice Today', *Expository Times* 118.4 (January 2007).

28 For situation analysis, see notes 11, 12 and 13 above.

29 For practice analysis, see *Outworkings*. I have tried this approach with the story of Jesus in Mark in *Radical Jesus* (rev. edn, Sheffield: Ashram Press, 2004).

30 For Endogenous Analysis, cf. my paper, 'Endogenous Theology', *Theology* (forthcoming).

31 For political analysis, see Ched Myers, *Who Will Roll Away the Stone?* and his classic commentary, *Binding the Strong Man: A Political Reading of Mark's Story of Jesus* (Maryknoll, NY: Orbis Books, 1988). Also see Timothy Gorringe, 'Bible and Subversion' in Rowland and Vincent (eds.), *Bible and Practice*, pp. 44–51.

32 Contributions may be sent to me at Urban Theology Unit, 210 Abbeyfield Road, Sheffield S4 7AZ.

4

The essays

JOHN VINCENT

Our essays come from widely differing people and places. Each of us comes at the text from our own viewpoint, though together we belong to a contemporary movement to see Mark in our own situations today, to 'use' Mark in one or more of the ways just indicated, to see Mark's 'action' picked up in our time.

We 'use' Mark as a companion in our own lives, vocations, communities and politics, each one of us in unique ways – some of us more in terms of discipleship, some of us more in terms of community and politics, at least as starting points!

Part 2: In discipleship and vocation

In the first pieces in Part 2, five of us in varying ways indicate how Mark's pictures of Jesus and discipleship have influenced the ways we have felt called to live our lives as disciples, and the ways in which we see our personal vocations; three of us then report on how Mark is heard within wider Christian groups.

Andrew Parker sees Mark's Jesus as someone calling others to join him 'on the road', on a journey to the margins, to participate in the divine covenant with 'those who fall or are pulled out of the net'. The parables are shown to be 'exposures' of the situation of the afflicted, the powerless, who cannot act, but who are merely 'reactive'. Jesus places himself in solidarity with the outcasts, thus fulfilling 'Israel's destiny to be the faithful servant of the God of the marginals'. To be a disciple today is to do likewise, and become, like Jesus, a grass-roots activist.

David Blatherwick identifies with the first disciples, leaving behind their careers, going into the unknown, being alongside the outcasts, giving themselves to the dream of a 'richer, fairer, more humane society'. Mark's Jesus does not found a church, but 'creates a body of people who will carry his message and continue his work – and do it with generosity of spirit, perseverance and great courage'. David, as a minister and a church person, reflects the agony, confusion and incompetence of Mark's first disciples, committed to bringing in a new world, which they only mess up.

John Fenton reflects on Mark's comment that 'the time for them to fast' suggests that Mark favours a view of discipleship as 'the *via negativa*, the renunciation of the world, the flesh and the devil'. Fasting is part of 'the cost' of discipleship. In Mark, 'the first half is the offer of healing; the second is the cost of it'. 'Losing life' is really 'destroying life'. 'Mark assumes that human beings have the ability to transcend themselves and to act to their own disadvantage.'

John Vincent battles with his innate commitment to 'do something useful in life', and relates this to the observations of Jesus about losing life and gaining life, and to Jesus' call to follow. Jesus also emerges as someone who has to 'do something useful in life'. So John follows Jesus in his 'journey downwards', his incarnation into the depths of his own society, down to a place where 'gospel insights and discernments might actually work in practice'. Could this be 'gaining life'?

Mary Cotes sees the strong, distinctive characteristics of the women who feature in Mark's account of the ministry of Jesus, and feels this to be a call to herself to see herself and other women as similarly people who are marginalized or victimized, but who through their initiative (what Jesus calls 'faith') become beneficiaries of Jesus' ministry. From this, she reflects how far this Jesus-style ministry to women on the margins now becomes a privilege for herself to exercise, being now not sociologically 'of the margins'. Do the women at the passion and empty tomb have a more positive picture of co-ministry with Jesus?

In all these five pieces, there emerges a Marcan spirituality of discipleship which the interpreters see as unique, demanding and significant for the world – Parker's life with the marginal, Blatherwick's revelations through service, Fenton's blast against obesity and world hunger, Vincent's unbelieving discoveries 'at the bottom', Cotes's walk with Mark's radical women. In each case, as the feminists say, 'the personal is the political'. The personal practice of gospel alternatives and gospel disciplines effect a double cure – the poor have the Good News, and the affluent self-indulgent world is rejected, at least in these parabolic particulars or people.

These discipleship 'uses' derive from a sense of 'call', coming from the text or parts of it. Can this be partly due to our own personal disposition or context?

Leslie Francis sees in the Marcan passages ways in which people of particular temperaments or personality traits can empathize with stories or characters within them, or even with Jesus himself. Through this empathy, they identify with certain people or actions in the stories, and see themselves reflected in them, and so feel it appropriate to enter into certain actions themselves, which have, they feel, comparisons with the actions that people 'like themselves' entered into in particular gospel passages.

The Bible study groups in Glasgow, described by John Riches and Susan Miller, recall that Mark was originally read by people together. So the study groups 'reunited the book with the community'. John and Susan wrote recently:

> What came out was surprising and enriching. First a call to engage more coura-
> geously and imaginatively in dialogue, creating new opportunities and seek-
> ing to improve the quality and openness of our discourse. Second, a search
> for the 'unconsidered gifts' which can be found inside and outside the church
> and which can help us to face the seemingly overwhelming tasks before us.
> That search is given fresh impetus as we seek the means to bring understand-
> ing and reconciliation to our multi-faith community in Glasgow in the after-
> math of the recent bombings.

Part 3: In community and politics

In Part 3, the prime elements in provoking our responses are in the areas of community and politics. Just as the personal is political in Mark, so also the political is personal. When we discern political or community elements that provoke us, personal stances are required.

So the mission of Jesus has clear implications for missioners today. Like Jesus, Geoffrey Harris finds himself as a missionary taken up by people in need, welcoming every glint of faith, using whatever people offer, rushing urgently to get the message out, calling a group of co-missioners, setting up activities which embody the Kingdom, facing opposition from threatened inter-ests, restoring true community, incorporating the marginalized. Harris sees this as the politics of liberation and community reconciliation – and finds it today in L'Arche and Corrymeela.

Christine Joynes shows how John the Baptist can appear as a model of political empowerment to people facing tyranny or injustice. John's death fore-shadows Jesus' sufferings, and the severed head on a dish signifies the sacred bread on the paten. The dancing girl is either innocent child or erotic provo-cateur. Reception history reminds us that we bring our own pre-assumptions to the text, which can be limiting, but also provocative and empowering, for us today as it has been in the past.

Susan Miller reads Mark as a tract for our ecologically conscious times. Upheavals in the natural world, earthquakes and famines in Mark 13, are 'apoc-alyptic signs of the intensification of the struggle between God and Satan', and culminate in the return of the Son of Man, with a new 'age' for the created world. Jesus' nature parables in Mark 4 preview a time of future abundance and sharing, of the fruitful fig tree and the dying corn bringing a harvest – powerful images and provocations for ecological politics today.

Ched Myers sees two fundamental 'moments' – the in-breaking of God's Kingdom (Mark 1.15) and the outbreak of the Roman–Jewish war (Mark 13). But only the first was the true *kairos* – the war only pretended to be. The first calls disciples to 'Listen!', the second to 'Watch!' Under the first, disciples must heed only the Kingdom of God and its secret workings. Under the second, they must refuse all bogus political leadership that claims that any empire (Caesar or Temple or USA) can pretend to be the Messiah. We need both disciplines for politics today.

Christopher Burdon argues that Mark 'provides a goad to the formation or reformation of community'. He sees the contemporary equivalents to Mark's community as 'small learning groups, activist organizations, local parishes and alternative religious communities'. There is hope for society, Burdon claims, when we have 'a community with no leader, where boundaries are transgressed and where power is exercised in waiting and looking'. An alternative politics appears in the praxis of disciples together.

Ian Wallis tells how a congregation in a deprived North East town took Mark's invitation 'to discover Jesus for themselves and to reach their own conclusions in a comparable way to when he ministered in Galilee and beyond'. Mark's Jesus story becomes the TV 'soap' – 'fast-moving, vivid in characterization, stylistically economical, graphic and eventful, free from introspection, raw and uncut, suited for serialization'. Once brought into the story, we discover 'a faith that won't stretch our humanity beyond where we are able to reach in his company'. We adopt 'Jesus' take on being human, his characterization of personhood, the habitus of faith he embodied'. By this, 'Jesus is reconstituted within the faith of his followers.'

Part 2

MARK IN DISCIPLESHIP AND VOCATION

5

On the road with Mark

ANDREW PARKER

My lifetime's companionship with Mark has not been without its problems. It has, for example, meant that instead of being free to concentrate on Jesus I have found myself increasingly concerned with what the evangelist himself was doing. For, in spite of everything said about 'experiencing the risen Lord', all I know of Jesus has evidently come through Mark or his fellow evangelists. I don't deny that Jesus' spirit can be encountered in people today. It's just that I can only identify this spirit *because* the evangelists have alerted me to what it is. Someone described the situation as rather like that of a driver who on enquiring about the road to Lincoln was told that to make such a journey she would best be advised not to start from where she was! Though the way to Jesus is without doubt complicated by its passage through the evangelists, nothing is gained by pretending there is any alternative route. So I make no apology for discussing this obligatory diversion.

Take Mark's account of Jesus' parable-making. To understand what he is up to we must remind ourselves what parable-making is all about. The parable, and its close relative the complex simile, were common speech forms used throughout the ancient Near East from time immemorial. We can trace them back with certainty to the Sumerian civilization (which is as far back as our records go), and in all probability people were using them much earlier still.[1] Both are members of the illustrative speech form family and, in consequence, are built on the 'one is like another' principle.[2] This being the case, an individual parable or complex simile functions to throw light on a matter which is obscure, by comparing it with some state of affairs which is self-evident. The implication is, of course, that the self-evident illustration and the obscure subject matter exhibit an intrinsic similarity. Thus, for example, a person may help a friend identify the particular flavour of a wine by suggesting that it tastes like blackberries. The only difference between an ordinary simile, like this, and your normal parable or complex simile is in the make-up of the subject matter under discussion. In an ordinary simile it is a mere *characteristic* – the *taste* of a certain wine. In a complex simile it is rather a *phenomenon*. For example, in the story of The Children and the Pet Dogs (Mark 7.27–28) Jesus is clearly talking about the phenomenon of *discrimination*, whereas in her splendid reply the Syrophoenician woman changes the subject to talk instead about the phenomenon of *opportunity*. In a full-blown parable the matter under discussion is even more complex still, being what I call a *logic*. This logic works along the lines that if such and such a situation pertains then common sense, based on everyday experience, dictates that so and so will follow. For example, in the parable of New Wine in Old Wineskins (Mark 2.22), the logic is that *if you put new wine into old skins, then common sense suggests that you are inviting disaster.* That basically is it.[3] Of course, spelling the situation out analytically, as I have just done, may make it sound a bit complicated but it really isn't, for even a child can appreciate when a parable is properly told since the whole object is to make something which is not obvious crystal clear.

Mark starts out well by describing how Jesus told the parable of The Place for a Doctor[4] to reveal how mistaken people were in criticizing him for associating with dubious characters. He continues in this vein, explaining that Jesus' activities stirred up powerful opposition, and how he dealt with the criticisms levelled against him, by telling parables which exposed his critics' bad faith. There are a number of minor problems of course. One sometimes gets the impression that Mark is struggling with his material and that occasionally he finds himself obliged to change or embroider a story to get it into the shape he wants. But on the whole the exercise holds together fairly well.

However, in chapter 4 all this changes. Mark starts brilliantly, for all that. He tells us that Jesus was as usual out and about meeting people where they naturally congregated – on this particular occasion, on the shore of Lake Gennesaret. He implies that Jesus was beginning to become known since he tells us that a fair-sized crowd had gathered, forcing his hero to take to a boat so as to speak to them more comfortably. The whole thing is thoroughly credible right up to the point where Mark tells us about the content of Jesus' discourse. He claims that Jesus taught the crowd from the boat *in parables* and he gives The Sower as an example of one story he used.[5] At this stage I have to confess Mark loses me completely since everything indicates that you can't use parables to address large numbers of people in an extended discourse. There are, of course, many kinds of stories which can be used in such a fashion,[6] but parables are not of their number. For parables function as highly compact and abrupt conversation-stoppers,[7] as Mark himself has already amply demonstrated on three separate occasions.[8] So, clearly, using parables in the sort of situation he now describes would have been utterly pointless. To put it baldly, Mark's claim that Jesus used parables to preach to people is absurd. No communicator would attempt to do anything so silly. Mark, however, tries to make a go of it by pretending that the parable of The Sower was in fact not a true parable but rather a mysterious coded message[9] designed to confuse outsiders. But this in itself is nonsense, first because coded messages are not designed simply to confuse outsiders but rather secretly to inform those in the know, and, second, because, as I have already pointed out, parables are designed to make matters perfectly clear, which means that it would be altogether counter-productive to encode them. Of course some scholars argue that what Mark had in mind was not coded messages but rather riddles, the inference being that Jesus' intention was to enable people to learn important truths by forcing them to solve riddles in which he had hidden them. But this is equally silly, since learning how to answer riddles does not lead a person to take the messages within them seriously. In fact the more I consider the matter the more I am convinced that in describing Jesus as preaching[10] by means of parables Mark made a terrible blunder. That said, I have to grant him one thing: his honesty in admitting that the disciples would have been terribly perplexed by such a performance. My concern, however, is less with what their reaction would have been as with what the Capernaum fisherfolk would have made of it. In my opinion they would quickly have become bored, and dispersed.

Having, for some as yet unknown reason, plumped for this untenable description of Jesus' parable-telling, Mark naturally finds himself in an increasingly awkward position. First he tells us that, when the mystified disciples came to ask Jesus what the story of The Sower was all about, Jesus explained to them that his parables were specifically designed so that people should *not* immediately understand them and that they were aimed at outsiders and not at people like themselves (Mark 4.10–12). However, he then contradicts himself first by going on to suggest that Jesus was disconcerted by their lack of understanding (Mark 4.13) and then by proceeding to tell his disciples three more parables, there being, as far as we can tell, no outsiders present (Mark 4.21–32)! Of course, I am aware that all sorts of ingenious explanations have been put forward to rationalize Mark's handling of the matter, but the fact is that the more I examine it the more I am convinced that *Mark's explanation of Jesus' parable-telling holds no water whatever way you care to look at it.*

There are, as I see it, three possible choices facing a person who comes to such a conclusion. Either you can pretend that Mark is speaking about a heavenly truth which defies human reason. Or you can bid him goodbye and search for better company. Or you can be honest with him as well as true to yourself and try to find out why he got himself into this fix. For my money, the third is the only honourable choice.

Though I found it rather annoying to have to concentrate on Mark rather than on Jesus, as soon as I started to do so I immediately found that the exercise paid dividends. I began to realize that whenever Mark's demonstrations of Jesus' parable-making fall flat it is always because of a mismatch between the story illustration and the subject matter it is supposed to illustrate. What is more, it is always the subject matter that constituted the problem, not the story illustration, for sometimes Mark provides no subject matters at all. This leaves the reader with the necessity of having to guess what it is – or, in the case of The Sower, for Jesus to provide the answer himself, making the whole parabolic exercise rather pointless! At other times Mark provides subject matters that are so general – as in the 'Kingdom parables' for example – that it is difficult for the reader to be sure what they consist of. On other occasions still, the fit between the subject matter that Mark provides and the parable seems to have been achieved only by doctoring the story – as, for example, in The Wedding Guests (Mark 2.19–20) where the bridegroom is inexplicably 'taken away'. All of this indicates but one thing: *people remembered Jesus' stories long after they had forgotten the situations they illustrated*. This meant that early Christian writers were obliged to reconstruct subject matters for them to illustrate (e.g. the stories in Mark 2.15–22 and 3.22–27) or, failing this, find some other non-illustrative way of using them – as allegorical stories for instance (e.g. The Sower).

This new realization helped me regain my trust in my companion Mark. I now realized that he had been working under considerable difficulties and that his strange and inconsistent theory as to why Jesus 'taught in parables' was not due to what he actually knew about Jesus but rather to the unfortunate way in which Jesus' parable sayings had been preserved in the tradition. After all, if you came across the story of The Sower devoid of any context, what would you make of it? In the absence of any obvious way of seeing it as illustrative of some situation in Jesus' life wouldn't you too, in desperation, be inclined to read it allegorically, by attributing symbolic meaning to the elements in the story?

Granted, therefore, that Mark's account of Jesus' parable-making as 'allegorical sermonizing' had more to do with the way in which he came across the parables in the tradition than it had to do with what he actually knew about Jesus, where does this leave us? My whole appreciation of Jesus began to change as soon as I started asking myself this question. To understand what I mean it is necessary to appreciate the huge difference between viewing a parable as an exposure and viewing it as a preaching. When a parable is understood as a preaching (as in Mark 4.2), a *proactive strategy* is implied since the parable-maker is clearly portrayed as setting his world-view (his spirit) up front and advocating a specific ideological position.[11] Alternatively, when a parable is understood as an exposure (as in Mark 2.17), a *reactive strategy* is clearly involved since the parable-maker is seen as taking it for granted that everyone shares the same spirit/world-view (in this case the Mosaic covenant). So here the ideological position is assumed, not advocated, and it is peoples' behaviour, judged in the light of this spirit/world-view, which is placed up front and exposed as either faithful or hypocritical.

So the position is this. Because Mark was unable to provide the parable of The Sower with a suitable subject matter to illustrate, he felt obliged to find some other way of using it. The solution he came up with was to understand it allegorically. This was in itself a very understandable move, but unfortunately it had an unforeseen consequence in that it led Mark to offer a *proactive* explanation (ideology up front) of Jesus' *reactive* parable-making (ideology assumed). This not only undermined the reconstruction work he had already done on the other parables.[12] It also went against thousands of years of parable-making, which itself was based on the foundational linguistic rule that parables and complex similes function reactively.[13]

How was Mark able to get away with something so gross? Well, the fact is that most people prefer to see their heroes performing *proactively* since a proactive performance is taken as a sign of strength. Only the weak are seen as acting reactively. This is not because they choose to do so but because, like 'the afflicted' of the Old Testament (whose only recourse was to cry out unto the Lord),[14] they have no alternative way of operating. There must in consequence have always been considerable pressure on Christians to see Jesus as having a proactive strategy – even though it flew in the face of the evidence.[15] To do him justice Mark seldom portrays his hero as making ideological pronouncements. Furthermore, when occasionally he does so it is usually only to show Jesus as reformulating the Mosaic tradition.[16] Indeed though Mark never follows the other evangelists in actually describing Jesus' typical strategy reactively, in terms of God's exposing light,[17] this is basically the line he too takes – as his *normal* handling of the parables demonstrates.[18] My conclusion is therefore that Mark offers us a portrait of Jesus as a man following a reactive strategy; his description of Jesus as teaching/preaching in parables being an unfortunate though understandable aberration.[19]

Like most twentieth-century Christians I inherited the Church's proactive portrait of Jesus in which the Saviour is pictured as going about preaching a new improved religion designed to supplant the Jewish faith; a heresy which caused the Jewish establishment eventually to put him to death. I have to say that as an unskilled manual worker living at the bottom of society I found such a portrait not only uninspiring but also of little use to me and my mates. Lacking power, or the hope of ever achieving any, we naturally found ourselves the butt of proactive announcements and decision-making rather than the originators of them. Reflecting on this I soon came to realize that the Church's Jesus looked uncomfortably like the sort of hero figure espoused by our managers: that is, the boss who with firmness and kindness persuades people to stop grumbling, behave properly, and get on with the job. From my perspective and that of my mates on the shop floor it was not difficult to see why such a proactive leadership figure would appeal to management or why the Church in its own struggle for power had found it necessary to fabricate such a hero figure for itself.

It was for this reason that Mark's reactive Jesus came as such a revelation to me, once I had recognized it for what it was. For the simple fact is that however powerless you may be, you can *never* find yourself in a position in which it is impossible to expose what is going on ('to cry unto the Lord', as the Psalmist puts it), though, of course, there is never any assurance that doing so will make a difference.[20] In this way it suddenly dawned on me that Mark's reactive Jesus was precisely the sort of person who my mates would recognize as 'their man', as well as being the sort of person who my bosses would reject as a troublemaker. Not that this would depend in any way on my mates or my bosses being Christians. Indeed it seemed to me that Christian mates and bosses would probably have more difficulty in recognizing Mark's reactive Jesus precisely because he did not look like the figure they had been told about in church. They would probably fail to recognize him because they would be looking for a respectable establishment figure, not someone who went about upsetting the apple cart by exposing the truth.

If my problems with Mark had ended here I would have been a happy man today. As it is I now find myself obliged to tell you about the sting in the tail of his reactive Jesus. There are two quite different ways of exposing situations only one of which is countenanced by Mark's reactive Jesus. In the first and most common approach the operator stands as it were behind the torch, hidden from its illumination, as he or she focuses the light on other people's lives. This, of course, is the manner in which investigative journalists work. The interesting thing to note is that though it is claimed that this approach is reactive and non-coercive (it depends for its effect not on forcing change on people but rather on getting them to see what is happening so that they demand change themselves), people nonetheless often judge its performance in proactive terms, as when they claim that the pen is mightier than the sword. This suggests that there is no guarantee that such a reactive approach will be any less manipulative than the more straightforward proactive one. Another interesting thing to note is that our present world is often quite prepared to applaud this journalistic approach because it is seen as an unmasking *which does not call into question the natural way in which our civilization (this world) operates*. As such it can be interpreted as nothing more than a tidying-up exercise, which highlights a mess some individual has made without drawing attention to the basic flaw in civilization which is causing it.

Mark's reactive Jesus shares little with this investigative journalist approach since in his case the light source is not something independent of himself and behind which he can shelter. Rather, the light source is what he shows himself to be: the friend of publicans and sinners. In other words, it is not by using some independently verifiable truth that Mark's reactive Jesus achieves an impact, but rather by demonstrating solidarity with the outcasts in everything he says and does.[21] Unlike the investigative journalist, Mark's Jesus cannot rightly be accused of manipulation; there is nothing to gain in demonstrating solidarity with the outcasts since civilization does not honour such behaviour. All that can be said is that he achieves or does not achieve his end. Either he manages to express this solidarity, or he doesn't. Either his activity shames men and women, or it doesn't. Likewise it cannot rightly be said of him that he seeks to highlight some mess while leaving its real cause unexposed. For in demanding that a person should constantly be ready to sacrifice his or her own advantage – in order to demonstrate solidarity with the dispossessed – Jesus' behaviour clearly constitutes a subversion of civilization's privileges at their very root:

> 'If anyone wants to come after me, let them deny themselves and take up their cross and follow me. For whoever would save their life will lose it, and whoever loses their life for my sake and the gospels will save it. For what does it profit anyone to gain the whole world and forfeit their life?' (Mark 8.34–37)

But here's the rub, for the truth is that however much this civilization-world of privilege disgusts me – and disgust me it does – I continue to find it miserably difficult to follow Mark's reactive Jesus by being happily prepared to sacrifice the many privileges I still possess in the name of solidarity. Why does Mark have to make my life so difficult? For the marginals it was not difficult, of course, since they were deprived of civilization's privileges. That was why they loved Mark's reactive Jesus, I suppose.[22]

Notes

1 Some scholars claim that Jesus invented the parable (e.g. J. Jeremias, *The Parables of Jesus* (London: SCM Press, 1954), p. 12. See also R. W. Funk, *Honest to Jesus* (New York: HarperCollins, 1996), p. 68); a curious suggestion, I find. Speech-forms are part of the basics of language. It is difficult enough to invent a new word and make it stick. To invent a new speech-form all on your own would have been some undertaking. Rather like inventing the adjective!

2 The word *parabole* means literally 'a setting beside'.

3 For a fuller account of how parables work, see my book *Painfully Clear: The Parables of Jesus* (Sheffield: Sheffield Academic Press, 1996). See also my earlier self-published cartoon books written for my workmates, which some would say are more helpful: *Digging up Parables Vol. 1* (Castlemilk, 1980), *Digging up Parables Vol. 2* (Castlemilk, 1981) and *Political Parables* (Castlemilk, 1980).

4 Mark 2.17.

5 Mark 4.1–2.

6 Fables, for example, or the kind of stories in the *One Thousand and One Nights*.

7 Even the longest parable in the synoptic tradition – the Prodigal Son – only takes a little over two minutes to read.

8 Mark 2.17, 19–22; 3.23–27.

9 Which no one had ever come across before, perhaps?

10 The word Mark actually uses of course is 'teach'. I have substituted 'preach' because teach is ambiguous and can cover both preaching truths and exposing truths. In Mark 4.2 the idea is clearly preaching truths.

11 Those who plump for this understanding imply that parable-making is a way of sugaring the pill; avoiding the impression of ramming things down peoples' throats when dispensing political truths. However, when it comes to ideological matters peoples' instinctive reaction is to judge such oblique approaches as sly and underhand. So if you want to sell an ideological position then it is best to behave

above board as Moses or Marx did: 'Blessed are the poor . . . Woe to you who are rich.'

12 In chapters 2, 3 and 12.

13 Like all illustrative speech-forms parables do not advocate truths but rather throw light on situations.

14 E.g. Psalm 140. See also Mark Antony's famous speech in defence of the dead Caesar after the coup, mounted by Brutus and Cassius, had caught him and his imperial party on the hop (Shakespeare, *Julius Caesar*, Act 3, Scene 2).

15 I am not, of course, claiming that Jesus never behaved proactively (e.g. the Beatitudes; see note 11 above). I am talking about his central strategy and claiming that it was reactive, not proactive; that in choosing to perform as the light to lighten the Gentiles he was fulfilling the Mosaic covenant not introducing a new religion.

16 E.g. Mark 10.11 – his pronouncement on divorce. Mark 7.18–23, where Jesus declares all foods clean, appears to be a case in which he does make an ideological pronouncement that contradicts the Mosaic covenant. However, it is doubtful that Jesus ever did such a thing since Peter clearly never took the idea on board until much later.

17 See Luke 2.32; Matthew 4.13–16; and especially John 1.4–5, 8–11; 3.19–20; 8.12; 9.5; 12.35–36, 46.

18 Mark 2.15–17, 18–22; 3.22–27; 12.1–12.

19 A mistake seemingly repeated in Mark 13.28.

20 Apart, that is, from the biblical assurance that God always answers the afflicted.

21 In doing this he fulfils the Mosaic covenant for it was this very same solidarity with the outcasts which Israel, as her part of the covenant agreement, had contracted to demonstrate as a strategy for shaming the Gentiles into changing their ways.

22 'But many that are first will be last, and the last first' (Mark 10.31).

6

Mark's Gospel in personal faith

DAVID BLATHERWICK

For fifty years I have lived with Mark's Gospel more than any other book of the Bible. It has shaped my picture of Jesus, given me an understanding of the gospel and informed my ministry. It has also become an intellectual challenge, although I am less sure that I understand it now than I was as a theology student armed with Vincent Taylor's mammoth commentary on it.[1] It is no longer a familiar text that speaks to me in the language of the Church and can be fitted neatly into the agendas of comfortable twenty-first-century Christians, but a strange text that speaks to me from the past and reflects the concerns, priorities, hopes and dreams of a man (I assume that Mark was a man) who knows the day-to-day reality of life in a world dominated by Rome and has no illusions about the fate of believers who speak out (13.9–13) or the large number of mainly Jewish people trapped in Jerusalem during its siege and at its fall (13.14–20).[2] It does not provide many answers to life's mysteries, but it asks a lot of questions.

Setting out

As a young man, I had no difficulty in identifying with those who had in 1.14—3.12 left their nets or tax-collector's table behind to follow Jesus. I could imagine Peter, Andrew, James, John and Levi listening and watching as Jesus spoke of the coming Kingdom, cast out unclean spirits, healed the sick or infirm, cleansed a leper, enabled a paralysed man to walk and restored a man's withered hand to full strength, and realizing that to be caught up in the proclamation of the good news would not just mean speaking to people but also offering them practical help in God's name (cf. 3.14, where Jesus appoints the twelve to be with him, to proclaim the gospel and to cast out demons, and 6.7–13, where they not only call people to repent but also cast out demons and heal the sick). Later, Jesus would explain his life's work to them in terms of serving people and seeking to set them free (10.45).

I could also identify with some of the problems the disciples had to overcome. It was natural to them to want to stay in Capernaum – a place where they were known, where they understood people's needs and could presumably be useful – but Jesus had his eye on the other towns or villages of Galilee, where people also needed to hear the gospel, have their faith in life restored and be enabled to stand on their feet (1.35–39). It would have been natural for them to avoid someone like the leper of 1.40–45 and to find nothing helpful to say to the paralysed man who was let down through the roof in 2.1–12, but Jesus wanted them to know that the gospel was as much for outcasts as for respectable people and that God's forgiveness was available to all who needed it, even if he (or they) had to offer it. Peter and his friends may have been as uncomfortable in Levi's house as the scribes wanted them to be (2.13–17) and may not have understood why they should feast when others fasted (2.18–20), but Jesus was determined to teach them a way of living that built bridges, not walls, celebrated hope rather than mourned the bitterness of the present or the loss of the past, mended the fabric of people's lives in ways that did not damage it further (2.21–22) and did not elevate the observance of God's commandments above simple humanity or concern for one's neighbours (2.23—3.6; cf. also 7.1–23).

The leper's challenge is haunting – if you want to, you can make me clean. He does not doubt Jesus' ability to heal him, but his willingness to do so. He suspects that he may find his appearance distasteful or his condition distressing and want nothing to do with him, or be guided by convention and refuse to help him for fear of what others will say. People's generally negative response to the news of his healing explains why Jesus might have thought twice. He is now unwelcome in their homes – but those who need to, find him. The challenge of the paralysed man is unspoken. Can you assure me that God loves me and forgives me? Can you put me back on my feet and give me the courage to face life? According to the scribes who are present, Jesus claims too much for himself when he does, arrogating to himself the right to offer forgiveness in God's name and give him hope. I suspect that they would have had no problem if he had told him, in God's name, that he was lazy and sinful, deserved everything that had come to him and should not expect miracles! In terms of this Gospel, the stories mark a turning point in Jesus' fortunes – at least in relation to the scribes, Pharisees and Herodians. It is downhill from here on! In terms of our own discipleship, they remind us that we too often act in ways other people will approve of, rather than those we have learnt from Jesus, let personal prejudices, or hang-ups about beauty, cleanliness, making an effort, etc., stand in the way of simple kindness, use social norms, moral standpoints or even words of Scripture to avoid contact with people in real need, and refuse to explore with them what is possible to those who have eyes to see, ears to hear and hearts to yearn – and the energy and imagination to follow a dream. There is a desperate longing for the improvement of people's fortunes and the emergence of a richer, fairer, more humane society in the story Mark tells that is too rarely reflected in the life and worship of our churches today.

The opening chapters of Mark's Gospel always raise for me, as a minister, the question of how far the Church I serve and represent is identified with the limitation of people's ambition, the suppression of their imagination, the maintenance of the status quo – teaching people to accept the hand life has dealt them, to conform to the rules of society and be suspicious of new ideas, not to draw attention to themselves or be seen as troublemakers. It is a strategy I understand because I was taught it as a child and a young man. It works well for most of the people who attend church, because they are, on the whole, those to whom life has dealt a good hand. They have their struggles and tragedies but, in comparison with most of the world's population or with many people in Britain, they have comfortable lives. The agendas of most churches I know are like the one I imagine the disciples creating to consider the development of Jesus' work in Capernaum, especially among people of their own kind! This troubles me deeply, but, in my attempt to remind people of Jesus' impatience with a world in which there were so many more losers than winners and where people's creative energies were stifled, I too often say things that disturb without effecting change or sound like the musings of an unappreciative, grumpy older man.

I was fortunate in the early days of my ministry to work with people who were ambitious for the Church and saw its future in terms of service to the local community. Three churches in South-East London united to create a church, youth and community centre, which still prospers. A church in Grimsby ran an open youth club, catering for 120 members with a wide range of activities and a regular Friday meeting – and had a Sunday school of nearly three hundred children. The four years I had with the British Council of Churches, working especially with people developing local ecumenical projects, also put me in touch with men and women who were quite convinced that they could make a difference in people's lives and make the communities in which they lived richer, or happier, for their involvement in them. In the last few years, I have been working with congregations that have become turned in on themselves, or been battling for survival, and where it has been very difficult to have any meaningful conversations about other people's needs and what we might do individually or collectively to encourage or help them.

Moving on

But there are other aspects of Mark's Gospel that have also made me think.

(1) At the heart of the Gospel is a message about the coming of the Kingdom – that God is about to do something dramatic that will shake the world. Jesus announces it in 1.14–15 and explains what will happen in 13.24–31. Mark may paint a vivid picture of Jesus, but it is the picture of a herald, the agent or embodiment of the Kingdom whose arrival he proclaims. It shows

him reaching out to people in their need, releasing them from sickness, infirmities, demonic possession and sin, and teaching his disciples to do the same. It also shows him prepared to confront the oppressive forces of his time and place, even at the cost of his life, in his pursuit of a dream and for other people's sake. The faith for which he calls is essentially faith in the gospel God has entrusted to him. It finds expression in a wholehearted commitment to the Kingdom and its values and a confidence that anything is possible to those who have it (9.23; cf. 1.14–15; 11.22–24).

In this it reminds us that the Church is not an end in itself, but part of a process whereby God seeks the world's renewal, the reorientation of human society, and gives people something larger than themselves to live for, something that cannot be realized in their own lives, or in their own lifetimes, but gives meaning to what they do. It also suggests that we cannot 'preach Christ' without talking about the Kingdom or combine faith in Christ with a deep pessimism about the future or the ability of ordinary people like ourselves to make a difference.

(2) Mark's narrative is quite breathless, especially in the early chapters. One event follows quickly on another. Jesus hurries out of Capernaum in 1.35–39, because there are so many more places in which the gospel must be preached, so many more people to help. He tries to walk past his struggling disciples in 6.45–52, because he has set his sights on Bethsaida. He is unmoved by their fears in 10.32–34, because he has to go to Jerusalem in obedience to God's will. We assume that when the disciples meet him in Galilee (16.7), he will speak of the other places in which the gospel must be preached, the other people who must be helped or given hope. As disciples they should be aware of people's physical pain or infirmity, their emotional despair and lack of faith and do everything in their power to set them free, just as he did (10.45; 14.25).

It reminds us that we should not judge the success or failure of a church on the warmth of its welcome, the liveliness of its worship or the number of people who take part in its activities, but on its creative impact on the community around it. It warns us not to idealize the past or see present success as a signal for self-congratulation, but to be aware at all times of God's love and other people's need. Even when we are unable to do anything ourselves – for lack of time, lack of resources, lack of understanding or lack of the appropriate skills – we must still try to give people hope, make them aware of their own gifts and encourage them to use them.

(3) Mark's is the least guarded of the Gospels. He is happy to describe Jesus trying to heal a man, but not getting it quite right (8.22–26), or a man slipping out of his linen cloth and fleeing naked from the scene of Jesus' arrest (14.51–52). He explains that, in Jesus' opinion, the Sabbath was made for people, not people for the Sabbath (2.27; cf. Matt. 12.8; Luke 6.5) and that all foods are clean, despite what we may read in the Bible (7.19; cf. Matt. 15.17).

Mark's Jesus is a carpenter, the son of Mary (6.3; not the carpenter's son whose mother is called Mary, Matt. 13.55, or just Joseph's son, Luke 4.22). He accepts John's baptism of repentance (1.9–11). He does not want to be called 'good teacher', because only God is good (10.18), and does not suggest that the rich man has a choice between being perfect (selling everything and giving the money to the poor) and carrying on as he is, keeping the command-ments (cf. Matt. 19.16–22). He may take a step too far when he calls Levi to be a disciple too (2.14) – he does not make him one of the twelve (3.16–19)[3] – but, unlike Luke's Jesus, does not stop to explain that his call to sinners is a call to repentance (2.17; cf. Luke 5.32). He expects disciples to treat people who use his name to help people or heal them as friends, even if they are not technically part of the group (9.40).[4]

It reminds us that the sense of Jesus' presence and power is not best con-veyed in tidy, conventional speech or doctrinally correct teaching, but in lively, colourful and occasionally disrespectful stories that are marked by stark contrasts and do not always toe the party line. At the centre of the Church's life is a story, or a careful arrangement of stories and sayings, not a theo-logical textbook. The story Mark tells must be retold by people who can give their hearers a sense of its life, its drama and emotion, but not stand in their hearers' way or prevent them from reaching their own conclusions about its meaning for them.

(4) Mark's Gospel is also a story about discipleship. It describes the calling of five disciples, Jesus' selection of the twelve and the tortuous process by which he prepares them and others to continue his work after his death and resurrection. Mark allows the disciples some successes (e.g. 6.7–30), but tends to see them as slow in the uptake and unwilling to stand on their own feet (e.g. 4.13; 7.17–23; 8.4, 14–21; 9.14–29), vain and quarrelsome (e.g. 9.33–41; 10.32–45), too easily discouraged (e.g. 6.45–52) and totally lack-ing courage in the face of danger (e.g. 4.35—5.1; 14.26–72). At the end of his story we can only hope that they will learn from their mistakes – and that we can learn from them too. It is not a story about Jesus founding 'a church', as we understand that term, but creating a body of people who will carry his message and continue his work – and do it with generosity of spirit, perseverance and great courage.

(5) It is a story in which the chief opposition to Jesus and his message comes from good people – the scribes, Pharisees, chief priests and elders. The Herodians play their part and Pilate signs the death warrant, but again and again the people who are against him are the teachers of the Law and the upholders of morality. It is not just the yeast of Herod that disciples should be wary of, but also that of the Pharisees (8.15).

We have no difficulty in identifying the dangers that Herod represents – greed, materialism, lack of moral scruples, the use of political or economic power for selfish ends, the ability to make other people do what we want them to do, using violence if necessary. But why criticize the Pharisees? Do we not all divide people into good and bad, nice and nasty, saints and sinners? Do we not all see religious practice as, among other things, a way of protecting ourselves from the evil influences around us, holding on to our self-respect and witnessing to certain basic moral values in a world where for many people what matters is profit, pleasure or expediency? Do we not all look to the churches, synagogues, mosques, etc. to lay down certain basic principles of public and private morality and invite everyone (not just their own adherents) to accept them and live by them – and, if necessary, use moral persuasion to secure their observance? The Pharisees were, after all, idealists, like the Puritans or early Methodists. Some of them may have wanted to get rid of Jesus (3.6), but, in simple terms, they wanted everyone to live as in God's sight and see themselves as accountable to him for the good or evil they did. They wanted to restore the dignity of the people and the purity of the land in the light of biblical teaching and in the face of real and perceived threats to both. They would not have expected to be placed alongside Herod in Jesus' two-name list of evil influences – and would certainly not have expected to be placed first!

But the only 'rule of thumb' with which Jesus is comfortable is that we should love God passionately and hold other people's lives and well-being as dear as we hold our own (12.29–31). He realizes how easy it is to turn moral guidelines into criteria for distinguishing between acceptable and unacceptable human beings, people we will eat with and talk to and those whose company we will avoid (2.13–17), and how easy it is to use moral argument to justify despicable acts – the son who dedicates everything he owes to his parents to God (7.9–13),[5] or the king who has an innocent man beheaded in order to keep a foolish promise made to a little girl at a birthday party (6.22–28). He is no doubt also aware that guidelines encourage conformity rather than independence of spirit, tend to set the limits of a person's ambition rather than become the springboard for brave or imaginative action in response to other people's need, invite comparisons between people and drive them apart rather than bringing them together, create a tick-list against which people can work out their chances of getting past the final examiner (10.18, 37) rather than rolling up their sleeves and doing what needs to be done now.

Sitting down

At a quiet day, in which we were invited to reflect on the story of Jesus stilling the storm (4.35—5.1), I was struck by two images – Jesus in a boat on the lake talking in riddles to the people on the shore, and his disciples separating themselves from the crowd to join him in the boat. There is a physical distance between Jesus and those who have come to hear him and be healed – a gap his disciples cross – and also a psychological distance of which he speaks (4.14–20). There are people, he tells those around him, whose response to the gospel will be determined by its immediate relevance to them, whether it meets a need and goes on meeting it. There are those who will be excited by it and very enthusiastic about it until they meet resistance and discover that believing in it can be risky. There are those who will be excited by it and continue to believe in it until they die, but they will have so many worries and so many other goals to pursue that they will be useless. The sort of disciples he wants are those who will not only believe in the gospel, but be prepared to act on their beliefs, to dedicate themselves to realizing God's dreams and, if necessary, to lose their lives in the service of others and in their longing for a fairer, kinder, more peaceful and humane world (4.20, 24–25).

We tend to recoil from this passage because we cannot imagine Jesus speaking about anyone like that – let alone those who have come especially to hear him. But he is training disciples. He is not interested in whether or not people are basically decent, but whether they have a vision of what the world might be and are convinced that God can use them to set other people free, offer forgiveness, healing and help in his name, be lights shining in a dark world and point towards that transformation of all things of which the gospel speaks (4.21–22). The call Abraham hears in Genesis 12.1–3 is not to be a nice man and obey God's commandments, but to be a source of blessing to others and to help undo the damage done by Adam (cf. also Gen. 15.1–6; Gal. 3.6–9). Similarly Jesus' call to his disciples is not to be spectators or cheerleaders in the battle between good and evil, life and death, kindness and cruelty, but to take up arms in it.

The crux of the problem between Jesus and the rich man in 10.17–22 is that the rich man is concerned about his own reward – 'What must I do to inherit eternal life?' In terms of that debate he is a decent, God-fearing man, he obeys the commandments, but he has no concept of using his gifts and resources to transform other people's lives and make a significant difference to the world in which he lives. He has no awareness of other people's pain and anguish or his ability to do something about it. He does not hunger and thirst to see right prevail (Matt. 5.6, REB). We see the same problem in the conversation between Jesus and James and John in 10.35–45. James and John want to know where they will sit at the messianic banquet, whether their importance will be recognized in the position they are given. Jesus wants them to realize what they can do now to help people and understand that they will need courage to fight the battles they will have to fight and deal with the suffering they are likely to face. He wants them to see themselves as servants, not lords, and dedicate themselves to setting people free to live as God's children, even in these harsh times and this cruel world. One day God's Kingdom will indeed come in power (9.1; 13.24–31). In the meantime there are people to be healed, imaginations to be stirred, lives to be turned around. I do not think Mark would have understood what we were talking about if we had complained that he paid too much attention to what disciples should do and too little to faith, because faith was 'faith in the gospel' (1.15) and the gospel was about God creating a new world, giving people a new deal, and he could see too many suffering people in his world for him to be overly worried about such theological niceties (cf. 9.38–40; 3.31–35).

What struck me as I watched Jesus' disciples leave the crowd on the shore and get into the boat with him was that the distance between myself and the people I grew up with had grown as I offered for the Methodist ministry, entered theological college and committed myself to a way of life that emphasized service rather than reward, that offered limited financial stability and limited comfort, that asked me to move my wife and children from one situation to another in accordance with the needs of the Church, and that demanded a wide range of skills, constant availability and hours and hours of work – at the end of which I was always more aware of what I had not done, the needs I had not met and the thoughtful preparation for which I had had no time, than of what I had been able to do! I sensed that my words had often been like those of Jesus to the crowd on the shore, riddles: not because the words themselves were strange, although that may sometimes have been true, but because I was standing somewhere different. I had become a different person, with different priorities and pursuing a different goal. To some extent I was expected to say things that people did not believe or agree with, because that is what ministers do. It was assumed that I would be soft-hearted, patient, understanding, although I had to stand up for what was right and defend moral values. But I was not expected to take Jesus' hope of the Kingdom seriously, to see significant change in the Church and in the wider world as not only desirable but also, with God's help, possible. Part of my frustration on retirement is that I do not think I ever realized I was in that situation or knew how to deal with it, although Mark's Jesus speaks of it.

Mark's Jesus seems to accept it and focus his energies on developing the gifts of those who do understand him and are prepared to share his dreams – although their progress is, as we have already noticed, painfully slow. But although Jesus chooses to focus his energies in the latter part of Mark's Gospel on training disciples, his vision still relates to the world, what it might look like if it were less cruel and more humane and what it takes for people to change it. He does not talk to his disciples, as ministers so often do to people, about the Church, invite them to have mystical experiences or provide them with rituals that will help them to cope with the day-to-day business of living. He tries to make them aware of the powerful effects of lives given in service to others – for the sake of God, Jesus and the gospel (8.34—9.1).[6]

Notes

1 Vincent Taylor, *The Gospel According to St. Mark* (London: Macmillan, 1952; 2nd edn, 1966).

2 Josephus estimates the casualties during the siege at 1.1 million and speaks of wholesale carnage on a scale not seen before (*Jewish War* 6.9.3–4; cf. Mark 13.19). But Tacitus estimates the population of the city during the siege at 600,000 (*Histories* 5.13).

3 Matthew calls him 'Matthew' (8.9) and identifies him with the Matthew included in Mark's list of the twelve (10.3). Luke agrees with Mark in calling the tax-collector 'Levi' (5.27) and including 'Matthew' among the twelve (and not calling him a tax-collector, 6.14–16). Strangely it is the second James who is described as 'son of Alphaeus' in all three lists (cf. 'Levi, son of Alphaeus' in Mark 2.13).

4 Matthew omits the story in which Jesus makes this point, but records the statement that anyone who is not actually with Jesus is against him (12.30). Luke records both statements (9.50; 11.23).

5 Presumably the disciples of Hillel and Shammai would have been equally horrified by such use of the Corban oath (cf. Mishnah, *Nedarim* 3.2).

6 I suspect that Mark's story of the transfiguration (9.2–8) is less concerned with God's revelation of the divine glory Jesus had before he was born, or will have at the end of time, than with the transformation (*metamorphosis*) that takes place following his willing acceptance of the role God has prepared for him (8.31–33). Philo also speaks of a metamorphosis taking place in Moses as he accepts his God-given role as 'champion of the weaker' (*Life of Moses* I.54–57; cf. Exodus 2.16–20) and Paul expects people to be transformed by the renewal of their minds in response to the gospel (Rom. 12.1–2) or to be gradually transformed into the image of God's glory by keeping their eyes fixed on Jesus (2 Cor. 3.18).

7

A time for fasting?

JOHN FENTON

When the Editor invited me to write on a practical aspect of Mark's Gospel, I chose fasting, not because I had any personal experience of it, but rather because I had not. Moreover it was clear to me from the start that it was not a subject to which Mark paid much attention explicitly (unlike Matthew); even the translation of Mark 2.20 in The Revised English Bible (1989), 'That will be the time for them to fast', could, as we shall see, be read, and has been read, to mean that believers would be fasting on one specific day only, the actual day on which Jesus was crucified in Jerusalem at the time of the Passover festival in the early first century CE.[1]

The reason I chose fasting was because it expressed clearly and unambiguously one aspect of Mark's understanding of what was involved in being a follower of Jesus – namely, the *via negativa*, the renunciation of the world, the flesh and the devil. This, it seemed to me, was an essential part of Mark's message, and a part which was not perhaps as obvious in today's church life in the West as it had been in the past, and is still, I am told, in the churches of the East.

I

From the earliest days of Christianity, the gospel that it has proclaimed has been a combination of the indicative and the imperative; for example: 'The Kingdom of God is upon you. Repent.' The indicative expresses the action of God; the imperative the corresponding action of the hearer. Fasting is one element of the imperative in Mark's Gospel.

At first sight, one would think it to have been of only marginal interest to Mark. If, for example, one were to look up the verb (*nesteou*) and the noun (*nesteia*) in a Greek concordance to the New Testament, there would be only one paragraph in Mark where the verb is used (six times), 2.18–20, and one other passage containing the noun (once), 9.29. But further research would show the word in 9.29 is a variant reading, and that it is regarded as a harmonizing insertion into Mark from Matthew (17.21) which is itself a scribal insertion into Matthew's text, and is now omitted by translators and editors of that Gospel (e.g. NRSV, REB). From this, one might draw the conclusion that

scribes copying the Gospels were more concerned than the evangelists themselves to draw attention to the need for fasting. It may be relevant to notice
that Mark's account of Jesus' forty days in the wilderness does not include
any reference to fasting, unlike Matthew (4.2) and Luke (4.2), but only the
statement that the angels attended to his needs (1.13), leaving it unclear whether
he thought that Jesus was fasting or not. The two later evangelists remove
that uncertainty.

Thus in the original text of Mark, insofar as we can reconstruct it from
the manuscripts etc., we are left with one paragraph only that refers to fasting (2.18–20). The question is asked why Jesus' disciples do not fast when
the disciples of the Baptist and of the Pharisees do. To which Jesus replies
that it is impossible for them to fast in the present, while the bridegroom is
there with them, but that there will be a time when they will fast, when the
bridegroom has been taken away from them.

This is the sense of the translation in the Revised English Bible, but the
literal meaning of the Greek is 'on that day', which some have taken to mean
the actual day of the crucifixion only,[2] and others the weekly commemora-
tion of this on Fridays.[3] The REB translation has the support of the Arndt
and Gingrich *Lexicon*, which compares John 14.20; 16.23, 26; where 'that day'
means the time between the resurrection of Jesus and the second coming.
The singular ('that day') in Mark worried the copyists: some changed it to
'in those days', which was also Luke's solution (5.35); Matthew omitted it
altogether, leaving simply 'then shall they fast', and the scribes of D and the
Old Latin versions harmonized Matthew's text with Luke's, adding 'in those
days' (Matt. 9.15). Rightly or wrongly, those who copied Mark took him to
mean that there would be fasting in the life of the Church, and that Jesus
had commanded it.

In all this uncertainty, we can be fairly certain of the following:

1 There were Christians, possibly as early as the end of the first century CE
who observed weekly fasts: 'Do not keep the same fast-days as the hypo-
crites. Mondays and Thursdays are their days for fasting, so yours should
be Wednesdays and Fridays' (*The Didache* 8).
2 Some of the first Christians, being all of them Jews, continued to observe
Jewish customs. Compare: 'I fast twice a week' (Luke 18.12): 'When you
fast . . .' (Matt. 6.16–18); 'Often fasting' (2 Cor. 11.27), and the references
to prayer and fasting in Acts (13.2; 14.23).
3 Paul, writing to the Christians in Rome around the middle of the first
century, gives them advice on how to deal with people who have different
customs and beliefs about food and keep special days (Rom. 14.1—15.13).
Though fasting is not mentioned here, he probably thought that it came
within the same category as dietary beliefs and the observance of special
days. His overall instruction here is: 'Keep your faith to yourself' (14.22),

and do not allow it to create divisions among believers. Charity is more important than religious customs.

4 *The Gospel of Thomas* (second century?) may be evidence that some Christians of a Gnostic kind were opposed to fasting. See, for example, saying 6: 'His disciples asked him (and) said to him: Do you wish us to fast?', to which there seemed to be no answer, and saying 14: 'Jesus said to them: If you fast, you will beget sin for yourselves.'

II

What we have seen so far concerning fasting in Mark's Gospel will scarcely answer the question, Did he think it important? Might one not conclude that it was later Christian writers and non-canonical writers that attached more importance to the custom and helped it to become an established element in Christianity for many centuries – in fact, until the nineteenth and twentieth centuries in the West?

What we must see now is that fasting is only one element in Mark's description of discipleship, and that it is one that alerts us immediately to his particular understanding of what would be involved in being a follower of Jesus. But in order to do this, we must first pay attention to the overall arrangement of his material in his book.

Mark understood and made use of the skills of salesmanship as they were explained to me by a former door-to-door representative of a well-known encyclopaedia some years ago. The first rule is to persuade the target customer that he or she really needs the product. (You want to help your children with their homework. You do not want to be the only people in the street who do not own it.) The second rule is never to reveal the total cost, until an agreement has been reached on the payment for the first volume. (It is important not to suggest that the initial payment should be multiplied by the number of volumes in the complete work.)

This is the explanation of the arrangement of the material in Mark's book. In the first half of it (1.1—8.26), he has placed fifteen of the eighteen miracle stories that he was to include in the Gospel; in the second half of it (8.27—16.8), he brings in the three predictions of the passion and resurrection, the prophecy concerning the destruction of the world, the narrative of the arrest of Jesus, the trials and the crucifixion, with the burial and the women at the tomb; the last three miracle stories are appropriate here, because they include references to death and resurrection (9.26f.), following Jesus (10.52) and the withering of the fig tree (11.12ff., 20ff.). The first half is the offer of healing; the second is the cost of it.

Mark makes it clear what he thinks evil is: it is parasitical, living off its host and eventually destroying it; after which it must move on to its next victim. The sick and incapacitated, in the first eight chapters, present one aspect

of the world we live in: it is in the process of being destroyed by the Evil
One and his minions, the demons. But Jesus is stronger than the strong man,
and is able to bring health to the sick, sustenance to the hungry, calm to the
storm and life to the dead. That is what those who hear this book being read
to them at the Sunday assembly want to hear, and the first half of the book
assures them of the ability of Jesus to deliver what everyone knows is needed.
The method is known as *captatio benevolentiae.*

There has been one strange and at first sight inexplicable fact in these accounts
of healing: Jesus has told some of the people healed not to tell anyone about
it (e.g. 1.44; 5.43; 7.36; 8.26, if the original reading was 'Do not tell anyone
in the village'). One wonders why. The second part of the book provides the
answer to the question that the first half has raised. The price to be paid is
total: the destruction of the Saviour and of those whom he saves. If part one
of Mark offers what everyone wants to hear, part two tells them what nobody
wants to be told. The cost is concealed, until the hearer is sure that it must
be paid; and then it becomes clear that there are no successful disciples in
Mark, neither male nor female; even Jesus himself goes out of the narrative
asking why God has forsaken him.

The key word here is *apoluo*, 'to lose' or 'to destroy'. The offence of the
gospel, as Mark presents it, is the paradox that evil, the destroyer, is overcome
by the destruction of its victim. Salvation from destruction is by means of
destruction. Providence is both economical and ironic: it makes use of the
thing to be removed, by adopting its own method. The destroyer is destroyed
by destroying (8.35). The fifteen miracles in the first eight chapters may have
given the impression that salvation would be by a word and miraculous, as
in the case of the healings. The silence that Jesus imposes on those whom he
heals prevents us from coming to such a conclusion too quickly. The only
way to save your life (from destruction) is to lose it (or destroy it) for Christ's
sake and the gospel's.

At this point we must notice another word that Mark uses in this crucial
paragraph (8.34–38) because of its subsequent history when the Gospel was
translated into English. The word is *aparnaomai*, and it is translated 'to deny'.
Its first occurrence in Mark is at 8.34: 'Anyone who wants to be a follower
of mine must deny himself [or herself].' Mark will use it again three times,
in each case in reference to Peter who says that he does not know Jesus (14.30,
31, 72). In English, 'to deny' can be used with a double object – a direct
object and an indirect object – as in the statement: 'He denies himself alcohol during Lent.' This is the context in which the expression 'self-denial',
meaning giving something up, is now most frequently used. *Aparnaomai*, however, could not be used in this sense. It can mean to disown or contradict a
statement, or to declare that one has no relationship with another person.
There are, as far as I know, no instances of the verb being used in connection with abstinence and asceticism. If we were able to ask Mark, 'What is it

that we are to deny ourselves?', if he could understand our use of the verb with direct and indirect object ('What' . . . 'ourselves'), the only answer he could give would be, 'The object of the verb is "ourselves"'. Mark assumes that human beings have the ability to transcend themselves and to act to their own disadvantage: they can hate themselves, or disregard themselves, or detach themselves from themselves. This is made clear in what follows immediately: take up the cross and follow me (8.34). The reference is to capital punishment of slaves in the Roman Empire and Jesus has predicted this three times, in 8.31; 9.31; and 10.33f. As far as we know, the use of the image of crucifixion for anything less than death ('This is a cross I must bear', etc.) had not taken place when Mark wrote; it happened soon after (see Luke 9.23: 'Day after day he must take up his cross').

As we shall see, fasting has now become a no-go area in some ecclesiastical institutions. The word itself has been dropped and replaced by 'self-denial', which can then be trivialized so as to refer to actions that will be performed on specified days; whereas what Mark meant by 'deny yourself' was to be characteristic of the whole of your life, and was understood as referring to capital punishment. This trivialization of Mark can be illustrated from changes that have recently been made in the Church of England's Book of Common Prayer and its new revisions. I could have taken examples from churches other than the Church of England, but I ask readers to accept this just as a convenient example.

III

There was, as far as I can see, no mention of days of fasting in the first and second Prayer Books of Edward VI (1549, 1552), but, in the next century, the revision of 1662 contained a Table of Vigils, Fasts and Days of Abstinence, and these included Lent, the Ember Days, the Rogation Days and all the Fridays in the Year except Christmas Day. In some years, this might have added up to a total of ninety days in one year, almost one in every four days on average. A similar list was included in the book proposed in 1928, but with a reduction in the number of Vigils. A major change was made in the *Alternative Service Book* of 1980, and here the title was altered to Days of Discipline and Self-denial, avoiding the word 'fasting', and again the number of these days was slightly reduced. A further reduction was made in *Common Worship* (2002) where, again, the title of the list was Days of Discipline and Self-Denial (p. 531).

It seems to be the case, then, that just as the majority of us in the United Kingdom have become more affluent and enjoy a more prosperous lifestyle, so also fasting has been abolished as the term used to denote certain days of the year, and has been replaced by Discipline and Self-denial, which one might have thought to be characteristic of every day of the year, not just some.

Would it be ingenuous to suggest that the opposite might have been what we should have expected to happen, particularly, in a time when we know more than our predecessors about obesity and world hunger?

IV

Of the four Gospels, Mark is the most rigorous and ascetical. John of the Cross in the sixteenth century had noticed this, and he said of Mark chapter 8: 'The more necessary it is for spiritual persons, the less it is practised by them' (*Ascent of Mount Carmel*, II.VII.4). The journey from Caesarea Philippi (8.27) to Jerusalem (11.1) is full of teaching about what it means to be a follower of Jesus. It is a *via negativa* involving not thinking as humans think, not putting Jesus on the same level as Moses and Elijah, the inability to heal without prayer, giving up the desire for precedence, becoming like a child (i.e. having no status), living without the comforting distinction between 'us' and 'them', caring for others, not resorting to divorce, selling everything, being subject to persecutions, sharing Christ's cup and baptism, being slave to all, having faith.

More or less in the middle of all this is a saying that those who made copies of Mark found problematic: 'Everyone will be salted with fire' (9.49). Both Matthew and Luke omitted it; some copyists added into the Marcan text a verse from Leviticus (2.13): 'Every sacrifice will be salted with salt.' The Marcan saying is clearly modelled on the Levitical instruction: under the Law, salt made sacrifices acceptable to God; in the gospel, the believer is the sacrifice (Rom. 12.1) and what makes him or her acceptable to God is fire which, in this context, refers to destruction (see verses 43, 48). This salt is good, because it promotes God's purpose by the destruction of self-will.

Fasting is a religious custom directed against the desires of the flesh that need to be resisted and eventually destroyed. In the setting of Mark's Gospel as a whole, and in his *via negativa* in particular, it makes excellent sense. 'Then will be the time for them to fast.'[4]

Notes

1 See, for example, Robert H. Gundry, *Mark: A Commentary on His Apology for the Cross* (Grand Rapids, MI: Eerdmans, 1993), p. 133.
2 See previous note.
3 Perhaps as in *Didache* 8, quoted below.
4 I am greatly indebted to Professor Eamon Duffy for his article in *The Tablet*, 31.01.2004.

8

Losing life, gaining life

JOHN VINCENT

The saying of Jesus reported by Mark in 8.35 sets up a contrast between two ways of wishing to live life: 'Whoever wishes to gain their life will only lose it, but whoever loses their life for my sake and the gospel's will gain it.' This contrast between 'gaining' and 'losing' is elaborated in verse 36: 'Is there any advantage if you gain the whole world but lose your own life?' Finally, Mark adds the not necessarily consequential saying of verse 37: 'There is nothing you can give to regain your own life.'

This last saying is somewhat odd, unless it simply makes the point that the lost life cannot be regained – it has led to too many inexorable consequences.

What could it mean to 'lose one's life'? There is surely an element of the ridiculous in the proposition. To lose one's life can only mean the psychological implausibility of pretending that one was not acting authentically, not working out the potential of one's inner *psyche* (the Greek word for 'life'). Indeed, the unlikelihood of a human being acting against what was ultimately their own interests, or perceived by them to be so, must be obvious. And would not such a person, seeking or claiming not to be living from their own life honestly and with due responsibility and even vocation, be a strong dissuader to others? Would not their inauthenticity speak too loudly?

Again, what could it mean to 'gain' one's life? Is not any life lived to its own fulfilment a life in some ways 'gained'? And does not everyone, by living their life to its full, in some way 'gain' that life, or at least achieve its significance within its own terms?

Whatever these passages originally meant in the mind of Mark, or in the words of Jesus, or in the understanding of the early Christians, they come to us as striking and challenging – or ridiculous and illogical.

What could they mean, then or now?

In the present piece, I shall attempt a threefold journey. First, I try to recall my own journey into this apparent mystery, in my own early life. Second, I journey within the text itself, to discern what might have been its original meaning. Third, I journey back from the text into my own life, up to the present.[1]

A journey into the text

My first encounters with Jesus were with a heroic figure, calling disciples. It was the Jesus of F. Warburton Lewis[2] and Leslie Weatherhead's *The Transforming Friendship*.[3] I discovered Khalil Gibran, G. K. Chesterton on St Francis, and the Journal of John Wesley – all human figures following an enigmatic but compelling Jesus.

During ministerial training at Richmond College, London, I was captivated by Vincent Taylor's *Mark*.[4] Then, in 1954–55, I spent a year at Drew Seminary, Madison, NJ. Whichever seminar or class I went into, I wrote papers on what by then I was convinced was the only true Christianity – notably, discipleship. So I wrote on discipleship in Mark for Howard Clark Kee, discipleship in Galatians for William R. Farmer, discipleship in John for Henry J. Cadbury, discipleship as theology for Bernhard Anderson, discipleship as systematics for Carl Michalson, discipleship and the Reformation for Paul Lehmann, discipleship and Wesley for Franz Hildebrandt. In the midst of this riotous theological adventure, Oscar Cullmann visited Drew and persuaded them to give me a little money to go to Basel, where I spend the year 1955–56, and ended up with a dissertation for Cullmann, Bo Reicke and Karl Barth, on 'Disciple and Lord: the historical and theological significance of discipleship in Mark's Gospel'. Cullmann one day sent me to learn from Eduard Schweizer, busy writing his *Lordship and Discipleship*.[5] Barth led me through his long section on 'Nachfolge',[6] and discussed Bonhoeffer's *The Cost of Discipleship* with me – a book I had disciplined myself not to read until I had done the gospel work for myself, for fear that I would be biased![7]

In 1956, I returned to England. I concluded that you could not get a doctorate out of Marcan discipleship, and then go off and teach it to others rather than try yourself to put it into practice. So I set myself to becoming an urban missioner rather than a New Testament professor, and to try to keep my gospel work going alongside my ministry.

As I saw it, to be a disciple of the Marcan Jesus meant that you had to follow Jesus in his mission to people at the bottom or at the fringes of society, to seek to bring some life to the outsiders of the world. So I went to see the superintendent of the nearest city mission – the Manchester and Salford Methodist Mission.

'Have you got a job for me?' I said to the dour superintendent, J. Morrison Neilson.

'All the good places have gone,' he replied. 'I have this place in Wythenshawe left. But I don't think you'd be any good for it.'

'Can I have it?' I pleaded.

Thus, my 'journey into the text' about discipleship as losing life and gaining life had determined a crucial stage in my life. I was to see my life as a follower, a disciple, one 'walking in his footsteps' in a practical, rather than an intellectual, or even a spiritual, way.

So now we need to follow that 'journey within the text', to see how far I was mistaken or self-deluded!

A journey within the text

My own early conclusions concerning the discipleship tradition were stated rather bluntly in two articles. In the first, I argued:

> Jesus does not substitute a new and better religion for an inadequate one; the greatest thing Jesus does for religion is to do away with it. No longer is the confessional 'Lord, Lord' the criterion for discipleship, but the doing of the deeds of Christ, of the coming kingdom, of the cross which *is* Christ and the kingdom. The disciple is not one who is looking for the coming kingdom, nor one who applauds the ethics of the Teacher, nor one who hails him 'Messiah', but one who stakes his life on the validity of the cross as the way of life of the kingdom.[8]

In the second article, I tried to make sense of my early studies on discipleship, up to 1960, and asked why the question of discipleship had so often been ignored in synoptic scholarship. I suggested that this was due to four basic current assumptions:

1 The preference for reading the Synoptics in the light of the Bible as a whole, more particularly in the light of Paul or Acts.
2 The suspicion of the 'Jesus of history' as over against 'the Christ of faith'.
3 The belief that 'the Gospel' dates only from the resurrection and is characterized by the gift of faith.
4 The fear that the words of Jesus have been so influenced by subsequent church situations as to be of little value.[9]

This seemed still the situation when I redrafted my 1960 dissertation for publication in 1976.[10] Contemporary scholarship sees the sayings as something like proverbs, around the meaning of 'life' (*psyche*). The first saying, about saving and losing life (8.35), is regarded as deriving its significance from the situation of disciples in AD 66–70, facing Roman persecution.

> It refers to Christians who, hauled up before a court, know that death awaits them if they do not curse Jesus. The saying calls on them to be prepared to give their lives for the cause of Jesus, as Eleazar and the seven brothers in 2 Macc. 6—7 gave theirs for the Torah.[11]

The second saying, about 'gaining the whole world' (8.36), uses the idea of 'gain' versus 'give up' – equivalent to 'save' versus 'lose' in the first saying – and the idea of 'the whole world' versus 'one's own life'. The riches of the whole world cease to be of importance for the owner from the moment he or she loses his or her life. Even the most precious object loses its value for a person at the moment the person ceases to exist.[12]

The third saying about the impossibility of regaining a lost life (8.37) seems an obvious comment, requiring little note.

'Gaining life' is in the Greek 'saving life' (*sozein ten psuchen*). It is in Mark similar to 'gaining the world' (8.36), 'being great' (9.35), and 'being lord over others' (10.43–44). People who 'gain life' are those who control the vineyard (12.1–12). They want top places, and devour widows' houses (12.38–40). They destroy others – John the Baptist (6.26), Jesus (14.7); they use others – witnesses (14.55), jurors (15.3) and the crowd (15.11).

The meaning of 'life', *psyche*, does not constitute any major problem. The word simply means 'human existence', 'the present life', or the biological phenomenon of life.[13] In terms of 'gaining life', it is significant that Jesus legitimizes the desire to be first: 'Whoever wants to be first must be last of all and servant of all' (9.35); 'Whoever wants to be great among you must be your servant, and whoever wants to be first among you must be the slave of all' (10.43–44). Normally, people desiring to be first (*protos*) are condemned. The scribes seek the first seats in the synagogues and places of honour at banquets (12.39). The 'first' people in Galilee are at Herod's banquet (10.21). 'Being first' is a synonym for 'gaining life' in Mark.[14] Generally, 'seeking to be first' is seeking to be like the people opposed to Jesus. Yet here, he assumes such an intention in his own disciples, and approves it, or at least claims that it can be met in a radically different way.

In the context, the sayings illustrate the demand for cross-bearing. The call to 'take up your cross' (8.34) has to be seen as one among a number of striking images used by Mark to describe the ways in which disciple practice has to continue the practice of Jesus. There is a 'cup' of Jesus which the disciples must drink, and which they say they can drink (10.38–40), a 'fire' with which they are to be 'salted' (9.49), and a 'baptism' with which they are to be baptized (10.38).

However, just as 'losing your life' is the porch to discipleship, but not the discipleship itself, so the cup, fire and salt are the possible results precipitated by discipleship, not the discipleship itself. Also, there is an element in the 'salt' which refers to the usefulness of disciples and of discipleship to the world. This is plain in 9.50:

> Everyone will be salted with fire.
> Salt is good, but if salt has become non-salty, you cannot season it.
> Have salt in yourselves, and be at peace with each other.

What, then, could 'losing life' mean in the gospel story?

Disciples in Mark do not simply 'lose things'. They often throw them away. Disciples throw down their nets (1.18), and desert their fellow-workers (1.20). The widow throws down (*ebalen*) all she has in the Temple treasury

(12.42). The woman breaks the whole jar of ointment (14.3). The sower throws around all the seed, even if only one in four will produce harvest (4.1–20). The woman with the bleeding has already thrown around all of her money (5.26), and grabs hold of Jesus from behind (5.27). The leper throws himself in front of Jesus (1.40). The Syrophoenician woman willingly loses her self-respect by going with the term 'dog' to get her daughter healed (7.28). Joseph loses his status to beg the body (15.43), and women lose their safety to anoint it (16.1–3). Self-abandonment is a mark of the response of people to Jesus, not least the disciples, who have 'lost everything' (10.28).

'Whoever loses their life shall find it' (8.35). Not 'know yourself' (*gnothi seauton*) or 'save yourself' (*sozon seauton*), but 'lose yourself' (*apoleson seauton*) is the method of discipleship. Rabbi Hillel says: 'If I am not for myself, who is for myself? But if I am only for myself, what am I?' (*Aboth* 1.14). Paradoxically, Jesus proclaims that I can only be 'for myself' by being 'lost', and by being 'for others'. Jesus cannot 'save his life' is the mockery at the cross (15.31). He has not to save it, but to give it up, lose it, for others, like a ransom (10.45).

So, 'giving up' is a necessity. It can be to the poor (10.21). Significantly, 'giving up' is not expected of those who already have little or nothing – slaves or women or children. Rather, the values of slaves, women and children are what those in authority are to aspire to, when they 'give up' what they have.[15]

Every statement about discipleship is also a statement about Christology. Jesus asks disciples to do what he himself has done, is doing or will do. Mark's picture of discipleship is his picture of Jesus either *in extenso* or in minia-ture.[16] Mark's word usage makes this clear. Jesus has 'left behind' his mother and family (cf. 3.31–35). So, too, the disciples have 'left behind' theirs. The disciple is not called to perform activities other than those which the Master performs. The Master does and says things which are to be replicated by the disciple. For Mark, Christology is the key to and the programme for disci-pleship. For Mark, equally, discipleship is the key to and the programme for Christology.

Significantly, the disciple is described as someone who has 'left behind' valuable elements of life. Interestingly, though the list of persons and things 'left behind' in 10.29 includes 'father', the list of things to be 'gained a hundred times' in 10.30 does not include 'fathers'. This intentional slip of Mark – or Jesus – could well indicate that the old patriarchal systems, and the old father-figures of established religion and politics, now have no place in the Kingdom community. Now, 'You are all brothers' (Matt. 23.8). The source of authority does not come from status or appointment, but from inward call, conviction and spirit-empowerment.[17]

Of course, disciples are ambiguous. They have indeed given up all. But they still want to be greatest (9.33; 10.41), try to prevent an outside exorcist (9.38), rebuke bringers of children (10.13), debate places of honour

(10.35–45). In all these, they exactly mirror the style of those who 'seek to save their lives'. In the terms of God's Kingdom, such conduct is rejected (9.42–48; 12.40; 14.62).

Yet Jesus' admission of the legitimacy of 'seeking to gain life' adds a mysterious element. Are all disciples – then and now – seeking to 'gain life', and seeing discipleship to Jesus as an inverted, impossible way of being at least a true disciple? Is the scandal of the request of James and John in 10.35–40 that it so explicitly violates the mystery of gaining by losing, that they think they can go for gaining directly?

Essentially, the functions of lordship and seniority are performed by servant-hood. Thus 10.42–44:

> Among the gentiles, rulers have power over other people,
> and leaders have complete authority.
> But this is not the way for you.
> Anyone wishing to be great must be the servant of the others.
> Anyone wishing to be first must be the slave of the others.

'Anyone' simply means 'Any Son or Daughter of Humanity' – any Human Being. And 'Human Being' or 'Son of Humanity' or 'Son of Man' is Jesus' self-chosen euphemism. So that 'anyone' or 'whoever' in Mark includes Jesus himself. He is simply and sufficiently the archetypical Human Being, who calls others to be 'with him' (3.14). He does not call others to do things other than he does himself. Indeed, the discipleship words are keys to understanding Jesus' own vocation.

Sayings about 'Any Person' thus have an intimate connection with sayings about 'Any Son of Humanity'. 'Son of Man' is a newly revealed secret or essential human being. Mark's language itself invites the comparison between Jesus and the disciple:

> The Son of Humanity must lose his life to gain his life.
> The Son of Humanity does not come to be ministered unto but to minister.
> The Son of Humanity loses his life that others gain it.

The point of the sayings is not some kind of quasi-psychological comment on how a person best fulfils themselves, but rather a clear policy statement about something which is grasped by a disciple of Jesus as being more important than fulfilling personal drive or ambition, because it relates to Jesus' great project to make present God's love and compassion, his will, his Kingdom, here upon this earth. The vital clue to the meaning of 8.35 is, of course, the phrase 'for my sake and the gospel's'. The Kingdom is Jesus' gospel (1.15). Jesus was totally driven by this reality, and lost himself in it. He gave every ounce of his energy to do it. He counted his own life as secondary to it – or rather, his own life expanded into it, so that he lived, breathed, spoke, practised, celebrated the immediacy and availability of the divine, 'the Kingdom', in the whole of life. He gained far more than he lost in his Kingdom-centred life and ministry.

This was what he called others to 'follow' him into, so that they also became God-bearers, images of divine performance, embodiments of love of God and neighbour, imitators of a loving heavenly parent. Such a life, says Jesus, might look so different from your own customary life as to make you say that you could only gain it by losing what you were or what you had before. But see, he says, I am doing this new thing – I do not count my own life as the dearest thing to me. I live for God's Kingdom, and in God's Kingdom – for and in the divine life. And it's great. It's OK. It's really not losing your life, but gaining it.

And, says Jesus, I gain life partly because through my losing life, other people gain fullness of life.

A journey back from the text

Today, we do not stand in the same position as Marcan disciples or readers. In terms of losing life, we are not faced with any threats to our lives, so that to 'lose life' has to mean something different from being killed. Equally, 'gaining life' cannot mean a compensatory future Kingdom existence, much less a 'going to heaven', such as some people still speak of.

What, then, could it all mean today? Again, I do not answer the question theoretically, but practically, experimentally and experientially – as a Marcan disciple would expect it to be answered!

For a start, I have to say that everyone is called to take these journeys for themselves. This is the theme of the 'Journey' programme.[18] It is all about 'explorations into discipleship', which all disciples must do for themselves. It seeks to answer questions like: 'Can we get together a plan for a series of experiences that might open up discipleship to Jesus as an exciting, worthwhile option for people?' 'Can we walk alongside friends, and make some discoveries about some important things – like what's worth believing, who's worth being with, what's worth doing?' The method implies three journeys:

- Jesus' journey – what Jesus did;
- our journey – issues in our lives;
- the group's journey – discoveries to make.[19]

Mark's Gospel is the central resource for all these journeys – as I believe it was intended to be.

From Marcan discipleship, I learned also a theology of unilateralism. The Son of Man had to act first, giving his life, so that the many might be saved (10.45). So people, and even a nation, had to act unilaterally, to release life for others:

Christ is the Prototype. He is the Person *and the Way, and the 'Technique'*, whereby blessing comes to the many. His is, in classic atonement theology, the 'trick' whereby Satan is disarmed and man brought to salvation. He is the 'necessary risk' (the Suffering Servant, the oppressed righteous, etc.) which turns the tables and sets the world free. He suffers and redeems *unilaterally* so that multilateral blessing may come.[20]

As the disciple was part of the Son of Humanity/New Humanity, acting unilaterally was part of the disciple's task also, so that 'multilateral blessing may come'.

What direction that unilateral initiative is to take has seemed a vital gospel question to me.[21] In 1977, I visited the Church of the Saviour in Washington, and found them reflecting much on Elizabeth O'Connor's *Journey Inwards, Journey Outwards*.[22] I preached to them what I felt were more essentially gospel 'journeys' – a journey backwards, a journey sideways and a journey downwards.[23] There, I reflected on ministry in the inner city: 'We got landed a bit nearer the bottom, and became parables in a tiny way of the Gospel Journey Downwards.'[24]

Christopher Rowland comments:

For John, the experience of 'the journey downwards' and 'the radical alternative' to the religio-political life of his day mirrors his own experience of seeking an alternative space for following and understanding Jesus Christ. 'Re-education' through 're-location' is what John and the Urban Theology Unit have offered over the years, and John finds this in the alternative learning space set up by Jesus, according to Mark's Gospel, in the house or intimate meal rather than synagogue or temple.[25]

Behind this was, of course, a contemporary educational implication of Jesus' 'losing life'. It was the willingness to take a chance that the method of Jesus would actually work. The method of Jesus seemed to be clear – to go to the bottom of society with a presence and a promise that Jesus was a 'down-goer', and that the happening, or dynamic, or 'Kingdom' of God would happen in that situation, once one had taken the initial step of 'going down'. Later, I used the shorthand of 'incarnation' for this.[26] But originally and essentially, it was the move from a position of privilege, understanding or knowledge, down to a place where these insights or discernments into the gospel might actually work in practice. Mark, I believe, encourages such an 'imitation of Christ'.[27]

There is, of course, an element of presumption in this. Who am I to presume that I am in a position so that my moving down from it to give what I have to others would actually work, even if it was an appropriate act of self-giving? Certainly, I do not in any way see urban ministry as some kind of heroic self-abnegation.[28] If there is any element of 'losing life', there is certainly much of 'gaining life'. The inner city has become for me a 'site' for the contemporary rediscovery of some essential aspects of the Jesus of the Gospels. It seems to me that Jesus is 'at home' there. And gospel discipleship is both needed there and appears there.[29] So what I sought originally – to follow Jesus – is there fulfilled a hundredfold, whatever might appear the losses, willingly or unwillingly sustained.

So, to 'gain life' is something about being given significance, staying long enough to see some harvest, and being there for others to grow on it and out of it. Jesus reveals the good news of the presence of the divine life here on earth, which can be participated in by anyone who wishes. The divine life – the Kingdom of God present on earth – replicates itself through Jesus-like practice and motivation. That Jesus practice is the practice of self-giving, of pouring out life for others and into others.

Precisely such a presumption – that my gift is of value to others' lives when poured out for them – is the presumption of Jesus, into which all disciples are called. Thus, the life gained is essentially a life only gainable in its utilization by others. If one is left alone (*solipsism*), then there is no flow of reality coming back from practice by and with others.

The sense of being someone significant or of doing something significant is the unexpected 'gain' from the life lost to oneself but treasured by others, the life 'handed over' (*paradidomi* – the fate of Jesus before his opponents, 9.31; 14.41). The life handed over – 'lost' – is then used by those to whom it is given, or by those who help themselves to it.

I have encountered elements of this myself. By giving oneself over to the people of the inner city, and especially inner-city Christian communities, it seems to me that dynamic forces are released which work for the redemption and salvation of others. By putting Urban Theology Unit and Ashram Community houses and projects in the context of the inner city, a style of 'losing life', or of 'downsizing', or of 'journey downwards' is facilitated, which leads to the growth and self-realization of those already in the context, and also a discovery of their own 'true selves' on the part of those who give themselves as living incarnations into that context and its community and projects.[30]

Notes

1 This method is that of the first two 'Models and methods' in the Introduction.
2 F. Warburton Lewis, *Jesus of Galilee, Saviour of Men* (London: Nisbet, 1945), *Jesus, Son of God* (London: Nisbet, 1950).
3 Leslie D. Weatherhead, *The Transforming Friendship: A Book about Jesus and Ourselves* (London: Hodder & Stoughton, 1936).
4 Vincent Taylor, *The Gospel According to St. Mark* (London: Macmillan & Co., 1952).
5 Eduard Schweizer, *Lordship and Discipleship* (London: SCM Press, 1960). The German edition was *Erniedrigung und Erhöhung bei Jesus und seinen Nachfolgern* (Zurich: Zwingli-Verlag, 1955). The German title translates as 'Humiliation and Exaltation in Jesus and his Followers'.

6 Karl Barth, *Church Dogmatics*, IV. 3 (Edinburgh: T&T Clark, 1961), pp. 588–601.

7 Dietrich Bonhoeffer, *The Cost of Discipleship* (abridged) (London: SCM Press, 1948).

8 John J. Vincent, 'The Evangelism of Jesus', *Journal of Bible and Religion*, XXIII.4, (October 1955), pp. 266–271, p. 267.

9 John J. Vincent, 'Discipleship and Synoptic Studies', *Theologische Zeitschrift*, 16.6, (Nov.–Dec. 1960), pp. 456–69, p. 460.

10 John J. Vincent, *Disciple and Lord: The Historical and Theological Significance of Discipleship in the Synoptic Gospels* (Sheffield: Academy Press, 1976).

11 Bas M. F. van Iersel, *Mark: A Reader-Response Commentary*, JSNT Suppl. 164 (Sheffield: Sheffield Academic Press, 1998), p. 189.

12 van Iersel, *Mark*, p. 189. See also Ched Myers, *Binding the Strong Man* (Maryknoll: Orbis Books, 1980), pp. 245–7.

13 'To cling to life (existence) is to lose one's real self.' Morna D. Hooker, *The Gospel According to St. Mark* (London: A&C Black, 1991), p. 209.

14 Cf. David Rhoads on 'Losing Life for Others in the Face of Death', *Reading Mark, Engaging the Gospel* (Minneapolis: Fortress Press, 2004), pp. 44–62.

15 Susan Miller, *Women in Mark's Gospel*, JSNT Suppl. 259 (London: T&T Clark International, 2004), p. 23.

16 Cf. Vincent, *Disciple and Lord*, p. 113; also in my paper, note 27 below. Morna Hooker sees Jesus performing 'dramatic actions', 'prophetic dramas'. *The Signs of a Prophet: The Prophetic Action of Jesus* (London: SCM Press, 1997), pp. 77–8.

17 However, Susan Miller, *Women in Mark's Gospel*, p. 23, observes that Mark uses *diakoneo*, 'to serve', only for Jesus (10.45) and women (Simon's mother-in-law in 1.31, the women who followed him in 15.41), but not for the male disciples.

18 John Vincent, *Journey: Explorations into Discipleship*, 4 Vols (Sheffield: Ashram Press, 2002–04).

19 Vincent, *Journey*, Vol. 1, p. 6.

20 John Vincent, *Christian Nuclear Perspective* (London: Epworth Press, 1966), pp. 21–2.

21 Cf. my comments on moving to Sheffield in *Into the City* (London: Epworth Press, 1982), pp. 10–15.

22 Elizabeth O'Connor, *Journey Inwards, Journey Outwards* (New York: Harper & Row, 1972).

23 Later elaborated in the Carl Michalson Memorial Lecture at Drew Theological Seminary: 'Christian Theology and the Challenges of our Times', *Drew Gateway* (Winter, 1976). Reprinted as *Alternative Journeys* (Sheffield: Urban Theology Unit, 1981).

24 Vincent, *Alternative Journeys*, p. 21.

25 Chris Rowland, 'The Journey Downward' in Ian K. Duffield (ed.), *Urban Christ: Responses to John Vincent* (Sheffield: Urban Theology Unit, 1997), pp. 35–46, p. 37.

26 John Vincent, *Hope from the City* (London: Epworth Press, 2000), pp. 126–34.

27 Cf. my paper 'A Markan Version of the Imitation of Christ', Institute for Methodist Theological Studies, Oxford, August 2002 (publication forthcoming).

28 For some highly suggestive reflections on the self-perceptions of urban ministry, cf. the comments of previous Sheffield colleague Jane Grinonneau, 'Incomers – and Jesus' Ministry of Incarnation' in my *Hope from the City*, pp. 126–34; or

Laurie Green's comments on 'Street Level Ministry' in his *Urban Ministry and the Kingdom of God* (London: SPCK, 2003), pp. 121–41.

29 So *Radical Jesus: The Way of Jesus Then and Now* (1st edn, Marshall, Morgan and Scott, 1986; 2nd edn, Sheffield: Ashram Press, 2004). Cf. p. 7: 'I have almost learnt as much about the Gospel stories from working in the urban wilderness of today as I have from studying all the books about the New Testament.'

30 See my *Theology from the City* (London: Epworth Press, forthcoming).

9

Following Jesus with the women in Mark

MARY COTES

I first fell in love with Mark's Gospel when I was 20 years old. As a student of modern languages I had been doing a placement in France and was returning home for a Christmas holiday. In my hand luggage I was carrying a novel and a little book on Mark's Gospel that a friend in France had asked me to pass on to someone I knew back in Britain. There was a terrible snowstorm, and the plane was delayed hours. Once I had finished the novel, I pulled out the book on Mark . . . and read it from cover to cover. I was enthralled then, and have been enthralled ever since, through years training for ministry, through my doctoral studies and through my ministry. At every corner, this Gospel has encouraged or challenged me and urged me to go in directions I might not otherwise have taken; and I suspect that its influence is not through with me yet.

When I first read Mark's Gospel with a special regard for the way in which it portrays women, I was captivated. Although the main thread of the plot of the Gospel was already well known to me, I had barely noticed before these powerful stories of female characters who, if only for a moment, are thrust into the foreground of the narrative. Simon's mother-in-law, the haemorrhaging woman, the Syrophoenician woman, the widow at the Temple, the woman who anoints Jesus, and the women, witnesses to Jesus' death and resurrection, who follow him from Galilee to Jerusalem – each in their own way mesmerized me as they burst on to the scene, demonstrating the attributes of exemplary discipleship.

What I would like to do in the course of this essay is to explain how the female characters who appear in the Gospel encouraged and influenced me back in those days, and then to describe some of the very different ways in which they continue to challenge me even now. I shall begin by considering how most of the women in Mark appear as models of discipleship within the gospel story.[1] Then I shall look at them as typical of the 'outsiders' who appear in the Gospel – examining particularly the first five – and see how their exemplary discipleship is related to their marginality. After this, I shall turn to the women who follow Jesus from Galilee to Jerusalem, who become the witnesses to the cross, burial and empty tomb. In each section I shall try to describe how a growing understanding of the themes of the Gospel has had an impact on my own discipleship and ministry, and I shall finish by reflecting on the challenges that the gospel leaves me with today.

Models of discipleship

Simon's mother-in-law (1.29–31): a model of servanthood

Simon's mother-in-law is the first woman to appear in the Gospel. Her presence occupies but three verses, yet her action has a significance which echoes through the whole of Mark's story of Jesus. The narrative describes how, raised by Jesus from her fever, 'she served them'. In one short phrase the narrative offers here an image of servanthood which is at the heart of Mark's understanding of true discipleship: as Jesus says, 'Anyone who wants to become great among you must be your servant' (10.43). In the Gospel as a whole, the word *diakonos* and its cognates is perhaps surprisingly used very little. The principal occurrence of the verb is in relation to Jesus himself (10.45).

Interestingly, the verb is never used to describe the actions of the twelve: they systematically fail in their discipleship. However, the word *is* used also to describe certain other characters in the Gospel. First, it occurs towards the beginning of the Gospel in relation to the activity of the angels, administering to Jesus as he faces temptation in the desert (1.13). Servanthood is the proper response of those who understand his true identity. Apart from this occurrence, however, the only human characters in the entire gospel story to whom the quality of servanthood is attributed are women: the women who watch the cross from a distance (15.40–41), and here, where it is used of Simon's mother-in-law.

The woman with the flow of blood (5.25–34): an example of faith

Whereas other healing miracles in the Gospel begin with a formula such as *kai erchetai*, 'and there came', and open the pericope with a verb after which the subject appears, this is the only case in the Gospel where the noun 'the woman' opens the pericope. This is unusual, and highlights right from the outset the significance of this character's femaleness. Meanwhile, the language in which her complaint is described clearly echoes the language of the Levitical purity codes (Lev. 15.19–33) and presents the woman as the one who epitomizes uncleanness in relation to the Law. Not only has she a flow of blood, but she has had it without stopping for twelve years. The number of years she has suffered not only makes it clear that her condition is permanent and desperate – as the narrative points out – but also highlights the particularly Jewish nature of the problem, as does the geographical setting of the story, on Jewish soil. The Levitical codes make it clear that any man coming into contact with her will be contaminated (Lev. 15.19). So her act in touching Jesus is a courageous one. She breaks the taboos and dares to believe that rather than her making him unclean by their contact, *he* will instead make *her* clean.

This woman is therefore the boundary-breaker who heralds the super-ceding of purity codes which enable the welcome of Gentiles into the Church. She throws cultural and religious norms out of the window – and as a result is congratulated by Jesus for her faith. In contrast to other healing stories in the Gospel where characters in need throw themselves at Jesus' feet and beg for a healing before any miracle takes place, here events occur the other way round. The woman starts by believing and by claiming a healing for herself, and only at the end of the narrative does she come forward and throw herself at Jesus' feet. She is thus the only character in the Gospel to 'claim' a healing without first asking for it, and Jesus warmly accepts and affirms her as he names her 'daughter'.

The Syrophoenician woman (7.24–30): a visionary theologian

In the first place, this woman has enormous tenacity. She will not give up without a fight and cares little for politeness and decorum. Even though Jesus is seeking peace and quiet, this woman dares to intrude on his rest in order to beg him to save her daughter's life. When at first Jesus refuses, she simply will not take no for an answer and persists. She has courage and persever-ance, which in the end win through.

However, there is more to this woman than what can simply be account-ed for by sheer perseverance, however praiseworthy it might be. Much fur-ther-reaching is her capacity to speak as a theologian. When faced with Jesus' initial refusal, her insights come into their own. She has a wide vision of God and she is unwilling to let go of it – in fact, the narrower the vision that Jesus presents to her of his own ministry to the children, the wider becomes her own understanding of the God whose care extends to those imaged and defined as the dogs under the table eating the children's crumbs. Such is her passion for this insight, she even adopts Jesus' derogatory language, describ-ing Gentiles as dogs, when she refers to her own people. She has the sense that God's care does not stop with the boundaries dividing Jew from Gentile, but extends to all who call on God. In naming Jesus as *Kyrie* she heralds the confession of faith of the Gentile Church responding to the vision of a God whose grace extends to all nations. Her determined engagement in debate with Jesus and her incisive wisdom win through. In the end she is congrat-ulated for 'her word'. She goes home to find her daughter well – evidence of the power and truth of her faith and understanding.

The widow (12.41–44): a foreshadower of Christ

The humble widow who puts her two small coins into the Temple treasury is also, in a sense, held as a model of discipleship. As the one who sacrifices all she has, her whole living, she foreshadows the Jesus who will give his life up, sacrificially, as a ransom for many (10.45). At many levels, the passion narrative is one that describes Jesus as an agent. He it is who takes actively the decision to go to Jerusalem, knowing what the outcome will be, and teaching those who come after him that they too are called to take up their cross (8.31–34; 9.30–31; 10.33–34). He it is who actively engages with the authorities even though he is aware of their opposition, and in a sense provokes their ultimate reaction to him (2.6–12; 2.15–20; 2.23–26; 3.1–6; 7.1–13; 11.15–18; 12.1–12; 12.13–40). Underlying the whole gospel narrative, then, is the sense of Jesus' self-sacrifice. The placing of the story of the widow at the end of the passion predictions and teaching about discipleship enables her to be seen as one who is ready and willing to leave self behind, as Jesus has been teaching.

However, Jesus' words about this widow are painfully two-edged. They immediately follow Jesus' condemnation of the scribes who exploit the poor (12.38–40), and stand in between Jesus' expulsion of the money-changers from the Temple and the condemnation of the fig tree on the one hand (11.15–21), and on the other the prediction of the Temple's destruction (13.1–2). Jesus' comment that the widow has given all she possessed into the Temple treasury is therefore hardly neutral. There is a sense in which she is portrayed, for all the quality of her self-sacrifice, as a victim of injustice. And to that degree, she also foreshadows Jesus, who equally is portrayed in the passion narratives as the victim of a corrupt system. The passion predictions make this clear: a series of passive verbs spell out the fact that Jesus' story is as much about what is done to him by his opponents as what he himself does. Within the narrative, he is both active and passive, both agent and victim. This is also true of the widow: she is both the generous giver and the one whose very last mite is squeezed out of her by a corrupt religious system. Emerging from the shadows, she foreshadows something of the truth of the passion: Jesus not only 'gives himself up as a ransom for many' (10.45), but has his life torn from him by those who unjustly condemn him to death (14.65) and crucify him (15.21).

The anointing woman (14.3–9): a prophet of the crucified King

Sandwiched inside the narrative describing the plot to kill Jesus, this story has a particularly chilling feel. Breaking the jar as might have been done in a burial chamber, the woman pours the perfume over Jesus' head. This woman both grasps and accepts the reality of Jesus' forthcoming suffering and death. Standing against the fury and criticisms of the onlookers, Jesus congratulates her for anointing his body beforehand for burial. Hers is a prophetic act. His use of the future tense and reference to the future in which he will no longer be there, coupled with the use of the term memorial, further heightens the significance of the act and the sense of the inevitability of his forthcoming death. Of course his reference to this is no surprise. On the way to Jerusalem Jesus has made it repeatedly clear to his disciples that his forthcoming death is inevitable (8.31–32; 9.30–31; 10.33–34). His reference to it here does not offer any new prediction, but occurring as it does immediately following the reference to the plot to kill Jesus, Jesus' words seem to seal the inevitability of the predictions.

At the same time, there are hints in the passage of something more. Throughout the story, Jesus' language in describing the woman's act is often both open and ambiguous. This is particularly true at the end of the pericope, where it is not clear whether the 'memorial' he speaks of refers to the woman's memorial to him, or the Church's memorial to the woman. However, this ambiguity is present not just at the end of the story but throughout. Jesus refers to the woman's action as simply 'a beautiful thing'; even at the very end of the story he simply describes the action as 'what she has done'. There is thus an openness about the terms he uses which offers the possibility of an interpretation of the woman's action which is wider than simply that of an anointing for burial.

In ancient Israel kings were anointed by oil being poured on their head (cf. 1 Sam. 10.1; 2 Kings 9.3, 6). The woman's act thus hints at a royal anointing, and the openness of Jesus' language leaves the space for such an implicit understanding. That there is nothing explicit in the narrative is hardly surprising. Although the royal theme is prepared throughout the Gospel, from the first passion prediction, it does not become explicit until the moment of Jesus' trial and death (15.1–18, 26). It is entirely fitting with this pattern, then, that no explicit mention of royal anointing appears in this story. It would be premature and inappropriate. However, this woman, whose action both reflects an anointing for burial and implies an anointing for kingship, points prophetically to the truth about Jesus which emerges as the narrative of the Gospel approaches its climax. The one who can be recognized only on the cross as the Son of God is also the one whose kingship can only be made fully known in death.

The women at the cross (15.40–41): servants and faithful followers

The women at the cross are also models in their way of discipleship. As those who have served, they stand with Simon's mother-in-law as those who have grasped the essentials of Christian living. As those who have followed, and followed right to Jerusalem from Galilee, they have done all that can be asked of a disciple. 'Come, follow me,' says Jesus at the very start of his ministry to the fishermen at the shore side (1.16–20), and to Levi at his desk (2.13–14). As the gospel narrative progresses, so the meaning of true following gains definition. During the Galilean ministry, discipleship allows Jesus' followers to engage in debate with opponents, it is true, but principally to share in Jesus' success. As the narrative progresses to the journey to Jerusalem, so the cost of discipleship starts to be made clear: it involves following a leader who will face public humiliation, arrest and execution (8.31–33; 9.30–32; 10.32–34), and this has radical implications for the followers (8.34–38; 9.35; 10.17–22, 28–31, 35–40). As Jesus' teaching progresses, so the need for disciples to understand the call to self-sacrifice becomes apparent. Once the group arrives in Jerusalem, the pressure upon the followers to remain faithful to the teaching of Jesus becomes even greater as the reality and ferocity of the opposition to Jesus builds up.

It is significant, then, that these women are described as those who have followed. They remain faithful to the last, remaining close enough to him to be able to witness his crucifixion, if from afar. Unlike the twelve who along the road vie for positions of power (9.33–37; 10.35–45) and eventually all desert Jesus (14.51), these women fulfil Jesus' demands, demonstrating by both following and serving that they have understood the crucial connection between the two (10.32–45).

The women at the empty tomb (16.1–8): witnesses to the resurrection

Of all the female characters in the Gospel, these are the women the nature of whose model of discipleship is the least clear. Entrusted with the news of the resurrection, they run from the tomb and say nothing to anybody, because they are afraid. However we are to account for this silence – and I shall return to this later on – the fact still remains that unlike the twelve who run away (14.51) these women are witnesses to the empty tomb and entrusted with the news of Jesus' resurrection, and with his promise to meet his disciples back in Galilee.

It is important for the proclamation of the faith that these women offer into the narrative the presence of the threefold witness – to the death and burial of Jesus and to the empty tomb. At another level, however, the gospel narrative implies that it is because of their faithfulness in following Jesus to the cross that these women are subsequently entrusted with the message of the young man at the empty tomb. As followers along the way, they have heard the threefold passion predictions. As followers to Jerusalem, they have proved their faithfulness through their service and through their witness to the suffering and death of Jesus and his burial. As followers to the point of going to the tomb with the intention of anointing his body, they are commissioned to be messengers, informing the twelve of the fulfilment of Jesus' predictions of his resurrection. Arguably more than any other character in Mark's story, they are called to proclaim the gospel!

When as a theological student taking a course in feminist theology I first looked carefully at the female characters in Mark, little did I suspect the impact such a reading would have on me! Although the individual stories were already familiar to me, I was excited to find the female characters as a whole so systematically portrayed as models of discipleship within the whole context of the gospel narrative. As a young woman, I had struggled to be accepted by and into the very male structures of the Baptist Church to train for the ordained ministry, and as a student of theology the wounds which such a struggle had inflicted were still open. For that reason, the reading of Mark's Gospel in the light of the insights of writers such as Elisabeth Schüssler Fiorenza[2] was for me a liberating experience. As I read of the Jesus who turned to the women in the Gospel and congratulated them either directly or implicitly for the quality of their discipleship, I felt my own discipleship affirmed and my own path as an ordinand upheld in ways that I had not heard before.

Discipleship at the margins

For all their model discipleship, however, the female characters in the Gospel of Mark are all, arguably, marginal in one way or another, given that by and large women in the ancient world had inferior status. As such, the female characters in the Gospel are typical of the 'outsiders' of the gospel narrative who show that they have understood the truth of the gospel when the 'insiders', those who should know better, are far from understanding it. If the 'insiders' are to make headway as disciples, they need to turn their eyes towards the people on the edges. It is there that they will find their inspiration. The outsiders will be their teachers.

In this section I shall be looking again at the first five of the women I examined above, all of whom are anonymous. In each case, I shall be pointing to their marginality and showing how the quality of their discipleship and understanding offers within the Gospel a contrast and a challenge to the failures and weaknesses of other, male, characters, such as the twelve and the religious authorities. It is in this way that these female 'outsiders' become examples where the 'insiders' do not. Because the women who follow Jesus to Jerusalem include some who are named, and because those particular women, as witnesses to the death, burial and empty tomb of Jesus, play an important role in the plot of Mark, they are arguably less marginal than the five I isolate here, and for this reason I do not include them in this section, but shall be considering them in a separate section later.

Simon's mother-in-law: challenging those who seek status

There is no doubt that this woman is socially on the margins of society, as would be any woman dependent on her family in the ancient world. We never know her name; we know her, as most women in the ancient world, only in terms of the relationship she has with a man. In her own right, she is anonymous; she is simply a mother-in-law. Equally, the Gospel places her geographically on the edge, in Capernaum, where Jesus begins his ministry, and in the private world of a home. She is no public figure. Like many of the women in the Gospel, she has no active part in the plot as such; she does nothing to push the action forward, nothing to change the direction the story takes. She appears simply as a cameo, a snapshot of true discipleship on the very edges of the narrative.

Yet the servanthood of Simon's mother-in-law offers a striking contrast to those characters whose area of activity lies, supposedly, nearer the centre. As the focus of the Gospel moves closer to Jerusalem, the place of influence and power, so examples of servanthood get harder to come by. Rather, the pictures of power-mongering become more frequent. Once they are on the way to Jerusalem, for example, the twelve spend their time not exceeding one another in acts of service, but in arguing as to who is the greatest (9.33–37) and vying for positions of power in the Kingdom (10.35–45). Once arrived in Jerusalem, the lack of servanthood becomes even more salient. Not only are we presented with the picture of the scribes who parade about and enjoy receiving the obsequious greetings of others, and who far from serving others rather exploit them (12.41–44), but we are also offered the desperate narrative of the failure of the twelve to serve faithfully: Judas betrays Jesus (14.10–11), Peter, James and John fall asleep praying (14.32–42), Peter denies him (14.66–72), and finally all abandon him (14.51). Nor are the Roman military exempt from criticism. The picture that the Gospel portrays of them is a cruel caricature of servanthood, as they place a crown of thorns on Jesus' head and fake gestures of servility while beating him and spitting on him (15.16–20).

The woman with the flow of blood: challenging the guardians of tradition

Even more so than Simon's mother-in-law, this woman is well and truly at the margins and even more anonymous. As a woman with continuous bleeding, she is unmarriageable, unable to have children, and unlikely to be in a relationship with a man. Her condition makes her permanently unclean according to the Law (cf. Lev. 15.25). Worse still, as the text informs us, she has spent so much seeking a cure that now she is destitute.

The painful truth of the Gospel is that it is a woman on the edge who has the faith to overturn the cultural taboos of her day, while those near the centre hold on to the boundaries tightly. In fact, the closer the characters' relationship to the religious establishment and the centre of power, the more heavily protected their boundaries become. Those who complain that Jesus and his disciples are breaking the Sabbath by picking corn are the Pharisees (3.23–28). When Jesus goes a step further and breaks the boundaries by curing a man with a withered hand on the Sabbath (3.1–6), the Pharisees start to plot with the Herodians; and not long after, we hear that scribes have come down from Jerusalem, with the accusation that Beelzebul is in him (3.22). By the time we get to the tricky issue of handwashing, the opposition has increased: Jesus' opponents number not only Pharisees but scribes who have come down from Jerusalem (7.1), concerned at the implications of Jesus' scandalous rejection of boundaries. Once in Jerusalem, Jesus is surrounded by interrogators who seek to catch him out on more subtle issues of boundaries (12.13–17, 18–27). In the end, of course, the establishment condemns Jesus not simply for having broken the traditional cultural boundaries but for breaking the boundaries of orthodoxy by the very identity he claims for himself (14.61–64). As the tearing of the Temple curtain shows (15.38), Jesus is the boundary-breaker par excellence. By his constant overturning of traditional boundaries, he represents the ultimate threat to those in power. This woman, daring to break the taboos of the purity codes, follows humbly in his footsteps.

The Syrophoenician woman: challenging the conservatives

Once again, this woman is very much at the margins: a Syrophoenician whose Gentile identity is emphasized by the description of the illness that her little daughter is suffering from as being possessed by an unclean spirit. The expression is repeated. As she comes to Jesus herself, the chances are that she has no husband, father or brother to represent her. Perhaps she is a widow.

As a theologian speaking from the edge, her vision of God is strikingly different from the theological insight or lack of it expressed by the twelve. Already in Galilee, the twelve never shine: they are accused of lacking faith (4.41), of having closed minds and not understanding the miracle of the loaves (6.52), and of lacking perception (8.21). As the journey to Jerusalem continues, so their closed-mindedness grows more pronounced. Despite his confession that Jesus is the Christ, Peter cannot accept that Jesus' path might take him to arrest and crucifixion (8.32–33) and, only a few days' later, misses the point entirely at the transfiguration of Jesus, wanting to create tents for the three participants (9.6). Still on the way to Jerusalem, the disciples are unable to cast out a demon (9.18), and despite having heard Jesus' teaching about children (9.37) nonetheless send the children away when they come to him seeking a blessing (10.13).

More entrenched still, however, are the theological perceptions held by those functioning on the inside, in places of power. From the very outset of the Gospel, authorities of the Law offer opposition to Jesus. The scribes are outraged that he forgives the sins of a paralytic man (2.6), the Pharisees are uncomfortable at Jesus' eating with tax-collectors and sinners (2.16) and picking corn on the Sabbath (2.24). The closer the explicit connection of the authorities with Jerusalem, the more entrenched the theology becomes, and the more threatening and dangerous the opposition. The Pharisees are so scandalized by Jesus' breaking the Sabbath that they start to plot with the Herodians against Jesus (3.6) and together with the scribes fail to understand Jesus' point of view on handwashing (7.1ff.). Meanwhile the scribes from Jerusalem go as far as to accuse Jesus of having Beelzebul in him (3.22). Once Jesus arrives in Jerusalem, the Temple personnel are determined to catch him out rather than share his vision (14.13–27). Most lacking in insight are the members of the Sanhedrin who cannot grasp who Jesus is (14.53–65) and who condemn him to death. Such is the portrait of the entrenchment of the authorities that it is no surprise that the Temple as a whole is accused of corruption (11.12–21) and that its destruction is foretold (13.2).

The widow: challenging the rich and powerful

It might be argued that here, at last, we have a woman who belongs not to the margins, but to the centre of power: to Jerusalem. The picture we have shows her amidst the crowds in the Temple treasury. She at least has come into the Temple, the heart of the Judaic cultural and religious world. Yet, as a widow, she remains very much on the margins of society, one of the little people representing the very poorest of the poor, and the text very deliberately contrasts her with rich donors (12.41). There is no sense in which she has a real place at the centre. On the contrary, by the end of the short narrative, having given her two small coins away, she is even more destitute than she was at the beginning and disappears into the background as quickly as she came.

Standing as a figure who is commented upon for giving up her money and livelihood, she is nonetheless surrounded by, and implicitly contrasted to, those who cannot give up either wealth or power. Already, on the way to Jerusalem, the text introduces the rich young man who, despite good intentions, cannot give up his wealth (10.17–22), and Jesus teaches his disciples that it is easier for a camel to pass through the eye of a needle than for a rich man to enter the Kingdom of God (10.25). In Jerusalem itself we are presented with the corruption of the Temple tradesmen (11.17), the corruption of the scribes (12.40), and those who participate in a death plot in order to keep their own power and authority secure (14.1). The few in power at the centre who do actually part with their money are, sadly, those corrupt chief priests willing to pay Judas for handing Jesus over to them (14.11). An implicit contrast equally exists between the widow and the twelve, none of whom are ready to risk all to follow Jesus and who in the end abandon him to save themselves (14.51). Even the young man in white linen, arguably dressed for death in a shroud, slips out of the clothing and runs away naked (14.52). Although his dress suggests that it is his intention to follow Jesus to the cross and the tomb, he is no more able to sustain his discipleship than Peter is (14.29; 14.66–72), and the nakedness that is revealed as he runs serves as a symbol of the sinfulness that in the end causes him to abandon Jesus.

The woman who anoints Jesus: challenging the denial of Jesus' true identity

Once again, rather as in the case of the widow, this woman might be seen as belonging somehow to the centre, offering hospitality to Jesus as he arrives in Jerusalem. Yet here again this woman belongs to the margins. The scene is Bethany, which is explicitly described as outside of Jerusalem (11.11), and the setting in which the woman performs her act is the house of a leper – one who represents all that is unclean, an outsider in a profound sense.

The insight of this woman, bringing together through her action both her perception of Jesus' forthcoming death and her understanding of his royal identity, puts to shame the limited understanding of Jesus' identity presented both by the twelve and by the Temple authorities. The twelve, represented by Peter, certainly have grasped something of Jesus' royal identity: Peter describes Jesus as the Christ, the anointed one (8.29). However, they fail to see how this identity could be linked to Jesus' death. When, immediately after Peter's confession, Jesus predicts his future suffering and execution, Peter remonstrates with him and is described by Jesus as Satan (8.33).

Those at the centre of power also lack insight as to Jesus' true identity. However, for them, the idea of Jesus' suffering is not a problem: rather, it is his identity as the Christ which is the stumbling block (14.61). Even though Jesus makes his identity known at the moment of the trial (14.61), the irony of the narrative is that the Sanhedrin cannot believe him, and therefore condemn him to death (14.64). With equal irony, the text describes how the Sanhedrin accuse him of claiming to be King of the Jews, and nail the title above him on the cross as a form of abuse, all the while unaware of the truth of their allegations. The irony is sustained as the title King of the Jews follows Jesus from the court of Pilate (15.2) to Pilate's questioning of the crowd (15.10, 13), to the torture of Jesus at the palace (15.16–20), and to the cross itself (15.26).

To me as a young minister of a church in the South Wales valleys, this 'inside-out' dynamic in the Gospel was a huge inspiration. A church seeking to be open to 'the outsiders' in the community, we opened a night shelter and a drop-in for homeless youngsters, initially in the church hall. The impact of this on us was startling. In the first place, we began to receive not only huge support on the one hand, but also, on the other, insulting calls and mail from members of the community who urged us to have nothing to do with 'layabouts', and on occasions we were misrepresented or vilified in the local press. Given the pictures of opposition that we are given in the Gospel, it perhaps should not have surprised us that we had our opponents! But more importantly, however, we started as a church community to be changed, not to say converted. The transformation that came upon all of us was wonderfully exemplified by one faithful church member, an older woman who volunteered to help in the drop-in. When she first started she could hardly 'say boo to a goose'. But my overwhelming memory of her is of the emboldened woman she became, making a speech to the members of the local Council, passionately and eloquently advocating the creation of a direct-access hostel in the very centre of town. Allowing the outsiders to be her teachers had changed her through and through.[3]

Models and margins: connecting the two

Reflecting the position generally of women in the ancient world, these women appear in the Gospel as marginal in every way. As we have seen in each case, they are in a marginal position. They are anonymous, described simply, as in the case of the women with haemorrhages, as 'a woman' (5.25), or described, as Simon's mother-in-law, in terms of a male head of the household. They live, mostly, in the private world of the interior, or, as the woman with bleeding, they remain hidden in the crowd and shrink from being identified in public. Little or no direct speech is accorded them in the gospel narrative, and certainly no public speech. Either their remarks are reported indirectly, or they are silent. Simon's mother-in-law says nothing either before or after her healing. The woman with bleeding is actually accorded some direct speech, but the narrative is careful to point out that these are words which she uttered to herself (5.28). The dialogue she has with Jesus at the end of the episode presents us with direct speech from Jesus, but what the woman has to say is merely summed up with the words 'she told him the whole truth'. The Syrophoenician woman offers an exception to this pattern, but both the widow and the woman who anoints Jesus' head establish it again. These are women who are talked about, commented on or criticized, but who do not speak for themselves.[4]

But these female characters are also marginal to the action of the plot. Although, as we have already shown, they are important to the Gospel as a whole in that they offer pictures of model discipleship in a narrative populated by characters who are far from exemplary, they nonetheless do nothing in terms of developing the plot. This role is taken by male actors who, in keeping with the social position of men in the ancient world, are the principal agents. The action in the Gospel is thus created and propelled by Jesus, his disciples and his opponents, and its development is charted essentially by the changing relationships between the three elements. The female characters stand apart; they merely offer cameos of discipleship, in general disappearing as quickly as they have appeared.

What is most striking, however, about these figures on the margins of society and at the edges of the story is that the exemplary discipleship which they model, or for which they are congratulated by Jesus, is actually connected to their marginality, and often *arises directly out of it, or contributes directly to it.*

Simon's mother-in-law, for example, undoubtedly offers a model of disciple-ship in the way she is raised from illness to serve others. Yet in the ancient world, servanthood was considered to be the hallmark of any virtuous woman.[5] So that the very servanthood which is held in such high regard in the teaching of Jesus is, in the case of this woman, simply a question of her fulfilling a trad-itional woman's role: the role of one who was socially inferior and subservient to her husband.

The great act of faith achieved by the woman with haemorrhages arises equally out of her marginality. The point is that this woman who is suffer-ing from a condition considered to be taboo in the ancient world is both so desperate for a cure and yet also at the same time so desperate to stay hid-den because of her condition, that she is pushed by her situation to a point of huge daring and courage, claiming a healing from behind without asking for it. This is identified as faith by Jesus, yet a character with a less cruel and socially unacceptable condition might well not have been pushed to such lengths.

The case of the Syrophoenician woman is not dissimilar. She too is des-perate for Jesus to offer a healing – albeit for her daughter – and she too finds herself, for reasons of birth rather than bodily condition, on the wrong side of the boundaries. Her vision of a God whose care and love transcends all that separates Jew and Gentile is born out of her fear and experience of exclusion, just as her naming of Jesus as *Kyrie* – the title with which the Gentile church shall come to know Jesus – arises out of her pressing, urgent need to be included in the sweep of his ministry. Her desperation pushes her to acknowledge her dependence on his power and authority and to challenge his thinking. Her identity and experience as an outsider, and the strength and revolutionary quality of her vision of God, are thus inextricably linked.

The way in which marginality plays a part in the picture of discipleship is perhaps slightly different in the case of the widow. While the great gen-erosity of the widow, foreshadowing the self-giving of Jesus, is not in ques-tion, here the extremity of the widow's social and financial position serves not so much to motivate the act of discipleship, as to strengthen the way it is portrayed. The widow has so little, and yet by giving her all makes herself entirely destitute. The pitifulness of her initial situation adds a powerful dimen-sion to her gesture and makes the contrast with the scribes who swallow the property of widows the more striking (12.38–40). Equally, when we under-stand the widow as a victim as much as an actor, the portrait of the extreme poverty of the widow enables Jesus' comments about her to be taken as a more scathing criticism of the corrupt Temple system. This is a system which devours even the little which remains to the destitute.

The woman who pours perfume on Jesus' head prophetically points to Jesus' identity not only through her act, but also by contributing *as a woman* to the scene in the house in which the act takes place. As we have seen, this scene has overtones of a royal anointing. But just as the kingship of Jesus will not be made known in power and glory, but revealed only by the cross, so also the scene in which the anointing takes place is one which turns on its head the traditional grandiose style of such an occasion and presents a deliberately alternative, humble setting consistent with the picture of a crucified king. The scene takes place not in the city of Jerusalem, but in a village; not in the Temple in the company of priests ritually clean, but in the house of the leper. The crowd of onlookers, far from crying 'Long live the King', offers only complaints. And at the heart of the picture, the one who performs the ceremony is not the high priest, at the top of the social scale, whose name is well known and charted in the history books, but simply an anonymous woman, a nobody off the streets.

These days, I find that relating to these five female characters in Mark in the light of this connection between discipleship and marginality is actually quite a painful business, and it presents me with uncomfortable questions that are a far cry from the initial sense of liberation that I experienced as a young theological student. While each of these figures may well be portrayed as a model disciple in some way, there is nothing explicitly to suggest that they become leaders, or that they break out of the traditional roles assigned to them as women, or that they escape their anonymity. By the faithful nature of their discipleship they serve as examples or present a telling contrast to those in power, but they never take on that power for themselves. As such, they would seem to offer very little encouragement to women like me who, believing that structures should embody justice for men and women, have struggled their way into the places of influence from which they have been excluded for centuries. Yes, two of these passages – the woman with haemorrhages and the Syrophoenician woman – offer encouragement to those at the edges desperately struggling against the taboos and traditions which oppress them; but the others – Simon's mother-in-law, the widow, the anointing woman – keep women securely in their traditional place and offer no prospect of any change in situation whatever. They are examples of discipleship by accepting an unjust status quo. Meanwhile none of these passages encourages me to hope that exemplary discipleship might, but just might, be attributed to women who have succeeded in escaping anonymity and marginality and have found their place in leadership roles. If anything, these particular women characters, acting at the margins, imply exactly the opposite.

Discipleship at the centre

The women who follow Jesus to Jerusalem, however, offer a different picture. When Jesus issues his many invitations to follow him, the implication is that following involves faithfulness all the way to the place of his arrest, condemnation and death, and these women show precisely that degree of faithfulness. They have come from the margins of Galilee and made their way, in obedience to Jesus, into the city with all its challenges and horrors and corruption. While many of them remain nameless, some of them are considered significant enough to escape anonymity, and have their names recorded in the Gospel (15.40–41) – a rare honour! Perhaps here I will find characters to whom I can more readily relate.

These women have witnessed the two sides of Jesus' ministry. As those who come from Galilee, they have known the region where, immediately after his baptism (1.9–11), Jesus has begun his ministry and started to proclaim the Kingdom of God (1.14–15). It is where Jesus has called disciples to him (1.16–20; 2.13–14) and appointed the twelve (3.13–19), and drawn the crowds. Jesus' ministry in Galilee has been a time of 'success': of miracles (1.21–28, 40–45; 2.1–12; 3.1–6; 4.35–41; 5.1–43; 6.30–44, 45–52, 53–56; 7.24–30, 31–37; 8.1–10, 22–26), of the crowd's flocking to hear his teaching (3.8–10, 32; 4.1), of word about him spreading far and wide (1.28, 37, 45; 3.20; 5.20). Galilee has been the place of Jesus' first encounters with the authorities (2.1–11, 15–22, 23–28; 3.1–6, 22; 7.1–23), and the siding of the crowds with him rather than with the figures of institutional religion (1.22; 2.12). The ministry in Galilee has been a time of encounters with ordinary, humble people on the edge; people of the land and the sea, people living far from the influence of the city, who are open to the possibilities and challenges that his whirlwind ministry represents.

But then these same women have followed Jesus on the way to Jerusalem and with the reluctant twelve have heard Jesus' predictions of his passion (8.31–33; 9.30–32; 10.32–34). In Jerusalem itself they have been surrounded by the messy and dangerous realities of power politics. Jerusalem is the place of Jesus' growing struggles with the authorities and where the entrenchment and lack of vision of the religious establishment is all too clear to see. The role of the Temple as the locus of true worship is compromised by its desire for status (13.1) and its focus on making money (11.15–19). Religious leaders enjoy dressing up for the show and the food, but are little concerned for the poor (12.38–40). Those in power are terrified of losing their status. Certainly at the centre exciting transformations do occur (12.28–34). But it is also the place where good and honest disciples are in danger of being corrupted (14.10), of betraying, denying (14.66–72) and abandoning their master (14.51). It is the place where public opinion is fickle (15.14) and the establishment conducts itself in such a way as to court the judgement of God (11.12–14; 13.2). The very people who imagine themselves to be great and good – bastions of the truth of God – end up pinning Jesus to a cross (14.64). So the women who follow from the margins to the centre walk a painful path. They know the glory and the joy of Galilee and the freedom of the gospel at the margins; they also know the failure and the sinfulness of Jerusalem.

The story of these women presents me with a challenge and, in certain ways, a kind of mirror to my own situation. Currently, I have a leadership role as the Ecumenical Moderator to what is known as the Mission Partnership of the Milton Keynes Churches' Council, a courageous and exciting experiment in regional ecumenism which draws together the traditional denominations into an unusually close relationship. I suppose it could be said that this is a senior position. No matter how marginal the Church may be in today's society, I find myself nonetheless in a place within the ecclesiastical centres of power and influence where I am playing a part alongside other women colleagues within the complexities of the Church's still predominantly male power structures.

Milton Keynes is an absolutely exhilarating place to be and I am very excited to be part of a church which is grappling with what it means to be an ecumenical Christian presence in a rapidly expanding city. However, the journey towards the centre is not without its cost. I cannot help but compare my working life today with my experiences in the South Wales valleys. Young people in the night shelter there had an uncanny way of seeing through the pretences of the many bureaucratic systems they had to be plugged into, and their passionate cries for justice and dignity, charged with unprintable words, used to ring daily in my mind. Then, as chaplain to my local mental-health unit, one of the questions I was most frequently asked was, 'Did you ever try to commit suicide?' And when I mumbled that no, I never did, the reply would instantly come back, 'Well, *why* didn't you?' These days however, as I attend meetings with denominational or city leaders I am asked different sorts of questions. Who is going to come up with the cash to fund such-and-such a post? How can we structure the constitution so as to satisfy the requirements of all the parties? How will the implementation of such-and-such a policy impact on the way we are seen by other bodies? Of course these are important issues in their way. But I notice that in my current environment few people ever rail at me about injustice or ask me why I bother to stay alive. At the centre of power, fundamental questions of life and faith which strip away the pretences and challenge the existing priorities of the system seem not to get on to the agenda. Perhaps they are too threatening. And there are days when I am scared that the sort of questions which confront me in my current post may deafen me and distance me from the compelling voices which cry at the edge.

While many words are often spoken about the way in which women's leadership can ultimately bring a new face to a principally male culture, I find that very often in practice the opposite is true: in order to survive in leadership roles in a male culture, women increasingly have to adopt masculine styles of working. I watch with interest the progress of some of my younger, very talented, female colleagues. I see them dressing in their smart dark suits, and I notice that as time goes on they start to pitch their voices on a deeper note and adopt ways of communicating that are strong and combative, not to say aggressive, highly rational and authoritarian. I observe the same tendencies in certain female politicians, and as I speak to women in management roles across the city they often tell me that their experience is largely the same. In the changes and accommodations to the male culture which I see other women making, I recognize elements of my own inevitable evolution, signs of my own strategies for survival as I have journeyed into the establishment, and often I grieve for the self I once was before I started out. On the path that I have taken, all too often the outsiders have had to conform to the insiders, not the other way round. It is hard to follow Jesus into the places of power.

Back to the margins

Yet for all the challenge and pain which they face in Jerusalem, these women have a crucially important role to play there: they are witnesses to the death and burial of Jesus, and on the third day they are witnesses to the empty tomb. But they are even more than that. Following their encounter with the young man at the tomb they are called to go and give a message to the disciples. This is the message that Jesus has already given to the disciples (14.28), but these women are charged with reminding them of it (16.7). The risen Jesus will meet his disciples in Galilee, back at the margins, in the place where the journey and the ministry first began. These women, who have journeyed into the centre from the edge are charged therefore with a mission: to urge the disciples to leave Jerusalem and all that it implies, and meet Jesus far from the centre of power, back in Galilee.

The thrust of this message, calling the whole group of Jesus' followers – even Peter who of all the twelve might traditionally most be associated with ministry in Jerusalem – to turn outwards rather than inwards and face the edges rather than the centre, is arguably the movement which characterizes the whole of the Gospel of Mark. The movement of Jesus himself traces a journey into the centre to suffering and death, and then, as the risen one, back out to Galilee. Even on the night on which he is betrayed, Jesus looks beyond death and announces that it is in Galilee that his risen glory will be made known (14.28), and it is there, we assume, that the disciples, forgiven for their failures, will begin their path of discipleship anew. The same movement again characterizes the teaching of Jesus in Mark: those on the margins are not so much invited to join up with those at the centre, as those at the centre are invited to be seen in the light of those who show true discipleship at the margins. The little people are not to grow to be like the important people: rather, those in power are to receive the truth from those excluded from power. In Mark's Gospel the insiders are outsiders, and the outsiders the true holders of the secret of the Kingdom. Here the last are first and the first last.

The difficulty with the resurrection narrative in Mark is of course that the women fail to pass the message on. They remain silent. In their silence, they actually conform to a social stereotype: the image of the virtuous woman in the ancient world was the image of one who was silent.[6] There is thus a subtle contrast between these women here at the empty tomb and elsewhere in the Gospel. Whereas in the case, say, of Simon's mother-in-law, her servanthood – the essence of true discipleship – emerges from her performance of a traditional role. Here at the empty tomb, by conforming to a traditional stereotype of women, the opposite occurs: these women fail in their calling. Whether or not their silence is understood as a religious response, the circumstances are essentially the same: the women do not accomplish the task. The challenge is left unfulfilled. It is left to the reader to assume that very challenge, and do what these women fail to do.

This is the radical challenge with which Mark's story of Jesus leaves me, and I find myself pulled in two directions – into the centre and back out to the edge. The Gospel of Mark reminds me that the women who, obedient to his call, follow Jesus into the places of power, are the ones commanded to tell the disciples who have struggled and failed to be faithful at the centre to return to Galilee. It is there that the glory of the risen Christ will be made known. And if these women are entrusted with such a message, then they too are left with the challenge of travelling themselves back to Galilee, following their risen Lord. These are challenges which these same women may not have the wherewithal – the courage or the freedom from social conditioning – to be able to fulfil. The possibility of failure and faithlessness is always there. But so also is the call to follow, its uncomfortable and challenging echoes constantly ringing in the heart and mind of anyone who dares to read Mark often. Falling in love with Mark's Gospel has serious consequences! As the narrative points out at every turn, it is not easy to be a follower of Jesus Christ. But then, he never promised it would be.

Notes

1 This essay was written before I had seen Susan Miller's book, *Women in Mark's Gospel* (London and New York: T&T Clark International, 2004). Miller argues that women are portrayed in Mark in three distinctive ways: as those who serve, as those who anoint, and as key witnesses to Jesus' death and resurrection. She points out that two women in particular offer contrasts to these portraits, namely Herodias and her daughter (6.17–29).
2 Elisabeth Schüssler Fiorenza, *In Memory of Her* (London: SCM Press, 1983), who argues that Mark offers evidence of the 'apostolic leadership of women'. See also Joseph Grassi, *Hidden Heroes of the Gospels* (London: Lamp Press, 1989), pp. 12–44.
3 Jane Grinonneau, in her MMin thesis, 'City Kids as Agents of the Gospel' (UTU/University of Sheffield, 2000), describes the similar and equally inspiring transformation which came over the congregation of Northfield Baptist Church,

Birmingham, in providing play facilities for children from the adjacent urban area of Allen's Cross.

4 This is also true of the women at the cross (15.40–41). They stand there watching, saying nothing. The women at the empty tomb are also silent (16.1–8). Rather than their telling the young man why they have come, it is instead the young man who pre-empts their speech and tells them: 'You are looking for Jesus of Nazareth' (16.6). When they run from the tomb and say nothing to anyone (16.8), they are behaving in a way that is consonant with nearly all the other female characters in the Gospel.

5 This theme is explored in my PhD thesis, 'Images of Women in the Gospel of Mark' (University of Manchester, 1993), ch. 6.

6 I discuss this more fully in my article 'Women, Silence and Fear' in George J. Brooke (ed.) *Women in the Biblical Tradition* (Ceredigion/Lewiston, NY: Edwin Mellen Press, 1992), pp. 150–66.

10

Mark and psychological type

LESLIE J. FRANCIS

Biblical hermeneutics

A major development in the theory and practice of biblical criticism in recent years has concerned the emergence of the crucial issue of perspective or standpoint in the reading and interpretation of biblical texts. The issue of perspective or standpoint takes seriously the role of the reader in interpretation. Within this tradition of biblical hermeneutics particular attention has been given to the formative influence of the social location of the reader, as so well illustrated by the title of the volumes edited by Segovia and Tolbert (1995a, 1995b), *Reading from this Place*. In their preface to this collection of essays, Segovia and Tolbert (1995a, ix) draw attention to the way in which the foundation was set by such movements as feminist criticism, literacy criticism, sociological analysis, and liberation and contextual theologies, all of which questioned the implied claims of the older and established exegetical and theological methods to promote universal and objective interpretation under the construct of an objective and scientific reader. Thus, according to Segovia and Tolbert (1995a, ix):

> Factors traditionally left out of consideration were now becoming areas of exploration – for example, gender, race, ethnic origins, class, sexual orientation, religious affiliation, and socio-political contexts – with a focus on real, flesh–and–blood readers . . . whose reading and interpretation of the texts were seen as affected by their social location.

In other words, concepts, theories and heuristic tools of modern sociology were becoming powerful instruments in the discipline of biblical hermeneutics.

The key perspective of sociology within the process of biblical hermeneutics is made explicit in an essay by Segovia (1995, 57–8):

> I believe that the time has come to introduce the real reader, the flesh–and–blood reader, fully and explicitly, into the theory and practice of biblical criticism; to acknowledge that no reading, informed or uninformed, takes place in a social vacuum or desert . . . with a view of all readings as constructs proceeding from, dependent upon, and addressing a particular social location . . . I should like to propose, therefore, the beginning of a hermeneutical framework for taking the flesh–and–blood reader seriously in biblical criticism, not so much

as a unique and independent individual but rather as a member of distinct and identifiable social configurations.

Psychological perspectives

Taking seriously the issue of the perspective or the standpoint of the reader, in their series of three books Francis and Atkins (2000, 2001, 2002) argue that the concepts and tools of sociology alone are insufficient to provide an adequate account of the horizon from which the text is regarded by the reader. They are in basic agreement with the position encapsulated by Segovia (1995) above that flesh-and-blood readers need to be taken seriously in biblical criticism not so much as 'unique and independent' individuals but rather as members of 'distinct and identifiable' groups. Their point of contention, however, is that such groups can be explained not only in socio-logical categories, but also in psychological categories. In other words, they propose that tools of modern psychology need to be taken more seriously in the discipline of biblical hermeneutics.

The particular tradition within modern psychology to which Francis and Atkins draw attention is the tradition of 'personality and individual differ-ences' (see, for example, Eysenck and Eysenck, 1985). This tradition main-tains, generally speaking, that individual differences can be characterized by a finite number of discrete personality factors, identifiable by mathematical modelling of human responses (say by factor analysis) and replicable across different cultures, across different age groups and across both men and women. Although there is no universal agreement within the psychology of personality and individual differences regarding the best mathematical solution to the problem of individual differences in human personality, some level of agreement has been reached at least in respect of acknowledging the value of a few well-tested solutions, including the three-dimensional model operationalized by the Eysenck Personality Questionnaire (Eysenck and Eysenck, 1975) and the Eysenck Personality Scales (Eysenck and Eysenck, 1991), the four-bipolar model of Jungian psychological type operationalized by the Myers-Briggs Type Indicator (Myers and McCaulley, 1985), and the Keirsey Temperament Sorter (Keirsey and Bates, 1978) and the five-factor model operationalized by the NEO Personality Inventory (Costa and McCrae, 1985).

Each of these different models of personality possess particular strengths which may render them particularly appropriate for specific purposes with-in the broad field of personality and individual differences. Reviewing these different strengths, Francis (2005) argues that the four-bipolar model based on the Jungian notion of psychological type has, for one reason or another, attracted the greatest level of interest and attention among theologians. It is on this model of individual differences that Francis and Atkins (2000, 2001,

2002) construct the SIFT method of biblical hermeneutics and of biblical preaching.

Psychological type

Shaped first by Carl Jung (1971) in his classic book *Psychological Types*, in its best recognized form, as popularized through works like *Gifts Differing* (Myers and Myers, 1980) and *Please Understand Me* (Keirsey, 1998), psychological type theory distinguishes between four bipolar psychological perspectives: two orientations, two perceiving functions, two judging functions and two attitudes.

The two orientations are concerned with where energy is drawn from and focused. On the one hand, extraverts (E) are orientated towards the outer world; they are energized by the events and people around them. They enjoy communicating and thrive in stimulating and exciting environments. They tend to focus their attention upon what is happening outside themselves. They are usually open people, easy to get to know and enjoy having many friends. On the other hand, introverts (I) are orientated towards their inner world; they are energized by their inner ideas and concepts. They enjoy solitude, silence and contemplation, as they tend to focus their attention upon what is happening in their inner life. They may prefer to have a small circle of intimate friends rather than many acquaintances.

The two perceiving functions are concerned with the way in which people perceive information. On the one hand, sensing types (S) focus on the realities of a situation as perceived by the senses. They tend to focus on specific details, rather than the overall picture. They are concerned with the actual, the real and the practical, and tend to be down to earth and matter of fact. On the other hand, intuitive types (N) focus on the possibilities of a situation, perceiving meanings and relationships. They may feel that perception by the senses is not as valuable as information gained from the unconscious mind as indirect associations and concepts impact on their perception. They focus on the overall picture, rather than on specific facts and data.

The two judging functions are concerned with the criteria that people use to make decisions and judgements. On the one hand, thinking types (T) make judgements based on objective, impersonal logic. They value integrity and justice. They are known for their truthfulness and for their desire for fairness. They consider conforming to principles to be of more importance than cultivating harmony. On the other hand, feeling types (F) make judgements based on subjective, personal values. They value compassion and mercy. They are known for their tactfulness and for their desire for peace. They are more concerned to promote harmony than to adhere to abstract principles.

Most operationalizations of Jungian psychological type theory (see for example, Keirsey and Bates, 1978; Francis, 2004) also make use of a fourth index, the attitudes towards the outer world, pioneered by Myers and Briggs. The two attitudes towards the outer world are determined by which of the two sets of functions (that is, perceiving, S/N, or judging, T/F) is preferred in dealings with the outer world. On the one hand, judging types (J) seek to order, rationalize and structure their outer world, as they actively judge external stimuli. They enjoy routine and established patterns. They prefer to follow schedules in order to reach an established goal and may make use of lists, timetables or diaries. They tend to be punctual, organized and tidy. They prefer to make decisions quickly and to stick to their conclusions once made. On the other hand, perceiving types (P) do not seek to impose order on the outer world, but are more reflective, perceptive and open, as they passively perceive external stimuli. They have a flexible, open-ended approach to life. They enjoy change and spontaneity. They prefer to leave projects open in order to adapt and improve them. Their behaviour may often seem impulsive and unplanned.

Jung's view is that each individual develops one of the perceiving functions (sensing or intuition) at the expense of the other, and one of the judging functions (feeling or thinking) at the expense of the other. Moreover, for each individual the preferred perceiving function or the preferred judging function takes preference over the other, leading to the emergence of one dominant function which shapes the individual's dominant approach to life. Dominant sensing shapes the practical person. Dominant intuition shapes the imaginative person. Dominant feeling shapes the humane person. Dominant thinking shapes the analytic person.

Personality and Scripture

Francis and Atkins (2000, 2001, 2002) build on the foundations laid by studies in practical theology and empirical theology in order to develop the SIFT method of biblical hermeneutics and of biblical preaching. They argue that the perceiving functions and the judging functions hold important keys to understanding the psychological perspectives or standpoints which individuals of different psychological types will bring to establish dialogue with biblical texts. According to this view, individuals who prefer sensing will approach Scripture in a very different way from individuals who prefer intuition; and individuals who prefer feeling will approach Scripture in a very different way from individuals who prefer thinking. Moreover, it is the dominant function which will inform the preferred perspective from which text is viewed.

Two important practical implications emerge from the SIFT (sensing, intuition, feeling, thinking) method of biblical hermeneutics and of biblical preaching. The first implication alerts the preacher to the communication problem which may occur between preacher and listener. Dominant sensers may find intuitive preaching leaves them confused and dissatisfied. Dominant intuitives in the congregation may find sensing preaching bores them. Dominant feelers may find themselves left cold by the analytic approach of the thinker. Dominant thinkers may find themselves frustrated by the warm engagement of the feeler.

The second implication alerts the preacher to the need to engage the biblical text with all four psychological functions (sensing, intuition, feeling and thinking). One psychological function alone is inadequate to the task of engaging the text in life-giving dialogue with the contemporary world.

It is for these reasons that Francis and Atkins (2000, 2001, 2002) approach the biblical text with the intention of systematically engaging each of the four psychological functions in turn. The SIFT method of biblical hermeneutics and of biblical preaching will now be illustrated by engaging dialogue between the text of Mark and the four psychological functions.

Sensing

The first step in the SIFT method is to address the sensing perspective. It is the sensing perspective that gets to grip with the text itself and that gives proper attention to the details of the passage and may wish to draw on insights of historic methods of biblical scholarship in order to draw in 'facts' from other parts of the Bible. The first question asks, 'How does this passage speak to the sensing function? What are the facts and details? What is there to see, to hear, to touch, to smell and to taste?'

When sensing types hear a passage of Scripture, they want to savour all the detail of the text and may become fascinated by descriptions that appeal to their senses. They tend to start from a fairly literal interest in what is being said. Sensing types may want to find out all they can about the passage and about the facts that stand behind the passage. They welcome preachers who lead them into the passage by repeating the story and by giving them time to observe and appreciate the details. Sensing types quickly lose the thread if they are bombarded with too many possibilities too quickly.

In approaching Mark 1.40–45, for example, from a sensing perspective Leslie J. Francis and Peter Atkins (2002, 35–6) pay close attention to the details that Mark makes explicit in his text and to the details left implicit but which would be so clearly recognized by the original audience in first-century Palestine. Then Francis and Atkins try to lead the hearers into the power of the narrative by developing their sense of being there at the time. They draw on all the senses of sight, sound, smell, taste and touch. So hear how a sensing preacher addresses Mark 1.40–45.

Sensing perspective on Mark 1.40–45

Awake from slumber and find yourself transported back in time, back, back to first-century Palestine. You are travelling the dusty road on a warm, warm day. Feel the sun beating down on the back of your neck, taste the dust from the road in the back of your throat, smell the parched atmosphere at the back of your nostrils, and see the scorching road running into the distance, peopled with fellow-travellers.

Out there, in the middle of nowhere, your ears prick up and catch a distant sound. You recognize the harsh croak of an untuned voice. You hear an indistinct, but distraught cry. Approaching you along the road is the well-known figure of the leper man.

As the leper man approaches, you see the disfigured unkempt figure. The awful disease has eaten away at self-respect. As the leper man approaches, you hear the distraught cry, 'Unclean, unclean'. The awful disease has eaten away at social relationships and distanced all uncontaminated human contact.

See your fellow-travellers avert their eyes and divert their path. Each traveller, in turn, avoids the leper man and reinforces his sense of loneliness, isolation and distance from the human race.

But there, in the crowd, is a fellow-traveller who disobeys the rules and runs in the face of convention. See Jesus of Nazareth stretch out his hand to touch the leper man who is himself untouchable. Hear the gasp of surprise, the gasp of incredulity, the gasp of horror, as Jesus makes himself unclean by such intimate contact with the leper man, whose disease is so readily communicable, physically, socially and ritually.

See Jesus take up the leper man's cry and shout out his own pollution. See the leper man lay down his leprosy, peel away his disfigurement, slough off his social isolation, and make his way to the priest to proclaim the cleansing and rehabilitation so freely offered.

You have been transported back in time, back, back to first-century Palestine.

Intuition

The second step in the SIFT method is to address the intuitive perspective. It is the intuitive perspective that relates the biblical text to wider issues and concerns. The second question asks, 'How does this passage speak to the intuitive function? What is there to speak to the imagination, to forge links with current situations, to illuminate issues in our lives?'

When intuitive types hear a passage of Scripture they want to know how that passage will fire their imagination and stimulate their ideas. They tend to focus not on the literal meaning of what is being said, but on the possibilities and challenges implied. Intuitive types may want to explore all of the possible directions in which the passage could lead. They welcome preachers who throw out suggestions and brainstorm possibilities, whether or not these are obviously linked to the passage, whether or not these ideas are followed through. Intuitive types quickly become bored with too much detail, too many facts and too much repetition.

In approaching Mark 2.1–12, for example, from an intuitive perspective, Francis and Atkins (2002, 41) find inspiration and light on four different themes. The passage sparks ideas about collaborative ministry, about the discipline of intercessory prayer, about individuals' responsibility for their own salvation, and about the Christian vocation to serve without seeking reward. Can you see how all these ideas can be sparked by the same story? Can you imagine how whole sermons can be preached on each of these themes? So hear how an intuitive preacher reflects on Mark 2.1–12.

Intuitive perspective on Mark 2.1–12

Here is a story about four people who brought their friend to Jesus. They were unaffected by the encounter themselves, but their friend's life was changed. So where does that leave you and me?

We, too, are called to bring others to Jesus. It is often not an easy task when we are working in isolation, one by one. Just one of the friends would never have got the paralysed man as far as the threshold. Four of them together raised the paralysed man to the rooftop and delivered him at the feet of Jesus. Collaborative ministry may achieve what individual ministry fails to do.

We, too, are called to bring others to Jesus. It is often no easy task to bundle our candidates on to a stretcher and to lug them lock, stock and barrel into the presence of Jesus. But we can, at least, begin by carrying them to the Lord day by day in prayer. And this may be more effective than carrying them to the rooftop of the church. The ministry of prayer may achieve what the ambulance ministry fails to do.

We, too, are called to bring others to Jesus. But note carefully, our calling stops right there. The real work takes place face to face, between Jesus and the candidate. We cannot negotiate healing and salvation on their behalf. In the story, the paralysed man takes responsibility for his own condition. He stood on his own two feet and accepted the gift of mobility.

We, too, are called to bring others to Jesus. But we must always be willing to do so for their benefit and not for our own. In the story, when the healing was complete, the four men vanished from the narrative, thanked neither by Jesus nor by the man who had been healed. They had performed their task and were happy to return to their home. Only hope that they had the courtesy to repair the roof before they left.

Here is a story about four people who brought their friend to Jesus. Pray that we may continue to do the same.

Feeling

The third step in the SIFT method is to address the feeling perspective. It is the feeling perspective that examines the human interest in the biblical text and learns the lessons of God for harmonious and compassionate living. The third question asks, 'How does this passage speak to the feeling function? What is there to speak about fundamental human values, about the relationship between people, and about what it is to be truly human?'

When feeling types hear a passage of Scripture they want to know what the passage has to say about personal values and about human relationships. They empathize deeply with people in the story and with the human drama in the narrative. Feeling types are keen to get inside the lives of people about whom they hear in Scripture. They want to explore what it felt like to be there at the time and how those feelings help to illuminate their Christian journey today. They welcome preachers who take time to develop the human dimension of the passage and who apply the passage to issues of compassion, harmony and trust. Feeling types quickly lose interest in theological debates that explore abstract issues without clear application to personal relationships.

In approaching Mark 1.29–39, for example, from a feeling perspective, Francis and Atkins (2002, 33–4) select one of the characters and recreate the experience from that individual's point of view. Having tried first to step into the shoes of the more obvious characters in the story (Simon, Jesus, and the sick mother-in-law), they prefer to adopt the perspective of the person who was crucial to the whole story but utterly marginalized by the gospel-writer, namely Simon's wife and daughter of the sick mother-in-law. So hear how a feeling preacher reflects on Mark 1.29–39.

Feeling perspective on Mark 1.29–39

Here is a tale of family life. Try to see it through the eyes of the woman whom Mark excluded from the tale. Grasp how things feel from the daughter's perspective, from the perspective of Simon's wife. Put yourself in the unenviable place of the woman caught between mother and husband. Feel that conflict in her soul.

The daughter's loyalty to her mother is deep and true. It is hard to forget the sacrifices mother made in bringing up her family. After all, times were bad and life was hard for the wife of the Galilean fisherman. Once the daughter was totally dependent on the mother. But now the tables are turned. Late, late in life, the mother is now totally dependent on the daughter. Once her husband brought home the fish, but now the home economy is supported by her daughter's husband.

How can a daughter loyal to her mother's needs see her way of life, her very security, threatened by a radical change in the home economy? How can a daughter but sympathize with a mother who retreats to bed in protest or confusion.

The wife's loyalty to her husband is deep and true as well. It is hard to forget the deep-felt love and tenderness that first attracted her to the young fisherman. After all, there had been many fish in the local sea. But the choice had been made and there had been, until now, little reason to regret it. Simon had supported her and her mother, too, through days when fish were plentiful and through days when fish were scarce.

How can a wife loyal to her husband's needs stand in the way, when he hears and responds to the call of God? How can a wife but understand when her husband takes time out to build the Kingdom of God?

Here, then, is a tale of family life. Try to see it through the eyes of the woman whom Mark excluded from the tale. Put yourself in the unenviable place of the woman caught between mother and husband. Empathize with the deep conflict in her soul.

Thinking

The fourth step in the SIFT method is to address the thinking perspective. It is the thinking perspective that examines the theological interest in the biblical text and that reflects rationally and crucially on issues of principle. The fourth question asks, 'How does this passage speak to the thinking function? What is there to speak to the mind, to challenge us on issues of truth and justice, and to provoke profound theological thinking?'

When thinking types hear a passage of Scripture they want to know what the passage has to say about principles of truth and justice. They get caught up with the principles involved in the story and with the various kinds of truth claims being made. Thinking types are often keen to do theology and to follow through the implications and the logic of the positions they adopt. Some thinkers apply this perspective to a literal interpretation of Scripture, while other thinkers are more at home with the liberal interpretation of Scripture. They welcome preachers who are fully alert to the logical and to the theological implications of their themes. They value sermons which debate fundamental issues of integrity and righteousness. Thinking types quickly lose interest in sermons which concentrate on applications to personal relationships, but fail to debate critically issues of theology and morality.

In approaching Mark 1.14–20, for example, from a thinking perspective, Francis and Atkins (2002, 26–7) are interested in trying to get inside the mind of the gospel-writer Mark and to identify his theological interests. Their analysis is that Mark begins the gospel narrative with the call of the disciples because his primary theological interest is in showing how Jesus established a new Israel. The old Israel was founded as twelve tribes, with the Levites sometimes counted as the thirteenth tribe. In the same way, Jesus calls and names twelve disciples, with Levi called but not counted among the twelve. So hear how a thinking preacher reflects on Mark 1.14–20.

Thinking perspective on Mark 1.14–20

The key question for the theologian concerned with gospel studies is this: why did Mark choose to open his gospel narrative with the account of the call of four disciples, rather than by relating some of the words of teaching or the acts of healing which would logically lead to people wishing to follow him?

The answer is that this opening call set the *structure* for what is to follow. Mark's primary interest is in showing how Jesus constructed around him a new Israel, a new people of God. The clue is given by the way in which the call of the first four followers (Peter, Andrew, James and John) is followed by the call of a fifth follower (Levi). Then there is a general commissioning of the twelve special disciples. The twelve are named and Levi is dropped from the list. The same thing, you see, so often happens in the Old Testament when the twelve tribes of Israel are named. There, too, Levi is often dropped from the list and the number twelve is kept alive by counting separately the two sons of Joseph, namely Ephraim and Manasseh. Mark's intention is clear.

For Mark, the words of teaching and the acts of healing are not there to attract the twelve followers, but to equip them. The teaching and the healing are the object lessons from which they are to learn. Then having learnt, they themselves are sent out to teach and to heal, the very activities that bear witness to the fact that the Kingdom of God has come near. Where God reigns, the words of the Kingdom and the new life of the Kingdom are free for all to receive.

For Mark, therefore, the call of the first disciples is indeed the proper opening act for the Jesus who comes proclaiming, 'The time is fulfilled, and the Kingdom of God has come near.'

Conclusion

This essay has examined the implications of psychological type theory for the interpretation of biblical texts and for reading and preaching Mark's Gospel. It has done so by introducing the SIFT method of biblical hermeneutics and of biblical preaching, a method developed on the basis of three principles. The first principle is that an understanding of the hermeneutical dialogue between the text of Scripture and the perspective or standpoint of preacher and listener properly involves the discipline of psychology as a key tool in the analysis and development of the place of reading, interpreting and proclaiming the Bible in the Christian community. The second principle is that the Jungian notion of psychological type provides an insightful and accessible model of the human psyche which is of practical relevance to the hermeneutical process. The third principle is that there is good theological justification for reading, interpreting and preaching the Bible to address all four of the psychological functions identified by Jung in response to the first of the great commandments to love the Lord God with all our heart, with all our soul and with *all our mind*.

References

Bassett, R. L., Mathewson, K. and Gailitis, A. (1993), 'Recognising the person in biblical interpretation: an empirical study', *Journal of Psychology and Christianity*, 12, 38–46.

Costa, P. T. and McCrae, R. R. (1985), *The NEO Personality Inventory*, Odessa, Florida: Psychological Assessment Resources.

Eysenck, H. J. and Eysenck, M. W. (1985), *Personality and Individual Differences: A Natural Science Approach*, New York: Plenum Press.

Eysenck, H. J. and Eysenck, S. B. G. (1975), *Manual of the Eysenck Personality Questionnaire (Adult and Junior)*, London: Hodder & Stoughton.

Eysenck, H. J. and Eysenck, S. B. G. (1991), *Manual of the Eysenck Personality Scales*, London: Hodder & Stoughton.

Francis, L. J. (1997), *Personality Type and Scripture: Exploring Mark's Gospel*, London: Mowbray.

Francis, L. J. (2004), *Francis Psychological Type Scales (FPTS): Technical Manual*, Bangor: Welsh National Centre for Religious Education.

Francis, L. J. (2005), *Faith and Psychology: Personality, Religion and the Individual*, London: Darton, Longman & Todd.

Francis, L. J. and Atkins, P. (2000), *Exploring Luke's Gospel: A Guide to the Gospel Readings in the Revised Common Lectionary*, London: Mowbray.

Francis, L. J. and Atkins, P. (2001), *Exploring Matthew's Gospel: A Guide to the Gospel Readings in the Revised Common Lectionary*, London: Mowbray.

Francis, L. J. and Atkins, P. (2002), *Exploring Mark's Gospel: An Aid for Readers and Preachers Using Year B of the Revised Common Lectionary*, London: Continuum.

Jung, C. G. (1971), *Psychological Types: The Collected Works, Volume 6*, London: Routledge and Kegan Paul.

Keirsey, D. (1998), *Please Understand Me: 2*, Del Mar, CA: Prometheus Nemesis.

Keirsey, D. and Bates, M. (1978), *Please Understand Me*, Del Mar, CA: Prometheus Nemesis.

Myers, I. B. and McCaulley, M. H. (1985), *Manual: A Guide to the Development and Use of the Myers-Briggs Type Indicator*, Palo Alto, CA: Consulting Psychologists Press.

Myers, I. B. and Myers, P. B. (1980), *Gifts Differing*, Palo Alto, CA: Consulting Psychologists Press.

Segovia, F. F. (1995), 'Toward a hermeneutic of the diaspora: a hermeneutic of otherness and engagement' in F. F. Segovia and M. A. Tolbert (eds.), *Reading from this Place: Social Location and Biblical Interpretation in the United States*, Minneapolis, MN: Fortress Press, pp. 57–73.

Segovia, F. F. and Tolbert, M. A. (eds.) (1995a), *Reading from this Place: Social Location and Biblical Interpretation in the United States*, Minneapolis, MN: Fortress Press.

Segovia, F. F. and Tolbert, M. A. (eds.) (1995b), *Reading from this Place: Social Location and Biblical Interpretation in Global Perspective*, Minneapolis, MN: Fortress Press.

11

Popular readings of Mark

JOHN RICHES AND SUSAN MILLER

Introduction

In the early part of 2004 the Contextual Bible Study Development Group in Scotland invited a number of partner groups to conduct and write up a series of studies on Mark's Gospel. Five texts were chosen: the call of Levi (2.14–17), the feeding of the five thousand (6.30–44), the story of the Syrophoenician woman (7.24–30), James and John want to be great (10.35–45) and the resurrection account (16.1–8). Seven groups agreed to take part in the project, and they all took part in at least three of the Bible studies. The groups were drawn principally from churches of different denominations across the central belt of Scotland. While the majority were from middle-class church groups, there was one group from a Roman Catholic parish in the East End of Glasgow and a women's group from Glasgow University.

The readings

We will start with a brief overview of one group's readings of the five passages and then compare that quite closely with the readings of the women's group. Finally we will pick up other points of contrast and comparison with the other groups who participated and seek to draw out some of the wider implications of these studies.

Lansdowne Parish Church/St Mary's Cathedral

This was a group which met during Lent, composed of members drawn from two adjacent churches in Glasgow's West End, one Church of Scotland, the other Anglican. The two churches have covenanted together and share a number of joint activities including regular worship. Most of the members of the group were academically trained, three had teaching responsibilities at Glasgow University. The group, which was on average 10–12 in number, had a quite wide age-range (late twenties to late sixties) and among the group there were clergy, religious and laity, Roman Catholics, Presbyterians, Anglicans and a Lutheran; there were US, UK and German citizens, English and Scots by birth.

In the first study of the call of Levi (2.14–17), what was immediately striking was its restless movement – 'the surprising change from the idyllic lake-side scene to the meeting with a load of unsavoury characters in Levi's house' – and the very public, open nature of the many exchanges which occur in the short space of four verses. This is not Jesus sitting down to instruct the crowds at length on some hilltop but Jesus mixing and meeting, engaging in the cut and thrust of conversation and debate. It's unplanned, spontaneous, quick-witted and animated. There's a sense of excitement, of something happening: people being caught up in some movement whose meaning they do not fully understand. But clearly huge expectations attach to Jesus: people are flocking to him, eager to hear him, ready to follow. 'Was this some kind of enthusiastic movement?'

The four verses contain many characters: Jesus, Levi, the son of Alphaeus, the disciples, the crowds, the tax-collectors and sinners, the scribes of the Pharisees. Jesus' interaction with people is complex, multidimensional, and the group was invited to choose one character or set of characters and consider how they might have reacted to the events Mark narrates. How, for example, would the tax-collectors have reacted to the fact that one of their number had just abandoned his trade and gone off after this wandering mendicant preacher, half-Messiah, half-peasant activist? True, they were sitting down and drinking with him, but one can imagine the subtle shifts of emotions and reactions: delight that they were being patronized by the local hero, but also uncertainty, a sense of not knowing where all this was leading. They 'would have been keeping a wary eye on Levi'. They may have seen Jesus as a 'destabilizing influence, stirring up the people and unsettling Levi'. How far were they willing to follow the crowd in their enthusiasm for Jesus? How comfortable was Levi with his decision? And how pleased would he and the others have been with 'the sting in the tail of Jesus' reply to the Pharisees'?

The group was then asked what these meals tell us about Jesus' understanding of God and of God's purposes for the world? Such meals were breaking the conventions, not restricting the meal to one's own (family, the Jews). They say, 'There is room for everyone in God's house.' At the same time, they give a practical image of God, signified by the contrast between teaching those sitting at your feet and engaging with people over a meal. As so often in Mark, we are told that Jesus teaches, but not what he says; we do get an account of Jesus' encounters with the crowds, the tax-collectors, the Pharisees. God through Jesus is involved in the physical world, is 'involved in people's communities, engaging with and cutting across contemporary concerns, meeting people through dialogue'. There's an easiness of approach: 'Dialogue leads to small changes, as contrasted with the kind of transformation which might come from mass preaching.'

All this tells us something about the nature of the God of Jesus. 'Jesus is getting involved at an intimate, risky level, mingling with the people, exposing himself to danger and infection'. Jesus' God deals with the 'greatest need, i.e. of the sinners and weak'. It's a kind of 'positive discrimination'. 'There is something nicely unstructured about Jesus' approach in this story: he just lets it all happen.' It's a very organic situation, 'things developing naturally and spontaneously as the occasion arises'. It's subversive, allowing the surprising, the unconventional, the unplanned, the unauthorized to happen.

This then led on into discussions about 'bringing the sacred into everyday life', whether in the form of chaplaincy work in supermarkets or 'through small intimate encounters and dialogue'. There is need to find space to allow significant dialogue. 'We catch the Spirit from being with other people who bring it to us.'

Similarly, the story of the feeding of the five thousand (6.30–44) was read principally as the story, not so much of the miracle itself (though this topic and its problematic for many in the group was also raised), as of the complex exchange between the disciples, returned from their mission and keen to spend time on their own with Jesus, and the crowd who demand his attention and compassion. In this case, after taking initial reactions to the story ('a sharp contrast with the temptation narrative where Jesus rejects Satan's suggestion of turning stones to bread'; 'an in-your-face miracle with lots of leftovers'), we asked the group to identify the various scenes in the story and then to say what they thought the emotional content of the scenes would have been. In this way, they could again plot the reactions of the various groups to Jesus' actions and words. If initially the disciples were 'happy and relieved to have Jesus for themselves, excited, euphoric, getting back to normality in the boat, looking forward to sharing their experiences with him', this mood quickly turned to 'disappointment, frustration and aggravation with the crowd – and, quite possibly, Jesus'. By contrast, the crowd was desperate to hear Jesus. It was focused, filled with a sense of urgency and excitement, driven by great need. All of this must have led to a strong sense of rivalry with the crowd on the part of the disciples, as they vied for Jesus' attention. Indeed the more Jesus was drawn to the crowds through compassion for their need ('sheep without a shepherd'), the more the disciples became 'helpless outsiders, rather than actors and participators'. Jesus' patience may have been tested by their attitude, but the disciples' 'confidence and sense of authority grows' as he involves them in the organization of the feeding. In this way, the story was read principally as a story about boundary crossing, about inclusion and exclusion. 'Insiders become outsiders and vice versa: the crowds are included; the disciples feel excluded but are brought back in to the meal.'[1] The boundaries of the Church need to be more permeable, but this openness to outsiders can bring with it its own problems. What if those who come in reject the values of openness and inclusiveness, the vision of the central importance of dialogue and the search for sacred meanings, which underlay the invitation they received?

The discussion of the encounter between Jesus and the Syrophoenician woman (7.24–30) again focused on the topic of the spontaneous and exposed nature of genuinely open dialogue. The woman here is driven by her desperation over the condition of her child to break all the normal rules governing relations between men and women, to approach Jesus and to engage him in debate, trumping his dismissive, 'racist' remarks with her own witty and smart reply. This willingness to argue with Jesus brought not only healing to her own child but also an opening of Jesus' mind which had been closed to the needs of the Gentile woman.

In this passage we looked first at the way in which Jesus and the woman are depicted. What is striking is, on the one hand, the generally positive portrayal of the young woman fighting for the health of her child with all the resources at her disposal, not least her sharp wit; and on the other hand, the largely negative portrayal (as it was seen of Jesus): harassed, rude, almost racist and sexist, though ultimately responding to the woman's wit. In Jesus' treatment of the woman, people saw a reflection of the marginalization of women in the Church down the ages. What is the effect on women today of women (except for some outstanding individuals) not having had a voice in the Church over the last two thousand years? How long will it take to overcome the effects of this kind of suppression?

However, the group saw the clash between Jesus and the disciples and the woman predominantly in racist terms. Jesus' saying, 'Let the children be fed first, for it is not fair to take the children's food and throw it to the dogs', has something of a proverbial ring to it, reflecting deep Jewish prejudice against Gentiles. But it is here that the woman's wit comes into play, for she turns the metaphor to her advantage. What was intended as a crude description of two absolutely irreconcilable groups is turned into the picture of a family household. The parents and the children are gathered round the table, while round them lie (just like the woman who is addressing Jesus) the household animals and wait for the leftovers. It is admittedly an extremely lowly position; nevertheless, the animals – dogs – have their place within the household, as the lowest members of the household hierarchy, but not outside, as in Jesus' saying, as something wholly alien and threatening. The brilliant twist which she gives to Jesus' saying transforms the situation. Jesus rewards her witty saying by releasing her daughter.

This reading of the story in turn led to an interesting series of reflections around the notion of 'arguing with Jesus': considering the benefits to those inside and outside the Church of challenging the tradition and received meanings and interpretations in order to discover the true graciousness of the gospel. The group fixed on a phrase which emerged from the earlier discussion: 'arguing with Jesus'. We need to engage in this way with Jesus. 'It brings out the real nature of the relationship with Christ: the relationship is closer with someone you can doubt.' Similarly we need to engage in critical dialogue with the 'accepted teachings' of the Church. We need to cut through the official teaching which can be repressive and prejudicial to the weak, as it has been to women, and to hear the voices of those who suffer under it. This also meant looking at class issues. Glasgow society is still sharply divided. Selective housing policy, the creation of social enclaves, selective employment policy, all bear heavily on the poor and create an underclass. There are great injustices in the treatment of asylum-seekers, which the Church needs to challenge. In the same way, we need to engage with other faiths, less from a 'critical point of view' than in search of understanding and of mutual illumination. Again, the liberating effect of open dialogue was stressed.

Similar questions were raised by the James and John passage in 10.35–45, where again the rivalrous relationships, this time between different groups of disciples, provide the dynamic of the story. These led into quite rich discussions of preferred models of leadership. Perhaps not surprisingly, considering the composition of the group, there was a good deal of discussion of the model of teaching and its ability to draw out people's hidden potential. Good teaching 'takes time', it 'gives sufficient knowledge and understanding to allow people to develop for themselves'. We need 'fighting teachers'. Good teachers 'share what they know is good'. They don't teach answers; like Christ and the Buddha, they teach a way. Bad teaching becomes simply an enforcing of orthodoxy, is didactic in style ('What if you're wrong?!') and 'denies people their history'.

Finally, the story of the women's visit to the tomb (16.1–8) was read as a series of scenes, each with its different emotions, culminating in an encounter with the other, the numinous, which broke through their routines of grief and left them speechless. There was discussion here about our inability to provide safe spaces for people to discuss such experiences, which had clearly been shared by many in the group. There was a danger that without any possibility of articulating such experiences they would wither away and remain unrelated to the rest of one's life. How do we recover the sense of conviction of the first-century Church? We need to be ready to recognize a sense of the numinous breaking in when not expected; to experience amazement when it happens – in nature, music, buildings, prayer. There is a difficulty of sharing the experience, of finding the right forum where one is not inhibited by fear of ridicule or dismissiveness. Such experiences are too precious; there is 'too high a risk in sharing them'. We no longer talk theology; we are awkward about testimonies, and in this we reflect the virtual silence of our wider culture on such issues.

In all this, it is striking how much the question of true dialogue, its nature and its benefits, dominated the discussions, and how far such topics could be seen as running through Mark's Gospel, something which would certainly not be apparent from many more scholarly commentaries. There was a generally high level of appreciation of the quality of the discussions within the group and a consistent level of attendance. In general the discussion did not move much in to questions of social justice and was much more concerned with the cultural isolation and the lack of opportunity for open dialogue within the Church and with those outside. There was a high level of participation and members brought a wide range of skills and experience. Questions were raised about contemporary political and social arrangements, notably in relation to Mark 2 and 7, but these were not seen as more than aids to the main process of reflection, which was much more concerned with the reading of the narrative and the interaction of the various characters and the implications this might have for the life of the group. Literary, social, even philosophical and political understanding and emotional intelligence drove the conversation along.

What theological issues and insights does such a reading of Mark open up? In formal theological terms one would say that important issues were being raised here about the doctrine of revelation and the Word of God: its reception in Bible and tradition and the need for constant reappropriation of the central insights of the Christian faith. Alongside this was the recognition that there are other sources of illumination, whether in the unexpected encounter with the numinous in nature, music, art, buildings, prayer or in 'catching the Spirit from being with other people who bring it to us'. Importantly, there was a sense both that such appropriation could occur in dialogue with the most unexpected of people (a Gentile woman) and also that it needed to be fostered by dialogue within the Christian community. Interestingly, despite the multicultural setting of the two congregations, there was not a particularly clear emphasis on the possibilities of such dialogue on a multifaith basis. Maybe that is because there is as yet not much experience of such dialogue within the group itself.

The women's group

The women's group met to share three of the Mark studies: the healing of the Syrophoenician woman's daughter (7.24–30), the request of James and John (10.35–45) and the account of the women's visit to the empty tomb (16.1–8). Around eight to twelve women attended each meeting, and most had previous experience of contextual Bible studies (CBS). Two women are members of the core CBS Development Group, and others had recently completed the CBS course for facilitators. The women represented several denominations in Scotland: the Church of Scotland, the Scottish Episcopal Church and the Roman Catholic Church, including two women who are Sisters of Notre Dame. Unlike the other groups, the facilitation of this group was shared by the members with different facilitators working at each meeting. This leadership came about partly through the aim to share facilitation with those who had recently completed the CBS facilitation course, but it also enabled a greater sharing within the group. There was little evidence of a desire for a leader to provide the 'correct' answer to the questions.

The CBS process adopts the methodology of liberation theology, and our discussions had several connections with feminist approaches to biblical interpretation. Several women mentioned that they appreciated the opportunity to read the Bible in a women's group. We felt free to discuss issues without worrying about causing any offence to men. Some women expressed more confidence in participating in discussions, and others mentioned that they could speak more openly about their emotional responses to the passages. At the same time we wished to continue our conversations within a mixed group of women and men, and acknowledged the richness of dialogue with men.

We noted the number of women's stories in the Bible studies, and the importance of women was highlighted in the account of the women as the first witnesses to the resurrection. Feminist approaches came out clearly in our analysis of the exorcism of the Syrophoenician woman's daughter (7.24–30). The group's initial responses to the passage emphasized Jesus' harsh reply to the Syrophoenician woman. One group member asked, 'Is Jesus testing her?' and another said, 'Is she resisting Jesus?' The Bible study questions called attention to the differences between Jesus and the woman according to race, religion and gender. In contrast to the Lansdowne group the women's group pointed out the social inequalities between Jesus and the woman. Jesus had higher social status as a male, and the woman broke social boundaries by approaching and addressing a man who was not a male relative. In addition, the male Jesus represents the Jewish children who inherit the promises to Israel, whereas the woman stands for the Gentile 'dogs'. Jesus also has the power as Son of God to heal the sick, while the woman is desperate for help for her daughter. One woman pointed out that the passage showed the woman's 'need in every sense'. In our reading we interpreted the Syrophoenician woman as a representative of marginalized groups in society.

The women's group looked at the ways these social barriers were overcome, noting that the woman initiated the discussion. She was witty and responded to Jesus' riddle. One woman proposed that the Syrophoenician woman was 'not overawed by Jesus' and another said that she was 'full of love for her child'. The group, moreover, highlighted the change in the woman in the course of the conversation. One member said, 'She moved from her knees to walking tall', and another commented, 'In the end she achieved what she needed.' Some pointed out that the woman's faith was the source of her liberation. Others emphasized that the woman changed Jesus' mind. The women's group, however, echoed the view of Lansdowne concerning the importance of dialogue and conversations. Although the woman approaches Jesus, the participation of both Jesus and the woman is necessary for the conversation to continue. They are both willing to engage in dialogue with someone of a different race and gender. The group noted that the dialogue itself enables differences to be overcome.

In the later stages of each Bible study we moved to a discussion of the role of women in the Church. Historically, church structures have been primarily shaped by men and women have not been able to contribute their views and participate in decision-making. The women's group felt that it is important to acknowledge the distinctive voice of women in church discussions. Women are excluded from the priesthood of the Roman Catholic Church, and are not fully represented in leadership positions in the Protestant churches. In 2004 the Church of Scotland appointed the first woman moderator, Alison Elliot, but this church has yet to achieve the equal participation of women at all levels of church structures. The women's group had a strong impetus for change in terms of church structures and in relation to the recognition of women's gifts.

The social inequalities within the account of the Syrophoenician woman were emphasized by her willingness to accept the crumbs that fall from the children's table. One woman pointed out that the negative associations of the crumbs were transformed. She noted, 'Crumbs were all that was offered but they turned out to be God's crumbs satisfying and fulfilling.' Another said, 'Little moves need to be encouraged, and they are like the crumbs in the story.' There was also a recognition that growth is taking place on the fringes of the Church. One woman spoke of her concern for future generations: 'We need to nurture the next generation as well as ourselves.' The account of the Syrophoenician woman was an impetus to the women's group to seek change. In the concluding discussion one woman pointed out that if we keep faith, 'We can move mountains.' New directions can emerge from those who take the role of the Syrophoenician woman.

The comparison with the Lansdowne group is enlightening. While both groups focus on the importance of the dialogue between the woman and Jesus (and the sense in which it enables Jesus to change), there is nevertheless a significant difference in focus in the readings. The women's group is more concerned with the social implications of the story; while the Lansdowne group focuses on the need for dialogue within the Church and with the Church's traditions. There is a fairly obvious correlation here between the different readings and the different rationale of the groups.[2] These differences should not be over-emphasized. Both groups take cognizance of the connections between the story and social issues in contemporary society and also of the light it can shed on the role and importance of dialogue within the contemporary Church. Nevertheless the voices that are strongest in each group are different.

In their study of the request of James and John for the seats next to Jesus when he comes into his glory (10.35–45), the women's group again examined the models of power in the passage, and asked questions about the part these models play in the way we operate with the individuals and groups with whom we live and work. We then concluded with a discussion of the role of these models of power in Church and society.

The women's initial responses to the passage highlighted the sharp contrast between secular power and Jesus' model of power. One woman pointed to the description of James and John who have a 'favour to ask Jesus'. She noted that they could be compared to those who approach kings to request 'favours'. Another woman pointed out that James and John expect Jesus to behave in the same way as worldly authorities. The women's group emphasized the subversive elements of the story. One member commented, 'Power is being subverted', and another said, 'Jesus shows himself as a servant.' The Lansdowne group raised questions about the biblical references to service, and discussed the ways that servanthood can be abused and forced upon people. One person noted that women are often expected to be the ones who serve. The women's group, however, took a positive interpretation of Jesus' teaching about service. One woman said, 'Christians should serve others', and another member emphasized that Jesus specifically mentioned that his followers are to be 'servants of all others'.

The women were then asked to choose one of the characters or groups of characters in the passage, and to note what they can tell about them from the text. Three groups were formed to discuss James and John, Jesus, and the slaves and servants. The first group looked at the portrayal of James and John, and their responses were initially negative: 'They come over as speaking as a pair with one voice and out of self-interest'; 'They ask the question about themselves'; and, 'They see themselves as superior, as the inner circle of Jesus' friends.' Then one woman pointed out that their question showed that 'They didn't really know Jesus. Their response was too shallow and reflected the secular view of life.' Other women were more sympathetic towards James and John, and one suggested, 'Perhaps they were young and energetic with a drive for life.' Another woman noted that James and John were 'loyal' and that 'they stayed with Jesus on the road to Jerusalem'.

The second group discussed the portrayal of Jesus, and highlighted his character as a good teacher. Jesus called the other disciples together and brought unity to the group that had been divided by the actions of James and John. One woman noted, 'Jesus asked questions, developing their understanding, and gave them hard choices.' Another commented that Jesus was on a journey, and that he knew where he was coming from and going to; and another said that Jesus did not come as a 'slave-master' but to give his life. The end of the passage had a hopeful note, since Jesus 'came to rescue many people'.

The third group looked at the references to slaves and servants in the passage, and pointed out that they were anonymous and had no voice – unlike James, John and Jesus. The slaves and servants were also identified as a collective group, lacking individuality. One woman, however, pointed out that the slaves were the ones particularly linked with the Son of Man. Another referred to the Jewish understanding of slavery, emphasizing that the Israelites were liberated from slavery in Egypt. Similarly, Jesus has come to rescue many people.

The discussion progressed to an analysis of models of power, and one woman noted that ultimate power belongs to God. Jesus' power was revealed in service. Slaves, however, were not powerless. One member noted that there is a model of power in slavery and in servant leadership saying, 'A slave can give his or her life.' Jesus was seen to overturn the 'common world-view of power' and his power is not 'hierarchical, authoritarian or despotic'. The women commented, 'Jesus gives people choice and hope', 'he opens up new possibilities'; 'no one should have full power over others'.

The Bible study concluded with reflections on the role of these models of power in the churches. The Scottish Episcopal Church was praised for trying out new models of lay and ordained leadership. One woman thought that good leadership was necessary for 'things to happen'. Another thought that 'change began from the ground up', and another distrusted hierarchical power because 'it makes people passive and dependent'. The charismatic renewal movement was seen as a challenge to traditional, hierarchical church structures because it aims to 'use everyone's gifts in the Spirit'. Vatican II was also regarded as instrumental in bringing about an emphasis on the 'priesthood of all believers'. The women's group liked this model of power but believed that it was hard to work out in practice. Finally, the women noted the importance of love in creating positive power relations.

There are again interesting differences of emphasis between the readings of the two groups. The woman's group, perhaps surprisingly in view of the way that the notion of servanthood has been used to exploit them in Church and society, explored the positive side of servanthood and the ways in which the metaphor may help the Church to critique existing models of the exercise of power in society and in the Church itself. On the whole the Lansdowne group was more critical. 'The role of servanthood can be abused, forcing it on others.' It is a 'difficult metaphor to apply'. Too often the servant is seen as 'a doormat', leaving the authority to take decisions in other hands. Too often its use has been linked with the expectation that it is women who should serve. On the other hand, the Lansdowne group did also recognize that there was a positive side to the metaphor. It spoke powerfully of our service to God, but even then we should be aware that 'it was used ironically by Jesus'. Even 'Jesus had to be his own man while attending to the needs of others'. True servanthood lay in 'helping others to be independent', in 'enabling as opposed to ministering directly to people's needs'. Again, one should not exaggerate the difference between the two groups. The readings are largely complementary and give clear expression to the wish for more collaborative, enabling styles of church ministry and of teaching and leadership in society in general. Underlying this is a clear perception of the great value in being brought to recognize the gifts that one has, in learning from others to develop one's own spiritual insight and knowledge. There is equally a strong critique of models of power which impose others' beliefs and ideologies on those with little or no power, not least on women.

The series of Bible studies concluded with the account of the visit of the women to the empty tomb (16.1–8). This Bible study focused on the emotional experience of the women characters. The questions about naming the emotions were instrumental in opening up the story in new ways. The women's group was comfortable listing a wide range of deep emotions. We spent time trying to understand the meaning of the women's fear, terror and amazement. The experience of *ekstasis* was seen as something outwith the normal range of emotions. The women were 'outside themselves', and this experience paradoxically involved a sense of loss. The final Bible study showed the importance of emotions as a means of understanding the passage. The members of Mark's audience have listened to the whole story of Jesus' passion and death. They share the emotional impact of the news of the resurrection when they identify with the women. In this way emotions are crucial for a full understanding of the passage. This insight led to a discussion of the role of emotions in our churches. One woman spoke of the joyful and lively experience of worship in African churches. We need more joy and celebration in liturgies and also more time for the expression of grief and turmoil. The focus on emotions was helpful in highlighting the desire to help people to see God's presence in the grim realities of life. Mark's Gospel ends with the fear of the women, and another member of the group noted the need to acknowledge scepticism and doubt in our church contexts.

Again, it is interesting to note the way in which in the two groups similar themes and concerns are given slightly different expression. Both groups are seeking for modes of expressing deep religious feelings and experiences which are presently either suppressed or marginalized within church communities and worship. The Lansdowne group concentrated more on the need for creating spaces for significant dialogue, where people could nurture their experiences of the transcendent; the women's group sought to create a place for such emotions in our acts of worship. Such approaches are clearly complementary.

Overall, the women's group found the Bible studies liberating in the way they brought to light the voices of the marginalized in the passages. The questions allowed the group to imagine and identify with the perspectives of the Syrophoenician woman, the slaves and servants of the Graeco-Roman world, and the women at the empty tomb. The women's group also acknowledged the importance of conversations as being transformative. The questions concerning emotions opened up new ways of reading the text which were different from more cerebral academic readings. The focus on emotions allowed the group to participate on a deeper level, and opened up a discussion of the role of emotions within a church context. The women's group emphasized that a deep understanding of the Bible involves both an emotional and an intellectual response. This emphasis on the emotional response to the text was certainly something less clearly articulated at the Lansdowne group.

The Mark Project conference

The project invited everyone who took part in the Bible studies to come to a conference to share responses, and representatives from almost all the groups attended. We reflected on the Bible studies that were most memorable, and then discussed each Bible study before moving on to the questions concerning Christian identity and the role of the churches in Scotland. The groups recognized a common experience of the diminishing role of the churches in Scotland. There were concerns about the war in Iraq led by Christian leaders. Many Christians participated in protests against the war, but the group felt that there was a lack of a strong Christian voice in Scotland and no identifiable church leader who could speak out on political and social issues. The Bible studies raised questions about how the Church can speak out when it no longer has the authority of the past.

The importance of the role of the conversations that arose in the Bible studies was again stressed. One person noted that in the past we have waited for directives for action but now we must be like the Syrophoenician woman and speak up. Another participant noted that Christian identity itself emerges through dialogue with others. Members from St Dominic's, a Roman Catholic congregation in one of Glasgow's peripheral housing schemes, emphasized that conversations enabled racial, religious and gender barriers to be overcome, and Lansdowne/St Mary's talked of the importance of arguing with Jesus. Many of the conversations described in the Bible studies take place at meals, including Jesus' meals, with tax-collectors and sinners and the feeding of the five thousand, and the meeting of Jesus and the Syrophoenician woman also focuses on sharing a meal. Members from St Bride's, an Episcopalian congregation in the West End of Glasgow, mentioned the significance of meals as a mission tool within the Church, and stressed that 'at meals interesting things happen'.

The Bible study on Mark 16 again raised questions about religious experience. The groups discussed the experience of the numinous and the difficulty of sharing these experiences in a church context. St Bride's mentioned that the Church has to be part of the grim and unglamorous side of life. The Church is present with the bereaved and with prisoners, but these conversations are hidden. It is difficult to talk about these experiences and to find a common voice to speak out at an appropriate level. The group discussed the ways in which Christians can find common ground with people of different faiths or no belief in God. The experience of the numinous forms common ground with people of no faith and people of different faiths. One participant emphasized the experience of the numinous in listening to music, and the experience of beauty. Dialogue could begin on the basis of what is common to us as human beings. This approach involves vulnerability and an openness to develop trust with one another.

Some concluding reflections

The Contextual Bible Study (CBS) group is an ecumenical group of laity, clergy and religious who have been operating from their base in the west of Scotland since 1995. It arose out of a visit by Gerald West from the Institute for the Study of the Bible (ISB) in Pietermaritzburg, South Africa, who had been using Bible study methods derived from base communities in Latin America in the apartheid period in South Africa. The CBS group in Scotland has developed this method for use in Scotland and for the last three years has worked together with the Scottish Bible Society on a Conversations programme to promote this way of reading the Bible and to train facilitators in the method.

This is a method which is designed to allow a close, communal and critical reading of the biblical text, and which can lead to personal and corporate transformation. In this process it is of the greatest importance that the biblical text is read carefully and closely. To this end, study groups are asked an initial series of questions, which take them into the text, sometimes focusing more on the narrative or the argument of the text, sometimes reading it against the background of the context out of which it sprang. A further set of questions are then asked to assist the group in naming connections between the text and their own situation and context. The groups are encouraged to enter into dialogue with the text, recognizing that there may be different voices in any given text, and with each other in such a way that the language and the narratives of the texts facilitate a theological conversation which enables members to reflect in faith on life issues of importance to them.

The groups are, as a rule, led by trained facilitators, some, but not all, of whom will have had an academic training in biblical studies. It is our practice to use two facilitators in order to encourage greater dialogue and to avoid suggesting didactic models of leadership. We encourage people to work in different sizes of groups, threes, sixes and the full group, partly to ensure greater participation, partly to undercut, as far as may be, the possibility of the facilitators becoming dominant. The questions asked are intended to be open questions which can be answered without specialist knowledge but which invite participants to read the text through their own eyes.

We have worked with a great diversity of groups over the last nine years. We have worked with groups in the peripheral housing estates of Glasgow and Newcastle; with people caring for substance abusers and for offenders. We have also read with church groups in more affluent areas and with various church leadership groups. We have a positive commitment to read the Bible with the poor and marginalized and with those groups who work with the poor and marginalized. We are committed to reading the Bible closely and to reading it critically, discerning the different voices in it and being ready to engage in debate with it. Above all we seek to read the Bible in such a way as to encourage personal and social transformation.

The impetus to the present studies came from an invitation to one of the group, John Riches, to contribute a chapter on Ephesians to the Global Bible Commentary. As this was intended to be a reading of Ephesians from a specifically Scottish perspective, it seemed appropriate to ask a number of groups across Scotland to read sections of the Epistle and then to collate the responses. This proved to be a fruitful exercise in two ways: in the first place, it was good to study one book in greater depth than is possible with simply taking individual passages from a series of books. (We had in fact experienced these kinds of benefits when we had read a series of psalms of exile in the East End of Glasgow, but had then not subsequently followed up this approach.) In another way Ephesians raised a series of topics – about ethnicity, about Christian confidence/pessimism, about church unity, about empowerment – which proved to be challenging in a number of ways and which suggested an interesting agenda for theological debate in Scotland, and indeed theological insights which could contribute importantly to such a debate. Unfortunately, the project as such allowed no opportunities for following this up. All this prompted us to consider a similar project this year, which might allow greater opportunity for the participant groups to meet and to begin to develop some kind of ongoing theological reflection.

In all this, various questions continue to intrigue and worry us about the nature of the work that we are doing. The first concerns the theological framework and goals within which we operate. One can put this somewhat simply as: are our principal aims to work for the emancipation of the poor and marginalized in Scotland or to seek to encourage the practice of 'dominance-free discourse' (Habermas)? Putting the question like that makes it clear that these are not sharp alternatives: those who live on the peripheral housing estates are just as likely to find participation in open dialogue as liberative and life-enhancing as people in the university district in the West of the city. Nor should one think of emancipation as something that occurs only in relation to the poor and marginalized. True dialogue and critical engagement with the ideologies which shape their lives can be just as liberating for those in the more affluent areas of the city.

Nevertheless, there are significantly different emphases: members of churches who live in the West End of the city may well feel culturally marginalized and have quite different agenda from those in the East who are faced with drugs, unemployment, sectarianism, criminality and vandalism in quite different ways. For the latter, really open discourse as opposed to either the platitudes of sectarianism ('tinny-rattle') or the ideological straitjacket of certain kinds of religious instruction (which produces minds 'closed by instruction') is a necessary step to liberation.[3] The latter point is also highly pertinent. A close, critical reading of the Bible can provide the context within which participants can articulate views contrary to and subversive of the official discourse of Church (and society) which may inhibit and control them in ways of which they are barely conscious. A similar point is made by the Lansdowne group in their discussion of 'arguing with Jesus'. They experience a need to establish a different relationship with the tradition which makes for a critical reappropriation. The question, however, remains whether this step can lead on to liberative praxis, such that the contextual Bible study process becomes part of a reflective process supportive of such practical engagement with the injustices of our present society. It is interesting to contrast the Lansdowne readings with those of the women's group with its concerns with women's emancipation and indeed of the Berlin group, reading out of its work with asylum-seekers.[4] The Lansdowne group express a desire to engage with those outside the Church, who include not only those embracing postmodern, post-Christian goals and values, but peoples of many different faiths. In the light of the last three years, such dialogue becomes increasingly important.

All this raises questions about the underlying framework that might bring together these different, though clearly related concerns. What view of Christian liberty and its contribution to the healing of the wounds of our society and of the wider world would serve to give coherence to these debates? What view of God emerges from the ongoing discussions? What is suggested here is a view of truth, 'the Word of God' as communicated through dialogue rather than through didactic and dogmatic teaching, as grasped in the challenging of long-held assumptions and the reappropriation of old truths.

A second question concerns the role in these conversations of the various participants. What in such readings was the role of the trained readers and the 'ordinary' readers? The phrase 'popular readings of the Bible' suggests a contrast between such readings and the professional, scholarly readings which one might find in academic commentaries. In practice, we increasingly find this sharp polarization less than helpful. There is clearly an issue about the amount of control exercised by the trained facilitators, who in practice determine the shape of the conversations on any given occasion. But when it comes to identifying the various skills which people bring to the reading of any text, the 'trained'/'ordinary' distinction suggests far too stark a contrast and emphasizes the importance of, for example, historical skills and biblical knowledge in ways that distort the description of the process. We are much more concerned to identify the wider range of skills that can serve to illuminate a text: emotional intelligence, literary skills, theological and moral intuition, political, psychological and sociological understanding, wit, humour, imagination, storytelling skills. The role of the facilitators may on occasion be to supply historical information which is not otherwise available to the group, but this is in practice far less important than their skill in identifying and encouraging the exercise of such other skills among the other participants.

Finally, there is an intriguing question about the naming of the readings themselves and the identification of their relationship to various kinds of more formal theological discourse. One could say that such theological conversations around the biblical text are somehow located midway between, on the one hand, popular religious discourse with its untidiness and complexity (though it could be argued that this is presently greatly reduced) and, on the other, the more systematized and formalized discourses of either church or academic theology. They are to be distinguished from popular religious discourse (Ricoeur's first naivety) because here there is already a critical and creative reflective moment as different readings of the text are identified and explored/fought for. They are also to be related to and distinguished from church and academic theologies. This is more difficult. Some have referred to such readings as 'incipient theologies',[5] others as local theologies.[6] These two labels point to two important features of such readings: first, that they raise questions and provide insights for further reflection which need to be taken up into more formal theological work. In particular, they may articulate insights which run counter to received theological teaching and writing. Second, they raise such questions out of a particular context and thus again suggest directions for theological work. There needs to be a good deal more thought about how such questions and insights can be most fruitfully engaged.

Future directions

The Mark Project was developed in order to bring groups together to read the Bible in relation to questions of Christian identity and the role of the churches in Scotland. Some of the groups who participated in the studies were gathered groups but others such as St Bride's, Lansdowne/St Mary's and St Dominic's, have previous involvement with CBS.[7] There is scope to continue working with these groups on a longer-term basis, and we would like to explore the ongoing relationship between the group's practical responses to the Bible studies and their later rereadings of the texts.

A second aim for our future work is the development of day conferences on political and social issues with the inclusion of contextual Bible study. Some members of our group have recently participated in a conference on 'Identity and Devolution', and the CBS process enabled an open engagement with the Bible in relation to these issues. We hope to incorporate contextual Bible study in discussions with groups engaged in social justice as a means of theological reflection and of gaining insights into future directions.

Notes

1 This was a theme brought out forcefully at a subsequent conference for members of the Scottish Episcopal Church. The conference was based on a series of Bible

studies on Mark 6. In his meditation on the passage, Rowan Williams remarked: 'The trouble with being in the church is that you collect all Jesus' friends', including 'the tiresomely righteous', those oppressed by guilt and hatred. We can't draw boundaries around our communities as we would like and keep out those who don't fit, not even those who aren't as open-minded as us. There's a real problem for an inclusive church, committed to openness, grace and generosity if it is confronted by those who deliberately seek to suborn such an ethos. How is it to manage power without excluding but without being drawn into intolerance and bigotry?

2 A similar correlation can be seen in another reading by a group of readers in Berlin, who were comprised of those working with asylum-seekers and child soldiers. They focused on the advocacy role of the woman, as she struggled for the well-being of her child. 'This old story, despite its age, speaks provocatively and not altogether without hope to the situation of those who work with migrants in present-day Europe. The story gives clear expression to the extreme need and helplessness of those who, because of their strangeness and because of nationalistic and racist prejudice are excluded and ostracized. But it also sheds light on the role of those who work as advocates on behalf of migrants, who have to counter the official language of civil servants and judges, who need the wit and imagination to be able to confront those in positions of power effectively with the simple humanity and need of the homeless and powerless in our society.' Jesuit Refugee Service website: campaign against detention centres.

3 The references are to a study of John 4, the Samaritan woman at the well, in the Catholic parish of St Dominic's, Craigend, which was part of an international research project, 'Through the Eyes of Another', based at the Free University, Amsterdam. The life-transforming nature of the conversation between the woman and Jesus (transformative for both parties) was taken as a model for liberative discourse in the lives of the group. This was contrasted with the destructive clichés of sectarianism and illustrated by examples from their own lives. One member told of a friendship with a member of the Protestant Orange Lodge, who had been to him 'an embodiment of Christianity', 'the epitome of kindness'. In his simple advocacy of honesty and integrity, this man had opened his eyes and made a new way of life possible for him, which he had not previously found through the inherited teaching of his church.

4 See n. 2.

5 James Cochrane, *Circles of Dignity* (Minneapolis: Fortress Press, 2001).

6 Robert J. Schreiter, *Constructing Local Theologies* (Maryknoll: Orbis Books, 1985).

7 The participating groups were from the Roman Catholic Archdiocese of Glasgow; Corstorphine Parish Church; St Dominic's Roman Catholic Church, Craigend; Lansdowne Parish Church/St Mary's Cathedral; St Bride's Episcopal Church, Glasgow; Stonelaw Parish Church, Rutherglen; Women's group, Glasgow University.

Part 3

MARK IN COMMUNITY AND POLITICS

12

Mark and mission

GEOFFREY HARRIS

I first saw Mark's Gospel in action in mission when, in 1986–90, I worked at the Faculty of Protestant Theology in Yaounde, the capital city of Cameroon. Most of the students were training for ministry, and were drawn from all over French-speaking Africa, from as far afield as Madagascar or Côte d'Ivoire.

Mark's Gospel is full of occasions when Jesus encountered people in need and with problems. There is the Gerasene demoniac of chapter 5 – an outcast madman rampaging naked through a graveyard. There is the paralysed man who had to rely on his friends to deliver him to Jesus through the roof of a house (chapter 2). There is the man whose blindness was so severe that even Jesus took two attempts to heal him (chapter 8). There is the woman whose disposable income amounted to two copper coins worth a penny (chapter 12). And so it goes on. There are also those who appear to be successful in life, but have terrible family concerns. The respected leader of the synagogue, Jairus, has a daughter who is dying (chapter 5). There is the Syrophoenician woman whose daughter is afflicted and oppressed in spirit (chapter 7). Through Mark we come across people with material problems like lack of food, emotional problems like rejection and spiritual problems like a sense of guilt or an emptiness inside.

All of these problems are evident on the very surface of life in Cameroon, whereas they are often hidden below the surface in Britain. They are problems so widespread in Africa that one is at a loss to know how to help or what to do. Yet, paradoxically, first of all I had to learn that, despite many disadvantages (in western eyes), the vast majority of Cameroonians have a rich life and great dignity. They are very ready to laugh and joke, are grateful for small mercies and are open to God. Mark's Gospel also reflects this lesson: the people mentioned above all without exception come to Jesus with hope and expectancy. The Syrophoenician woman is ready to banter with and outwit Jesus; the haemorrhaging woman (5.25–34) is audacious enough to claim Jesus' healing without asking; the synagogue leader shows implicit trust in Jesus (5.22–24). One of the most common phrases on Jesus' lips in Mark is a word of respect – 'Your faith has made you well.' Thus, I needed to learn that it is not wise to be patronizing towards those in need. All people have worth and value, even when they own very little or face hardship. Any help offered must be as an equal to an equal, with a willingness to receive as well as to give.

The other lesson I came to learn – and this is also prominent in Mark's Gospel – is that when we do offer a little, especially when we give of ourselves, our time and our love, then God can take up this 'little' and multiply it. Surely this is one of the most important lessons of the feeding miracles in Mark (chapters 6 and 8). Jesus does not simply perform a miracle. He first says to the disciples, 'You give them something to eat' (6.37). They reluctantly agree (after some sarcasm) and then to their astonishment discover that the whole crowd has been satisfied from their few loaves and fishes. Like the disciples, Jane and I learnt to understand that 'a little' was not a drop in the ocean or a waste of time, but was something God could make use of. If we gave of our material or spiritual goods, we would often end with more than we bargained for. To take one example, once we contributed towards the cost of an operation for Marie, who cleaned and cooked for us. We went on holiday, and on our return were welcomed by frantic relatives banging on the door. One explained that the operation had gone badly wrong and that Marie was very sick and would die without a further operation. Gritting my teeth I passed over more money, and, thankfully, Marie's life was saved and she eventually recovered. Ever after, she was devoted to us, and all her family members regarded us as their benefactors! Good relations were forged, and, believe it or not, we still managed on my stipend throughout our time in Cameroon.

It is difficult to locate a single text which deals with Mark's Gospel as a missionary document; and yet even a cursory look at Mark shows that mission is a primary concern of the author. The very first verse of the Gospel bears this out: 'The beginning of the good news of Jesus Christ, Son of God' (1.1). There are debates over the interpretation of this verse, and over whether 'Son of God' was in the original manuscript,[1] but this proclamation, however we see it, is clearly the spreading of news about an auspicious event or arrival. And this announcement is linked with the only editorial quotation from Scripture, which speaks about the messenger who will prepare the way for the coming of 'the Lord': ' "See I am sending my messenger ahead of you who will prepare your way; the voice of one crying in the wilderness: 'Prepare the way of the Lord, make his paths straight.'" '[2]

This passage appears to be saying that a new day will dawn, a day when 'the Lord' will return in power to right wrongs, cleanse the land and establish his reign. Mark bears this out by going on to show, in narrative form, the heavens torn asunder for God 'to come down' (1.10); the Spirit descending upon God's chosen agent Jesus (1.10) and the time for a new intervention in history – the coming of the Kingdom of God (1.14–15). All of this demands an immediate response from those who hear it: 'Repent and believe in the good news' (1.15b).

What exactly this good news is we will be examining shortly, but suffice to say that the urgency and imminence of the coming of this new age is made clear throughout the Gospel: Jesus is constantly portrayed as 'a man with a mission'. He moves from one situation to another with almost unseemly haste – from exorcisms to healings, from preaching to debating. Mark sums up: 'He went throughout Galilee proclaiming the message in their synagogues and casting out demons' (1.39). There seems to be little time for stopping still or for teaching and reflecting; little time for drawing apart and praying. We read that Jesus was constantly harassed by crowds and pressed by needy people. Just to take a few examples from the first chapter:

> They brought to him all who were sick and possessed with demons. And the whole city were gathered around the door. (1.32–33)

So, as Richard Burridge has it:

> Jesus rushes about just like a bounding lion. It all happens 'and immediately', 'at once' or 'straight away', which are translations of *kai euthus*, which occurs eleven times in chapter one alone . . . This pace continues, with *euthus* occurring over 40 times in Mark, about as often as the rest of the New Testament put together.[3]

The Spirit 'drives' Jesus out of the wilderness (1.12) and into his mission, and thereafter the action is fast and furious!

Another clear sign that Mark is a book about mission is evident from Jesus' creation of a band of disciples. This is a motley crew, admittedly, and Mark is at pains to point out frequently that the chosen ones are nevertheless singularly obtuse, obstinate and obdurate. Yet Jesus singles them out for special teaching and training, and in chapter 6 the Gospel reaches a new point of departure when Jesus commissions these 'apostles' – those he 'sends out' – for a mission of their own:

> He called the Twelve and began to send them out two by two, and gave them authority over the unclean spirits. He ordered them to take nothing for the journey except a staff: no bread, no bag, no money in their belts; but to wear sandals and not to put on two tunics. (6.7–9)

Their task is summarized in the following way:

> They went out and proclaimed that all should repent. They cast out many demons, and anointed with oil many who were sick and cured them. (6.12–13)

The phrase 'began to send them out' could be significant; we could infer that this is the inception of a missionary activity which will continue into the time of the Church, and the full flowering of mission to the world at large. The preaching seems to have little real teaching content. It is also closely linked to the proclamation of good news at the beginning of the Gospel, being the announcement of a new 'act of God'; the possibility of a new start in life. Also, the exorcisms seem to have an earlier reference point, for Jesus' first action was to cast out an evil spirit; something which caused amazement and rejoicing among the ordinary people who witnessed it: 'They kept asking one another, "What is this? A new teaching – with authority! He commands even the unclean spirits, and they obey him." ' (1.27)

The contrast with the rabbis of Jesus' own time could hardly have been more clear-cut. They were constantly busy discussing the form of words which might be suitable at an exorcism, and were for ever quoting past precedent to justify one point of view or another. But Jesus' teaching was nothing like that: it was more a demonstration of power. Perhaps the crowd had an inkling that the overcoming of evil spirits was a mark of God's new age: in other words, it was an eschatological sign that the age of the Messiah had come. If those Jesus sent out were also able to cast out evil spirits, then surely a 'new age' had truly arrived.

Unfortunately, however, the success was not to last. Even after the twelve had witnessed other miraculous events, and had seen Jesus transfigured on the mountain, they found themselves incapable of helping a man whose son was possessed. The man tells Jesus, 'I asked your disciples to cast it out, but they could not do so' (9.18). Jesus rebukes the disciples for their lack of faith (v. 19) and then later tells them, 'This kind can come out only through prayer' (v. 29). Clearly, the disciples were not yet ready to take over the work of mission from Jesus.

The other mark of mission for the twelve is that of healing in general, and, interestingly, we read that they 'anointed with oil many who were sick and cured them' (6.13). Anointing was primarily a ceremony of consecration in the Old Testament; a king or priest was anointed to equip them for their office and to confirm God's blessing upon them. Occasionally, elsewhere we read of its being a blessing,[4] but rarely an aid for healing. Even in the New Testament the only two references to anointing with oil for healing are here and in James 5.14. Perhaps Mark is reflecting a later practice which became common in the Church's life. Another explanation could be that the author wishes to show that the disciples had been commissioned and blessed by God for this task, and the oil was an indication that the Holy Spirit was with them for the duration of that particular work. Later on, however, we do not read of healings by the disciples. Again, it seems their times were not yet. The mission of chapter 6 is therefore a kind of anticipation, a foreshadowing, of what will come in due course, when the time is right, after the resurrection.

Now it is time to consider what Mark means by the proclamation of good news, in terms of mission. The good news is clearly linked to the Kingdom of God in the very first words of Jesus in Mark: ' "The time is fulfilled, and the kingdom of God has come near; repent, and believe in the good news" ' (1.14). Mark never actually spells out what he understands by 'the Kingdom', but as is often the case in the Bible generally, and especially in this Gospel, the meaning becomes clear through narrative examples.[5] 'The Kingdom' is explained through the events which demonstrate the coming of the Kingdom. Thus, Mark highlights an exorcism (1.21–27), a healing (1.29–31), the rehabilitation of an outcast leper (1.40–45), the forgiveness of sins (2.3–12), table fellowship with sinners and tax-collectors (2.15–17), breaking the binding nature of the Sabbath day (2.23–28). All of this comes to a head in the summary words:

> Hearing all that he was doing, they came to him in great numbers from Judea, Jerusalem, Idumea, beyond the Jordan, and the region around Tyre and Sidon . . . He had cured many, so that all who had diseases pressed upon him to touch him. Whenever the unclean spirits saw him, they fell down before him and shouted, 'You are the Son of God!' (3.8, 10–11)

Immediately after this summary, Jesus has to face opposition – from his own family (3.21, 31–35) and from the religious leaders, the scribes from Jerusalem (3.22–30).

Several things become clear from the content of Mark's narrative. First, the Kingdom is essentially *liberation*. People are released from crippling and disabling illnesses; people are freed from the oppressive grip of evil, and have their past sins forgiven and their guilt lifted. Those who have been marginalized and demonized are drawn back into the mainstream of community life and are thus liberated from isolation and condemnation. Those who have been treated as pariahs and kept at arm's length are brought back into fellowship as God's children and members of the Covenant people.

The bonds of excessive and oppressive restrictions placed on people's lives are broken and the Sabbath day becomes a time for refreshment and rejoicing once again.

Mark's Gospel is revolutionary in the sense that Jesus is viewed as the liberator from all the forces that oppress and restrict human life – even from religious traditions which bind and create heavy burdens. He will not tolerate the notion that some people can be shunned because they are 'unclean' (7.15); he will not allow the Sabbath to become life-denying (2.27–28; 3.4); he confronts and banishes the spirits which seek to manipulate and control a person (3.5; 10.14); he will not allow blood ties and family loyalty to exclude reaching out to others (3.33–35), and he severely warns those who threaten to destroy a child's innocence or faith (9.42; 10.14). He works to release people from pain and suffering, and he will not even allow death to cut short a life – especially the life of a child (5.41–43). Anything that restricts and hampers growth and human development he confronts and opposes.

The Marcan narrative also discloses another radical understanding of the Kingdom of God. Not only is the Kingdom revealed by Jesus, like a mystery which is being unveiled or brought into the open, but Mark is clear that the

Kingdom is actually incarnated in Jesus and is activated through his mission and work. The Kingdom is seen in the person and in the power of Jesus. The subject of the very first verse of Mark is Jesus: 'the good news of Jesus Christ, Son of God'. The powers of the Age to Come are present in his coming. The miraculous deeds and the authority evident in Jesus' teaching and commands are signs that God is active in the world in a new way. For those with eyes to see, the charismatic presence of Jesus in Mark reveals the coming of the Holy Spirit – or, alternatively, the coming of God's glory (*shekinah*) into this world with new intensity. So it is Mark's intention to demonstrate that the Kingdom is both revealed *by Jesus*, and revealed *to be Jesus*.

The key to the Kingdom in the Gospel is thus Christological – that is, how people respond to and understand and relate to Jesus Christ. Part of Mark's task is to highlight the truth that most people – including the inner circle of disciples – fail to grasp who Jesus is or to perceive the significance of his mission. The disciples have the secret of the Kingdom offered to them, but they repeatedly fail to grasp its truth or import.

In the authority (*exousia*) of Jesus one encounters the authority of God and his Word. In the actions of Jesus one sees the will of God becoming a reality in the world. The Kingdom is seen to be a place of healing, compassion, mercy, new life and fulfilment. The oppressed are released, the outcast restored to the mainstream, the sick healed and the despairing given new hope. All this has as its focal point the work and witness of Jesus himself.

Third, the Kingdom is shown to be a restoration of harmony and community life.

It is commonplace to observe that the Marcan Jesus associates himself deliberately with outcasts and the marginalized. But there is more to it than that. He associates with them in order to restore them to the life of the mainstream community; that is, he brings such people back into fellowship with society at large. Mark demonstrates this intention through his remarkable stories of table fellowship. Jesus becomes known as 'the friend of sinners' by mixing with all the wrong people, as though they were quite normal people to mingle with. He befriends women and shows that there should be equality between the sexes.[6] He shows that children are worthy of respect and draws them into adult company, going so far as to say, 'To such as these belongs the kingdom of God' (10.14). He takes up the cause of the poor – that is, the powerless, those without a voice – and makes sure that they are heard and notice taken of them (9.42; 10.24, 30).

The most astounding aspect of this is that Jesus will not treat Gentiles as any different from Jews. They are in his time considered by Jesus' compatriots to be ritually impure as idolaters and eaters of pork, a people living in land infested by evil spirits (see 5.1–2). Yet Jesus goes out of his way to reach them and to restore them to fellowship with God and with God's people. In chapters 5—8 of Mark we read a series of narrative accounts centred on a Gentile mission.

First, Jesus lands 'on the other side of the lake' (5.1) in the land of the Gerasenes. He confronts a man tormented by evil spirits, who lies among the tombs of the dead and who cannot be restrained, even with chains and shackles. This Gentile territory is the habitation of demons; the place where the living dwell among the dead (5.3) and where people are fearful in the presence of a man of God (5.15). Jesus leaves this demoniac in his right mind, restored to normal society, but the Gentiles are not yet ready to receive him as Son of God (5.17, 20). Later, in chapter 7, Jesus goes to the region of Tyre. Again he encounters someone who is oppressed by an evil spirit – this time, a little girl whose mother is a Syrophoenician woman. Jesus at first resists the woman's insistent pleas, but after some conversational banter, he decides to heal the daughter, and then compliments the mother (7.29).

Then, in the region of the Decapolis (the ten Hellenistic cities), Jesus comes across the deaf-mute. The symbolism of this is clear: the Gentiles are about to have their eyes opened, their ears unstopped and their tongues released, in order to become aware of the work of God and the presence of God's agent among them. Finally in this section, the mission among the Gentiles concludes with the feeding of the four thousand (8.1–10). This story complements the earlier feeding of the five thousand (6.34–44). The location, as well as the number symbolism, indicate that the first feeding is for the lost sheep of the house of Israel, who are 'like sheep without a shepherd' and who need to be taught many things (6.34). The twelve disciples feed the twelve tribes, and twelve baskets are left over, full of pieces of bread and of fish. The second account has four thousand, to represent the four corners of the earth. The seven loaves indicate a number of completeness or fullness. In this case Jesus takes the loaves, breaks them and then gives them to the disciples to distribute. He does the same with the fish. With these few choice words, the Marcan community is reminded of the Eucharist or Lord's Supper when, as Jews and Gentiles together, they gather round the Lord's Table, one community reconciled together in Christ. In this simple, but marvellously evocative way, Mark is able to demonstrate how Jesus has created one new community from those who were previously separated, even at loggerheads, sometimes kept at arm's length, often treated as enemies. Now there is a community which is open to all, treating all on terms of equality, willing to use the gifts of each and of all, empowering all to serve in the community and placing on each and every one real value and worth in the sight of God.

The incorporation of the marginalized – even of Gentiles – into the community of God's people is not only a mission theme in Mark's Gospel: it is also a universalizing of the mission of God. What began with a chosen race, a holy nation, a covenant people in Israel, is now being widened and extended to all people who respond with faith in Jesus. This broadening of mission is therefore laid out in the Gospel in the form of a pattern or sequence.

The way in which Mark presents this pattern of mission is through the literary device of a geographical movement. Jesus is shown to begin his work to the west of the Sea of Galilee, at Capernaum (1.21), moving around the local area from his home base. Then, we read of a new development (3.7), as people come to him from the south – the Jewish heartlands of Judaea and Jerusalem, and also from the mixed race areas like Idumea and 'beyond the Jordan'; then finally from Gentile-dominated towns like Tyre and Sidon.

Moving on, Jesus teaches 'by the lake' (4.1) and gives a message in parables. Then, late in chapter 4, he determines to 'go to the other side' (4.35). This phrase is a coded way of saying 'to the Gentile territories'. Accordingly, we next find Jesus in the country of the Gerasenes (5.1) and then in the Decapolis region (5.20). In verse 21 he 'crossed again . . . to the other side' and ministered among the Jewish people to one of the synagogue leaders, Jairus. Later, he also teaches *in* the synagogue on the Sabbath day (6.2). Still remaining in a very Jewish setting, he sends out the twelve two by two (6.7). This is clearly a mission to 'the lost sheep of the house of Israel'. The feeding of the five thousand also has a Jewish setting, but we are in a wilderness, with people who are 'like sheep without a shepherd'. Jesus has moved from the heart of Jewish life – the synagogue – to the margins of Jewish society: to outlying deprived villages and to the wilderness.

Next we read that he takes a boat 'to the other side' (6.45) – to Bethsaida – but then, after a storm, which perhaps serves as a warning of impending danger, they land at Genessaret (6.53). Chapter 7 introduces a new theme, that of ritual purity. Jesus has no regard for a tradition which separates people from one another, which encourages spiritual prejudice and which leads people to treat others as pariahs. This all serves as an introduction for the extension of Jesus' mission into Gentile territories. He sets out for the region of Tyre (7.24) and there meets a woman of Gentile origin. Mark emphasizes her 'foreign-ness' by adding that she was 'of Syrophoenician origin' (7.26). Then, moving from Tyre to Sidon and then into the Decapolis on the east side of the Sea of Galilee, Jesus encounters the deaf-mute. After this dramatic episode, Jesus again meets a crowd of people in a desert place, this time counted as four thousand (8.4). He has compassion for this crowd, since they had had nothing to eat for three days. In this Gentile territory, the symbolism is clear: there are no villages around with food to offer – material or spiritual. Nor have the people any resources with them; only the disciples have a handful of loaves (seven) and a few small fish. Spiritual food comes from Israel, where the knowledge of God is kept alive.

Then in 8.22, they come again to Bethsaida, and Jesus rather tentatively heals a blind man. This whole section culminates with Peter's confession at Caesarea Philippi. Interestingly, this location has received little attention from critics. It is surely significant that it is a new Hellenistic city built by Herod the Great. Jesus is thus proclaimed Messiah in the sight of both Jews and Gentiles.

Immediately after this, the Gospel takes a new direction, as Jesus warns the disciples of his impending suffering, rejection, death and subsequent resurrection (8.31). This subject, of the necessity of Jesus' death, becomes a dominant theme in the Gospel, and even the disciples have to face the fact that following Jesus means losing one's life in order to save it, denying oneself and taking up a cross (8.34–35). Up to this point, the whole of the Gospel has been a story of mission. The geographical place names are a coded description of a mission which crosses boundaries – from Jewish territories west of Lake Galilee to Gentile territories to the north and east of the lake. This crisscrossing motif is a clear sign that Jesus intends to reach out to all people and all kinds of people.

Even the parables of chapter 4 are parables of mission: the sower and the seed (4.1–9, 13–20); the parable about shining one's light clearly (4.21–23); the parable of the seed growing secretly and spreading (4.26–29); the parable of the mustard seed which is like the expansion of God's work or mission (4.30–32). At the end of this parable, Mark includes a mysterious phrase: 'It grows up and becomes the greatest of all shrubs, and puts forth large branches, so that the birds of the air can make nests in its shade' (4.32). This is an oblique reference to the fact that even the Gentiles will find shelter in the new mission of Jesus Christ. In Ezekiel 31.6 (LXX version), this phrase will be used to denote all the nations of the earth, and, as Joel Marcus points out,[7] in a Greek commentary on Daniel 4.18, a similar phrase is used to describe Nebuchadnezzar's kingdom stretching to the very ends of the earth.

Conclusion

There are therefore two key aspects of mission in Mark's Gospel. First, mission is conceived as a form of *liberation*. Jesus is regarded as the one who, through the power of God, liberates human beings from all the forces which oppress and restrict life and fulfilment. The idea that some people are 'unclean' and somehow under the judgement of God already, and are to be avoided and shunned, is an idea vigorously and vehemently opposed by the Jesus of Mark's Gospel. He will not allow certain people to be pushed aside or even demonized in this way. Nobody should be cast right out of normal human society and concourse. Whoever treats others as non-persons or as those with no claim to God's blessings is the one to be challenged, even if it be members of one's own family or leaders of the religious establishment. Only those who do the will of God can be considered as truly brother, sister or mother (3.33–35). Jesus condemns the love which is too narrowly focused on family or clan and which is apt to exclude people outside a small circle of 'those like us'.

Liberation is of course also freedom from crippling illness or disability, and Jesus' work of healing affords ample proof of his desire to liberate people in this way. Even death is not permitted to stand in the way of human fulfilment and wholeness, which are other words for salvation – *soteria* in Greek.

Wealth is also regarded as a weight holding people back in Mark's Gospel. It breeds worry and anxiety and denies freedom to move or respond to a call to new life (10.21–22). Indeed, to leave one's possessions and earthly ties behind is regarded in Mark as a way of entering the Kingdom (10.29–30). Also, by forgiving the sins which haunt and hold back through guilt and fear, Jesus releases people from everything which causes a spiritual obstacle, cutting people off from God and preventing spiritual development. He restores hope and makes it possible for people to break down the barriers holding their life in thraldom. After healing the paralysed man, he declares that 'the Son of Man has power on earth to forgive sins' (2.10).

Faith in Mark is therefore universally portrayed as that which liberates. But Mark does not regard liberation as merely 'freedom from'. He sees it rather as 'freedom for'. Sometimes the search for freedom can end up meaning simply 'freedom of choice' or even 'the freedom to do as I like' or 'freedom to follow my feelings or desires'. This freedom can lead to an unending search for more material possessions, or the 'good life' or 'having a good time', or a self-centred personal fulfilment, sometimes at the expense of concern for the neglected, lonely or downtrodden. But in Mark liberation is, by way of contrast, freedom for a life of service and discipleship; sometimes even a life of self-sacrifice – in short, a disciplined life lived to bless and benefit others and to bring about their liberation. This is a freedom which might involve suffering and personal cost and even risk to one's life.

A vivid illustration of the life of service and self-sacrifice, bringing about the liberation of others, is provided by L'Arche ('The Ark') communities, founded by Jean Vanier in 1974. These communities were set up to care for people with learning disabilities. From humble origins, there are now eight ecumenical L'Arche communities in the UK and no less than 124 in different countries.[8]

In the beginning Jean Vanier invited two young men with a mental handicap to come and live with him in a small house in Trosly. They were not so severely handicapped as to require hospital care, but were not able to live in society at large without support. Jean Vanier realized that the state could not cater adequately for such people, and also that they could be integrated into the life of the community and actually enrich that life – the lives of others. Jean was convinced that our modern society had become over-intellectualized and needed to relearn 'the language of the heart', that is, how to relate to other people at the emotional and affective level. He believed that the men and women with mental handicaps could teach the members of 'normal' society how to love one another, how to demonstrate affection and how to enjoy life.

In this manner, L'Arche communities would be engaged in a two-way liberation. The members of L'Arche would release members of the wider community to be more caring and mutually supportive of one another. This would be a liberation for them, and could result in a rediscovery of how to live life and how to serve God. On the other side, the members of L'Arche would discover that they are valued and valuable members of society, capable of helping others, doing useful work and blessing other people.

The men and women (i.e. those with handicaps) therefore work normal office hours in workshops, carrying out a variety of tasks, from sorting screws for factories to craft workshops making pottery; from market gardening of fruit and vegetables for local shops to the forging of metal figures and sculptures of high quality. Each community has a shop 'on site'. Outside office hours the celebration of the Eucharist lies at the heart of the communities' life, and a 'house of prayer' is a permanent focus for contemplation and quietness before God. Many of the assistants working in the communities spend four to six hours a day in prayer and in some houses a 24-hour prayer vigil is maintained. It is understood that the spiritual life and the power of the Holy Spirit is the engine which enables liberation and creates true community life. L'Arche does not see duty and self-sacrifice as the goals;[9] rather, the visitor is struck by the smiles, the laughter, the carefree sense of fun and togetherness. These are signs of liberation in themselves.

Jean Vanier is realistic and hard-headed about the huge size of the task of running the communities, and the problems in overcoming past and present suffering and pain; but nevertheless out of the experience of the cross, L'Arche has managed to forge many experiences of new life and liberation. This is clearly very much in line with the teaching of Mark's Gospel. It is visible in the L'Arche prayer, which begins:

> Father, through Jesus Our Lord and Our Brother, we ask you to bless us. Grant that L'Arche may be a true home, where the poor in spirit may find life, where those who suffer may find hope.

The second major theme of mission in Mark is that of reconciliation and the creation of community life. When viewed from the outside, the most significant aspect of Mark's own church must surely have been the bringing together of disparate groups of people: Jews who believed Jesus to be the long-awaited Messiah; Samaritans who resented past mistreatment by Jews and who were viewed in their turn as half-caste and heretical; 'unclean sinners' who had practised outlawed professions before conversion, such as tax-collector or prostitute. Others had been marginalized through leprosy or supposed demon-possession. Then there were the Gentiles, who often feared and reviled one another if they belonged to different races. The reconciliation forged in the Church to bring all these different groups together – with their varying cultural and religious backgrounds, their differing outlooks and lifestyles – this reconciliation almost defies belief. We have become all too blasé about the facts of the case because we are so familiar with them. But this reconciliation of groups often at loggerheads was without doubt the most significant achievement of the Christian community in its entire history and it leaves us today with a great legacy – an example to follow and a pattern to imitate.

We struggle today – at international level and equally at local level – to bring together in harmony different groups and factions that have up until now misunderstood and perhaps feared one another, creating myths and pre-judices about one another as a result. And of course the Christian Church con-tains this very problem within its own life – the problem of a fragmented community with different denominations, ethnic divisions and histories of the oppression of minorities, even the oppression of the whole female sex by a male-dominated hierarchy through history.

Reconciliation might seem an impossible or unachievable task. But it happened before! In the Marcan church and in the early Church as a whole, reconciliation was not only about people being prepared to tolerate one another and to live side by side for the sake of a higher good: it was much more than that. It was about different groups with different agendas agreeing to lay aside their differences and to give up their individual ambitions in order to forge a new identity and to create a new community in the pursuit of a common ideal and vision.

The Church's achievement through its mission is thus a beacon of hope for the whole world: for it shows that those previously at daggers drawn can be united; can find peace and harmony in a new life together. Cultural dif-ferences can then become a rich mix of cultural expressions and traditions. But more than that, this reconciliation can be the way to overcome the evils of racism, sexism, nationalism and all other forms of exclusive behaviour, as well as the way to overcome the demonization or marginalization of particu-lar people or groups.

Under one and the same umbrella, the life of the most diverse commun-ity – a mixture of ethnic identities, different age-groups, sexes and cultures – was able to come together in faith to flourish through their common goal of worshipping Jesus Christ and serving their neighbour. Surely this lesson from Mark's Gospel is a lesson for the whole world in the twenty-first century.

A contemporary example of this kind of reconciliation and building of new community is Corrymeela in Northern Ireland. This organization had its beginnings even before the recent troubles. In 1946, Ray Davey became Presbyterian chaplain at Queen's University, Belfast. He had previously been involved in a YMCA venture in North Africa which acted as a meeting point for Jews and Christians of many denominations. The sense of unity and fellowship forged there became for him an ideal for life at Queen's. So Ray acquired a house near the university and began to build a community there. He strengthened the links between people by taking them in groups to the Agape Community in Italy, Taizé in France and Iona in Scotland. This took the students out of the sectarian atmosphere of their upbringing and exposed them to new ideas and to people from every country and background.

At a one-day retreat in 1964 these new ideas came together when the community bought a property on the Country Antrim coast. It had been a Holiday Fellowship Centre, and was now renamed Corrymeela, 'The Hill of Harmony'. It would later be the focus for a much more widely dispersed community (or series of 'cells') which grew out of these small beginnings. The centre has now become a settled group of about a hundred and fifty souls, but they resource a much wider number of supporters. They are a mixed bunch of Roman Catholics and Protestants, and have become a beacon of hope, a pointer to a better future in Ulster.

As the conflict in Northern Ireland escalated after 1968, so the community's thrust towards the work of reconciliation became more central. It was thrown into a series of crises – most especially helping Protestants and Catholics who had become the victims of violence. Corrymeela also began work among families and people at risk, developing programmes that addressed the problems of conflict and violence in divided communities. Many groups came visiting who were embroiled in the hatred and sectarianism of one side or the other in Northern Ireland.

The soul of Corrymeela is firstly, however, 'commitment to Christ, *and therefore* concrete commitment to some work of reconciliation' (my italics).[10] This means that Corrymeela is far more than a retreat centre. For some, this work of reconciliation is a full-time job; for others, it might involve teaching in a school, running a youth club, engaging in peace education, administering justice or working for prison reform. The overriding aim in every circumstance is the reconciliation of people previously at loggerheads. It is the struggle to bring people together through prayer and action in the power of Jesus Christ. There is for every member of Corrymeela a daily discipline of Bible study and prayer, with passages assigned each day and a 'prayer rota' listing names and areas of concern. Dispersed members ('Friends') meet together in cells and organize a programme of action. Major events take place at Ballycastle and at Belfast, responding to the needs of the day: perhaps a weekend on conflict resolution; perhaps exchange visits between young people from Ireland and Germany; perhaps bringing Catholic and Protestant teenagers from a certain area together; perhaps a conference for sixth-formers; perhaps unemployment workshops.

When groups with a history of mutual hostility meet together, they are encouraged to share their feelings with people on the other side of the divide – not accusingly, but 'saying how they feel'.[11] Many problems gradually come to be seen as the 'demonizing' or 'stereotyping' of people who actually share similar hopes and fears, dreams and anxieties. Corrymeela's 'Seed Groups' bring together young adults for four or five weekends spread over several months. The changes in attitude and the reconciliation brought about send ripples into the wider communities to which they return.

Corrymeela is not in the business of reconciliation alone: it seeks to build new communities of love, understanding and mutual respect under the banner of Christian faith. The last word ought to go to Ray Davey himself:

> For the first time, there is a very large body of people who want something different. It includes people in the churches, a lot of communities, and different groups and networks. That is a new thing: it has never happened before in Irish history. Maybe we are not being as effective as we might be, but we are here and we won't go away.[12]

With these robust words, Ray Davey sums up the great conviction of Mark's Gospel, that those who had been strangers and enemies could become friends in Christ and be united through the goal of seeking God's Kingdom.

Notes

1 See J. Marcus, *Mark 1—8* (London: Anchor Doubleday, 2000), pp. 141–7 for an exhaustive discussion of this verse.
2 This is a composite quotation from Malachi 3.1, Exodus 23.20 and Isaiah 40.3. All other quotations in Mark occur on the lips of characters in the story (mainly Jesus himself).
3 R. Burridge, *Four Gospels, One Jesus* (London: SPCK, 1994), p. 36.
4 See, for example, Exodus 30.22–33; Deuteronomy 28.40; Ruth 3.3; 2 Samuel 14.2; Psalm 141.5; Daniel 10.3; Amos 6.6; Micah 6.15.
5 In a similar way, after the disobedience of Adam and Eve in taking fruit from the tree of knowledge (Gen. 3.1–7), an explanation of 'sin' is never elucidated in Genesis, but becomes understood through a series of narrative examples, in chapters 3 through to 11 in particular.
6 See on this 1.30–31; 5.25–34, 35–43; 12.41–4; 14.3–9; 15.40–1, 47; 16.1–8.
7 J. Marcus, *Mark*, p. 324.
8 See *Methodist Recorder*, 20 May 2004, p. 4.
9 Assistants only receive 'pocket money' for the first two years, after which they become 'salaried' – that is, receive the minimum wage laid down by French law.
10 See J. Hinton, *Communities* (Guildford: Eagle Publishing, 1993), p. 99.
11 In Hinton, *Communities*, p. 102.
12 In Hinton, *Communities*, p. 107.

13

John the Baptist's death

CHRISTINE E. JOYNES

Mark 6.17–29 is frequently dismissed as an irrelevant legend or a time-filling device, but does the gruesome story of John the Baptist's demise have more to contribute to our understanding of Mark's Gospel than we give it credit for?[1] This essay aims to illustrate the story's potential for interpreters today by appealing to its reception history. Through an exploration of this prolific and diverse reception history we gain a better awareness of the narrative's rich significance.[2] We discover that Mark 6.17–29 provides us with a model of political empowerment, a vivid illustration of suffering and sacrifice, and a challenge to reflect on motives, actions and their consequences in the gospel narrative.

A cursory glance at the reception history of Mark 6.17–29 reveals its immense impact. This impact, ranging from the period of the early Church to the twenty-first century, comes from both inside and outside of the Church, including interpretations of the text in art, music and literature. We are thereby reminded that understanding the biblical text occurs not simply through elucidation of its statements but by engaging all the senses and involving the whole human being. The reception history of our Marcan text reveals significant interpretations of John the Baptist, Herod and Herodias, as well as the dancing girl.[3] However, for reasons of brevity we will sample some interpretations of just two key characters in the narrative: John the Baptist and the dancing girl.

Different versions of the same story

We should note at the outset that the beheading of John the Baptist is not a passage found only in Mark, a shorter version also occurs in Matthew (14.3–12), though it is not recounted by Luke or John. Since Mark was the earliest Gospel, Matthew is our first commentary on the Marcan text, to which he makes some interesting alterations. For example, Mark refers to Herod protecting the Baptist from Herodias's intentions to dispose of him:

> And Herodias had a grudge against him, and wanted to kill him. But she could not, for Herod feared John, knowing that he was a righteous and holy man,

and he protected him. When he heard him, he was greatly perplexed; and yet he liked to listen to him. (Mark 6.19–20)

Matthew's omission of this Marcan detail significantly alters the focus of culpability in his narrative, placing the responsibility for the Baptist's death more squarely on Herod. Matthew also corrects Mark's misrepresentation of Herod as a king, and instead designates him as a tetrarch. Further Matthean changes include abbreviation of Mark's explanation for John's challenge to Herod and Herodias, omitting the detail that Herod had married his brother's wife (Mark 6.17).

The synoptic nature of the gospel material often makes it difficult to determine whether an interpreter has the Marcan text in view. One could argue, pedantically, that where an interpreter explicitly refers to Herod as a king rather than a tetrarch he or she has Mark in mind, though I doubt whether this is actually the case. Indeed sometimes interpreters refer to Herod as both king and tetrarch interchangeably, harmonizing the gospel narratives.

Where there is no clear indication of an interpreter's biblical source, for example in Jacob Cornelisz van Oostsanen's painting of *Salome with the Head of John the Baptist*, there is a strong likelihood that Mark's narrative concerning the beheading of the Baptist is in view, particularly since Mark gives the most detailed account.[4] Some scholars might argue that such uncertainty about gospel sources makes any attempt to investigate the use and influence of Mark's Gospel impossible, but we suggest that it is feasible to discuss instances that could be labelled 'Marcan' where certainty about sources is unattainable. Hence the examples cited below include both implicitly and explicitly Marcan examples.

John the Baptist: a model of political empowerment

The reception history of John the Baptist's death illustrates a variety of themes, not just the Baptist's role as forerunner of the Messiah, but also how he has been regarded as a representative of monastic asceticism, a model of outspoken opposition to tyranny, a figure of virtue, or as a polemicist. We will focus here on interpretations which highlight the political significance of the Baptist's beheading.

The political import of the account of the Baptist's death was recognized at an early stage. Church Fathers such as John Chrysostom and Augustine regarded John the Baptist as a figure of bold prophetic protest and encouraged Christians to follow his example in courageously confronting wrongdoing. John Chrysostom comments: 'For the sacred laws which were despised he laid down his head.'[5] This approach is later adopted by Calvin, who extracts a general principle from reflecting on the Baptist's confrontation with Herod's court. He remarks: 'In almost all dynastic courts reigns hypocrisy and slavish admiration, and the ear of the ruler accustomed to flattery will tolerate no word which tackles his mistakes.'[6]

Political readings of the narrative are also to be found in several sixteenth-century dramas which reflect an anti-papist perspective in their interpretations of the narrative: thus George Buchanan's *Baptistes*[7] and James Wedderburn's *Tragedy of the Beheading of John the Baptist* used the account of the Baptist's death as a biblical allegory to dramatize the plight of oppressed reformers.

It is worth elaborating a little further on Buchanan's interpretation to illustrate the application of Mark's Gospel to particular historical concerns.[8] The prologue to his play makes its contemporary application clear when it describes the

> ancient tale in modern dress
> How John the Baptist to a monarch's lust,
> And subtle slanders of his spiteful foes
> Fell innocent prey, and died a guiltless death.[9]

Buchanan (1506–82) himself had a turbulent career in which he was frequently attacked for acts of political provocation. He was imprisoned at St Andrews in Scotland, as a result of satirizing the Franciscans. After escaping to the Continent, he became professor at the Collège de Guyenne in Bordeaux. Buchanan subsequently moved to teach at the University of Coimbra in Portugal, and while there he was imprisoned by the Inquisition (1549–51). He later returned to Scotland as a professed Protestant, and became tutor to James VI and I, to whom his Latin play *Baptistes* is dedicated. This background may suggest a certain autobiographical interest on the author's part, influencing the political emphasis found in his play about John the Baptist.[10] This highlights the close involvement of the interpreter in any act of biblical interpretation: as readers we inevitably bring our own contextual pre-assumptions to the text.

It is noteworthy that the play *Baptistes* functions as entertainment, as a drama to be performed in a secular context.[11] This of course does not prevent the author from making a political statement through this medium. Buchanan's play develops the theme of John the Baptist's determined stance against tyranny, especially through its focus on what constitutes good kingship. Herod's deliberations on this theme in many ways make his final decision to kill the Baptist even more blameworthy, since he is aware of what merits good government. This is evident in his debate with Salome at the conclusion of the play:[12]

Herod: But what the King commandeth should be just.

Salome: That which aforetime was unjust, the King,
          By his commanding it, can render just.

Herod: The law sets limits to the King's command.

> Salome: If that be right which gratifies the prince,
> Then does not law impose its bounds on kings,
> Rather the King sets limits to the laws.
>
> Herod: Report will vouch me despot, not a king . . .
> The fear of force,
> But poorly wards a State.

The emphasis on the theme of just kingship is particularly distinctive in Buchanan's reading of the Marcan text. The model of the 'divine right of kings' portrayed in the play mirrors the model of kingship recognized in Buchanan's own day, indicating again the contextual nature of biblical interpretation.

Buchanan was called to account for the political content of *Baptistes* in his trial before the Lisbon Inquisition, where he swore that his drama represented Thomas More's defiance before Henry VIII, not a Protestant objection to the abuses of the Catholic Church. Buchanan testified:

> As soon as possible when I had escaped thence, I recorded my opinion of the English in that tragedy which deals with John the Baptist, wherein so far as the likeness of the material would permit, I represented the death and accusation of Thomas More and set forth before the eyes an image of the tyranny of that time.[13]

In the context of a trial before the Inquisition, Buchanan's denial of an anti-papist agenda in the play is unsurprising. As with the biblical text, the multivalency of his play permitted a range of possible interpretations. It is, however, worth noting the constraints of the biblical text which Buchanan claims restricted his literary appropriation of the narrative.

As we have seen, a political reading of John the Baptist's death had a long heritage and this continued to be influential long after Buchanan's application of the episode to his own context. To take another more recent example, the political dynamics of the Marcan text were also recognized by the Nicaraguan peasants of Solentiname. Through both art and textual commentary they clearly appropriate the Marcan narrative to their own situation in the aftermath of the Nicaraguan revolution.[14]

In the application of Mark 6.17–29 to their own context, the peasants identify key characters in the biblical text with the central figures that led to the revolution in Nicaragua, so Herod is presented as the dictator Somoza. The contemporary appropriation of the story is clearly apparent: the artistic representation of the narrative presents the characters in modern dress, surrounded by contemporary furnishings and the textual commentary further develops the parallelism between the biblical account and recent events:

> *Manolo*: 'John was killed because he reproved the governor not only for his adultery but also for all his tyrannies and his crimes . . . He couldn't preach about a change of attitude without touching the person of Herod.'

Felipe: 'And when the priests and bishops keep prudent silence in the face of the crimes that happen in this country, because they say it is not proper for them to get involved in politics, they simply aren't following this example from the Gospel.'[15]

In contrast to Buchanan's reading of the text, this example comes from a religious context, as believers in Solentiname discuss with their priest, Ernesto Cardenal, how the biblical text is relevant to their life situations. We discover how the account of the Baptist's beheading has resonated with a marginalized group, who liken their own situation to that faced by John the Baptist and find themselves empowered by his stand against tyranny. The Marcan narrative provides a model for the believers in Solentiname to emulate when challenging perceived injustice.

These political readings of John the Baptist's beheading reveal particular historical preoccupations and striking continuities of interpretation in very different social and political circumstances. They remind us of the contextual nature of biblical interpretation, and how as interpreters we inevitably bring our own pre-assumptions to the text. They also alert us to the significant political implications of Mark 6.17–29, which we can apply to our own contemporary context.

An image of suffering and sacrifice

Another illustration of the significance of the Baptist's death emerges when we turn to examine Hinrik Funhof's 1483 altar painting from the Johanniskirche in Lüneburg, Germany.[16] Funhof's visual representation of our text confronts us with the repugnance of the Baptist's death, challenging us with aspects of the story that we probably prefer not to stop and think about. Moreover, his depiction of John's head on a platter also draws our attention to the food imagery in the story by the striking similarity between the severed head and the meat joint on the table; Herod holds a knife and prepares to eat. Too readily, I suspect, we gloss over the detail that the dancing girl demanded the head on a platter. The banquet setting of the story – at Herod's birthday feast – is also easy to overlook. However, once we pause to reflect on the feasting imagery of Mark 6.17–29, the significant connection with Jesus' feeding of the five thousand, which immediately follows our passage (6.30–44), becomes apparent.

The feeding of the five thousand is widely interpreted as a prefiguration of the messianic banquet and of Jesus' sacrificial self-giving, symbolized in the Eucharist (Mark 14), but the connection between the food imagery in 6.17–29 and 6.30–44 is less frequently noted. However, the eucharistic associations of Mark 6.17–29 are suggested both by the internal evidence of the Gospel, and its reception history.

Mark's Gospel draws significant parallels between the deaths of John the Baptist and Jesus, such as the arrest, seizure and binding of both figures, delay in disposing of them until an opportune moment occurs, and recognition by their captors that they do not deserve death. These parallels have prompted some commentators to note that in Mark's Gospel John the Baptist's death foreshadows Jesus' own. This understanding of the Baptist's death was developed in the medieval Church where the severed head came to be interpreted as a symbol of the Eucharist. So for example Pseudo-Jerome, an early commentator on Mark, allegorizes John's separated head and body to represent the division between the spirit and the letter. He comments: 'The body of John is buried, his head is laid on a dish: the letter is covered with earth, the spirit is honoured and received at the altar.'[17] Here then we see Pseudo-Jerome extending the comparison between John the Baptist and Jesus, suggesting that the dish on which John's head is carried is a reminder of the paten used at Mass. This interpretation is also reflected in the late-fifteenth-century York breviary, which reads: 'Caput Johannis in disco: signat corpus Christi: quo pascimur in sancto altari' ('St John's head on the dish signifies the body of Christ which feeds us on the holy altar').[18]

The eucharistic interpretation of the Baptist's death identified by Pseudo-Jerome was popular in the medieval period, reflected by sculpture, seals, paintings and domestic ornaments of John's head on a platter.[19] This veneration continued throughout the fifteenth and sixteenth centuries, with the widespread circulation of what became known as St John's heads, alabaster tablets depicting the head of John the Baptist on a dish. Stuebe comments on these alabaster tablets: 'Such an affinity between the veneration of St John's head and the cross or crucifix is entirely possible in view of the role of St John as the precursor of Christ, so much stressed in the fifteenth century.'[20]

So the reception history of Mark 6.17–29 clearly indicates that far from being an irrelevant time-filling device, John the Baptist's end was regarded as a highly significant foreshadowing of Jesus' sufferings, with the food imagery playing a central part in this parallelism.

The dancing girl: moral warning or innocent victim?

The dancing girl who gains the head of the Baptist in Mark 6.17–29 has attracted enormous attention from interpreters both inside and outside of the Church.[21] A survey of the reception history of this figure reveals that representations of 'Salome', a legendary name for the dancing girl, vary considerably.[22] Is the girl innocent or does she perform an erotic dance to arouse the guests? Mark does not tell us, but commentators have been swift to fill in the gaps in the text to reflect both these positions. We are thereby challenged to adjudicate between competing interpretations of the Marcan narrative.

It is striking, given its incidental occurrence in the narrative, that the girl's dance has been the focal point for so much reception history. In less than a sentence Mark reports only that 'when Herodias' daughter came in and danced, she pleased Herod and his guests' (6.22). The reason for an explosion of interest in the dance may derive in part from the momentous result that it brings: the beheading of the Baptist. For as Ched Myers points out, Mark 6.17–29 is in fact a political parody where 'among all these powerful men a dancing girl determines the fate of John the Baptist'.[23] But it also provides an opportunity for commentators to fill the textual gap in the light of their own contextual pre-assumptions.[24]

In support of the view that the girl is innocent, performing an honourable dance that charms the king, some commentators appeal to the Greek vocabulary used by Mark, where terminology such as *korasion* (which can mean 'apple of my eye' as well as being the diminutive 'little girl') and *aresen* (which according to many commentators means 'pleasure' but not of a sexual nature) is used. Following this reading of Mark 6.17–29, the reader is then extremely shocked when the girl asks for the head of the Baptist after consulting with her mother.

However, this construction of the text has not been the most widespread. To take an early example of an interpreter that viewed the dancing girl as a moral warning, an evil figure whose reprehensible actions are to be condemned, we can cite Ambrose who comments:

> Is anything so conducive to lust as with unseemly movements thus to expose in nakedness those parts of the body which either nature has hidden or custom has veiled, to sport with the looks, turn the neck, to loosen the hair?[25]

He appeals to a saying from Cicero ('No one dances when sober unless he is mad') and concludes that the story of John's beheading provides a caution concerning the allures of dancing. Chrysostom reflects a similar point of view in his assertion, 'For where dancing is, there is the evil one.'[26] Calvin continues this interpretation, describing the dance of the girl as a mark of lasciviousness and harlotry.[27]

We should note that the dancing girl has also been the subject of attention beyond the confines of the Church, making an extensive impact in the secular sphere, particularly in art, music and literature.[28] These interpretations of Mark 6.17–29 frequently portray the girl with amorous feelings towards John the Baptist and as acting on her own initiative rather than at the behest of her mother when she asks for his head. This can be contrasted with the Marcan text, which presents the girl as an instrument for her mother's ambitions. The biblical account is thus transformed into a gruesome love story, expressing the chaos of emotions and the triumph of the irrational.[29]

To further illustrate the two contrasting ways in which the dancing girl has been interpreted, we might compare Picasso's *Salome*,[30] a riotous scene of nude characters delighting in provocative poses, with Caravaggio's *Salome*, where she receives the head of John the Baptist, the (fully clothed) girl turning her head in revulsion when handed the Baptist's head on a plate.[31] These artistic representations illustrate the same ambiguity about the girl's behaviour (moral warning and innocent victim) as has been recognized by theological commentators.

The reception history of the girl's dance in Mark 6.17–29 therefore challenges us to adjudicate between very different interpretations. In so doing, we discover significant gaps in the biblical narrative. The contrasting ways in which the girl's dance and the request for the head have been presented prompt us to think about the motives, actions and consequences of the characters in the biblical story and to ask to what extent the gaps in the text are filled in legitimately. Indeed, in many instances the elaborations on the biblical narrative directly contradict its content (for example, where the girl is portrayed as in love with the Baptist, and as acting on her own initiative rather than at her mother's behest). The text can therefore provide some boundaries for interpretation.

Conclusion

Our investigation of the reception history of the Baptist's beheading has illustrated that, far from being an irrelevant legend or a time-filling device, this passage has significant implications for our interpretation of Mark today.

A model of political empowerment

We discovered that Mark 6.17–29 can provide political empowerment to those facing tyranny and challenging injustice. From Buchanan's sixteenth-century literary drama to the interpretation of the text in twentieth-century Nicaragua, the powerful political import of the text has been recognized. Its scope for similar appropriation in the twenty-first century is readily apparent.

An image of suffering and sacrifice

Artistic portrayals of our Marcan text vividly highlight the repugnant nature of the Baptist's death and the significance of the food imagery in the story. We are thereby alerted to the strong connections that Mark draws between the Baptist's death and Jesus' sufferings. The suffering that the Baptist faces as a result of his convictions is also an important image for our reading of the Gospel today.

A challenge to reflect on motives, actions and their consequences

Interpretations of the dancing girl in Mark 6.17–29 have portrayed her as either a moral warning or an innocent victim. These contrasting positions

prompt us to reflect further on how to adjudicate between competing interpretations of biblical texts. We are challenged to consider the motives, actions
and consequences of the characters in the biblical narrative. The extensive
elaborations on the text, importing features into the Marcan account, lead us
to rediscover the gaps in the Marcan story. This can be a liberative experience, enabling one to reject some offensive interpretations of the text.

A reminder of the contextual nature of biblical interpretation

Finally, our brief survey of the reception history of Mark 6.17–29 illustrated
the multivalency of the text. It also highlighted the role of the interpreter in
the act of interpretation, leading us to reflect on our own pre-assumptions
which we bring to the biblical text. As Mary Callaway comments, reception
history 'can keep us alert to the limitations of our own readings and especially to the moral consequences of absolutizing our own horizon'.[32] So by
reading Mark 6.17–29 through the lens of reception history we are pointed
to the rich interpretative potential of Mark, thereby widening our horizons.

Notes

1 Morna D. Hooker, *The Gospel According to St Mark* (London: A&C Black, 1991),
   p. 158, regards the passage as a 'somewhat artificial insertion [which] provides
   an interlude for the disciples to complete their mission'.
2 I should stress that I am not suggesting as a general principle that an extensive
   reception history necessarily correlates with valuable insights, but merely argue
   that in this particular case this is true.
3 For details of interpretations of the story as a warning about the evils of feasting and swearing oaths, and how the issue of culpability in the Marcan narrative has been variously interpreted by commentators, see Christine E. Joynes,
   Mark's Gospel through the Centuries (Oxford: Blackwell, forthcoming).
4 See <www.textweek.com/art/death_of_john.htm> for van Oostsanen's painting and other images of the beheading incident.
5 John Chrysostom, 'Homily I: Concerning the Statues' in Philip Schaff (ed.), *Nicene
   and Post-Nicene Fathers, First Series, Vol. 9* (Peabody, MA: Hendrickson, 1999),
   p. 343.
6 Cited by Joachim Gnilka, *Das Evangelium nach Markus, Vol. 1* (Zürich and
   Neukirchener-Vluyn: Benziger, Neukirchener Verlag, 1998), p. 253. My
   translation.
7 The full title attributed to the play's seventeenth-century translation is *Tyrannicall
   Government Anatomised, or A Discourse concerning Evil Counsellors, Being the Life and
   Death of John the Baptist, and Presented to the King's Most Excellent Majesty by the
   Author.*
8 Buchanan's play is implicitly Marcan rather than being explicitly based on Mark.
9 George Buchanan, *John the Baptist: A Drama,* trans. A. Gordon Mitchell (Paisley:
   Alexander Gardner, 1904), p. 19. My italics.
10 See P. Hume Brown, 'Reformation and Renascence in Scotland' in A. W. Ward
   and A. R. Waller (eds.), *The Cambridge History of English Literature, Vol. 3*
   (Cambridge: Cambridge University Press, 1932), p. 161, who comments: 'It is

in the *Baptistes*, however, that we find the fullest and hardiest expression of the convictions which, frequently at his own peril, [Buchanan] consistently proclaimed throughout his whole career. The principal character, John the Baptist, is the fiery apostle of precisely those doctrines of political and religious liberty which were then perturbing Christendom, and his death at the hands of Herod is pointed as the moral of all religious and political tyranny.'

11 It was written to be performed at the school where Buchanan was teaching.

12 Buchanan, *John the Baptist*, pp. 104–6.

13 Steven Berkowitz, *A Critical Edition of George Buchanan's Baptistes and of Its Anonymous Seventeenth-Century Translation Tyrannicall-Government Anatomized* (New York and London: Garland Publishing, 1992), p. 114.

14 This example is explicitly based on Mark 6.17–29.

15 Philip and Sally Scharper (eds.), *The Gospel in Art by the Peasants of Solentiname* (Maryknoll, NY: Orbis Books, 1984), p. 24.

16 Reproduced in Friedrich-August von Metzsch, *Johannes der Täufer: Seine Geschichte und seine Darstellung in der Kunst* (München: Callwey, 1989), p. 107.

17 Beryl Smalley, *The Study of the Bible in the Middle Ages* (Oxford: Blackwell, 1952), p. 1, n. 3.

18 York Service Book of the Guild of Corpus Christi. Cited by W. H. St John Hope, 'On the sculptured alabaster tablets called St John's Heads', *Archaeologia LII* (1890), p. 705.

19 Cf. St John Hope, 'On the sculptured alabaster tablets', p. 675, who describes the popularity of this image.

20 Isabel Combs Stuebe, 'The Johannisschüssel: From Narrative to Reliquary to Andachtsbild', *Marsyas* (1968–69), p. 6.

21 For examples of the reception history of this passage, see the collection by Hugo Daffner, *Salome: Ihre Gestalt in Geschichte und Kunst* (Munich: H. Schmidt, 1912), which includes over two hundred sculptures, illuminations, engravings and other art based on this story.

22 The identification of the girl as Salome originates from the account by Josephus in his *Antiquities*, Book 18.5.4.

23 Ched Myers, *Binding the Strong Man: A Political Reading of Mark's Story of Jesus* (New York: Orbis Books, 1988), p. 216.

24 See further Janice Capel Anderson, 'Feminist Criticism: The Dancing Daughter' in Janice Capel Anderson and Stephen D. Moore (eds.), *Mark and Method: New Approaches in Biblical Studies* (Minneapolis: Fortress, 1992), pp. 121–2.

25 Ambrose, 'Concerning Virgins: Book 3' in Philip Schaff (ed.), *Nicene and Post-Nicene Fathers, Second Series, Vol. 10* (Peabody, MA: Hendrickson, 1994), p. 385.

26 John Chrysostom, 'Homily XLVIII on the Gospel of Saint Matthew' in Philip Schaff (ed.), *Nicene and Post-Nicene Fathers, First Series, Vol. 10* (Peabody, MA: Hendrickson, 1995), p. 299.

27 John Calvin, *A Harmony of the Gospels Matthew, Mark and Luke, Vol. 2* trans. T. H. L. Parker (Edinburgh: Saint Andrew Press, 1972), p. 142.

28 Salome became especially popular in the literature of the nineteenth century, featuring in works by Flaubert, Heine, Huysmans, Mallarmé, Renan and Wilde among others. Note that she also appears musically in the works of Strauss, Massenet and Hindemith. Strauss's opera, which is based on Wilde's *Salomé*, is the most influential of these. Its continuing popularity is indicated by the scheduling of

excerpts from the 'Dance of the Seven Veils' at the BBC Last Night of the Proms 2000.

29 See further Ewa Kuryluk, *Salome and Judas in the Cave of Sex* (Evanston, IL: Northwestern University Press, 1987).

30 <www.tamu.edu/mocl/picasso/graphics/1905/opp05–53.jpg> (accessed 4 November 2005).

31 <www.nationalgallery.org.uk> (accessed 4 November 2005).

32 Mary Callaway, 'What's the Use of Reception History?', p. 13, at <www.bbib-comm.net/news/latest.html> (accessed 27 February 2005).

14

Mark in ecological consciousness

SUSAN MILLER

In recent years there has been a growing awareness of the cost of the human denigration of the earth through the effects of industrialization, pollution and climate change. The development of chemical warfare and nuclear weapons, moreover, threatens the survival of the earth. The present ecological crisis has brought new questions to biblical interpretation. Has biblical interpretation contributed to the exploitation of the earth? Are there any insights into the Bible that may give new directions to address this situation? The Earth Bible series has begun to examine the Bible from the perspective of the earth.[1] The scholars in this project have drawn up a range of principles emphasizing the intrinsic value of the earth, and the interconnectedness of all living things. They have noted that the Christian tradition has been associated with a series of dualisms between heaven and earth, the soul and the body, and God and humanity. In these dualisms the terms associated with materiality, the body and the earth have lower status than those linked to the spiritual or heavenly sphere. Frequently, the Christian tradition has understood salvation as an escape from the earthly realm.

In Mark's Gospel Jesus prophesies the imminent end of the world: 'Truly I tell you, there are some standing here who will not taste death until they see that the kingdom of God has come with power' (9.1). In his end-time discourse Jesus states: 'Truly I tell you, this generation will not pass away until all these things have taken place' (13.30). Jesus, moreover, predicts the dissolution of heaven and earth in the following verse: 'Heaven and earth will pass away but my words will not pass way.' Keith D. Dyer proposes that biblical interpretations of eschatological texts such as Mark 13 have been influenced by modern understandings of apocalypticism.[2] These interpretations have focused on the end of the world, and have supported current political beliefs that ignore ecological issues and disregard the fate of the earth. Mark's apocalyptic world-view, however, is illustrated by the prologue. At the baptism of Jesus cosmic events are described: the heavens are torn apart, the Spirit descends and a voice from heaven declares Jesus to be the beloved Son (1.9–11). Immediately after his baptism the Spirit casts Jesus out into the desert where he is tested by Satan for forty days. During this time he is described as being among the wild animals, and he is served by angels (1.12–13). The prologue inaugurates a conflict between God and Satan, and this struggle continues on a human level in the remainder of the Gospel. Jesus is tested by his human enemies (8.11; 10.2; 12.15), and he warns his disciples that they will also face a time of trial (14.38). The conflict between Jesus and Satan culminates in the account of his crucifixion in which he gives his life a ransom for many (10.45). Mark's prophecies of the end-time, therefore, reflect his apocalyptic eschatology in which Jesus struggles against the forces of evil. This essay will explore Mark's portrayal of the earth in the context of his expectations of the end-time. Is the earth devalued in Mark's apocalyptic eschatology? What will be the role of humanity in the end-time? To what extent may a reading of Mark's Gospel contribute to current ecological debates?

Jesus' teaching of the end-time

Towards the end of Mark's Gospel Jesus gives an extended account of the events of the end-time to his inner circle of four disciples who have been present with him throughout his mission. This period will be a time of increased suffering such as has not been witnessed since the beginning of creation (13.19). Apocalyptic writings, such as 1 Enoch and 4 Ezra, view the last age of the world as a time of increased suffering. Morna D. Hooker proposes that Jesus' speech is intended to prepare the disciples for a 'long struggle'.[3] Jesus, however, prophesies the end of the world within the present generation (13.30). He instructs his disciples about these events so that they may stand firm, and he encourages them with his promise to return and gather them from the four winds.

Jesus' prophecies focus on the events that will take place before the end rather than upon the end itself. False prophets will arise. Nations will rise up against nation, and kingdom against kingdom. There will be earthquakes in various places and famines (13.3–8). The disciples will be brought before councils and synagogues, governors and kings. During this time the gospel must be preached to all nations. Families will betray one another to the point of death, and the disciples will be hated by all on account of Jesus' name (13.9–13). When the desolating sacrilege appears in the Temple those in Judaea are told to flee to the hills. False Messiahs and false prophets will threaten the community (13.14–23). The culmination of Jesus' prophecies is the return of the Son of Man. He will appear coming in clouds with great power and glory, and he will send his angels to gather the elect from the ends of the earth and the heavens (13.24–27).

The upheaval of the natural world in the accounts of earthquakes and famines corresponds to the disruption of human relationships in which human beings persecute and betray one another. This passage illustrates the connections between wars and the devastation of the earth, since wars often lead to famines. Fields are destroyed, and crops cannot be sown or harvested. Mark also points out that the most vulnerable members of the community are the ones who suffer most during wars (13.17). Pregnant women and women nursing small children would experience the greatest difficulty in seeking to escape from areas of conflict.

Mark thus depicts turmoil in both the natural world and in human communities. Some scholars, such as Hooker, note that wars are sometimes attributed to the judgement of God upon humanity (Jer. 4.16–18; Zech. 14.2).[4] In Mark's Gospel, however, these events are not depicted as the retribution of God. In Mark's apocalyptic world-view the earth is ruled by Satan, and God intervenes to liberate the world. The conflicts are thus apocalyptic signs of the intensification of the struggle between God and Satan. The events described are characteristic features of prophetic and apocalyptic writings. Wars occur in Daniel 11.40–42, Zechariah 14.1–6, 4 Ezra 9.2 and 2 Baruch 29.2–5; earthquakes and famines are described in 1 Enoch 1.7, 4 Ezra 9.2, 2 Baruch 27.6–7 and Revelation 6.8. They indicate that the old world order is in the process of being torn apart, and evil appears to prevail during this time. In chapter 13 the description of the desolating sacrilege in the Temple suggests that the Temple itself is possessed by evil. The neuter phrase *to Bdelugma tes eremoseios* (desolating sacrilege) is used with the masculine participle *estekota* (standing), implying a personal agent. As Hooker proposes, the account of the desecration of the Temple points to the figure of Satan who represents the forces of evil at the end of the age (cf. 2 Thess. 2.3; Rev. 13.11).[5] The term *eremoseos* derives from the noun *eremos* (desert). The desert is associated with the abode of demons (Deut. 32.17; Isa. 34.14), and it recalls the testing of Jesus by Satan in the desert (1.12–13). The cosmic conflict of the end-time continues on a human level with the persecution of the disciples. They are persecuted on account of their mission to preach the gospel to all nations (13.10). The disciples will be hated by all because of their allegiance to Jesus: 'You will be hated by all for my name's sake' (13.13).

The series of catastrophic events culminates in the return of the Son of Man, and he is accompanied by cosmic signs. The sun darkens, the moon gives no light, the stars fall and the powers are shaken (cf. Isa. 13.10; 34.4). This account indicates that all powers are shaken in relation to the authority which belongs to the Son of Man. Dyer suggests that the falling stars refer to the demise of the leaders of the East in the aftermath of the fall of Jerusalem, and they are the ones who will see the Son of Man in heaven.[6] He argues that there is no allusion to the parousia or the second coming in Mark 13. In addition he suggests that the Son of Man is vindicated before the Ancient of Days in heaven as in Daniel 7, whereas the gathering of the elect corresponds to the emergence of the discipleship community on earth. Daniel 7.13–14, however, refers to the ascent of the Son of Man whereas Mark describes the descent of the Son of Man (13.26–27). Those who 'see' the Son of Man are more likely to be those who wait on earth for his return. Similarly, the chief priest is told that he will 'see' the Son of Man 'seated at the right hand of power and coming with the clouds of heaven' (14.62). The final parable of the return of the householder also alludes to the imminent end of the world, and points to an allegorical interpretation of Jesus in the role of the householder (13.32–37).

Mark's account of the end-time, therefore, reflects a cosmic struggle between God and Satan. Unlike other apocalyptic texts, such as 1 Enoch, there is no description of the judgement and punishment of those who oppose God. In Mark, God does not seek to judge the world but to liberate humanity from the power of evil. In Mark's apocalyptic world-view God moves from heaven into the earthly sphere through the return of Jesus. Mark, moreover, does not denigrate the earth, but is concerned to show that there are signs of hope in the midst of the horrific events. Natural metaphors are employed to counteract the predictions of devastation. Paradoxically, these events are depicted as the beginning of birth pangs (*arche odinon tauta*, 13.8). The metaphor of birth pangs is a standard apocalyptic term for the beginning of the new age (cf. Isa. 26.17; 1 Enoch 62.4; 4 Ezra 4.42; Rev. 12.2). The suffering of childbirth is overcome at the joy of the birth of a child. In Mark the birth pangs refer to the destruction of the old age. The metaphor of birth suggests that a new creation will emerge from the tearing apart from the old. The new age is incompatible with the old in the same way that new cloth will tear an old garment, and new wine will burst old wineskins (2.21–22).

The term *arche* (beginning), moreover, recalls the opening verse of Mark's Gospel, '*arche tou evangeliou Iesu Christou*' ('The beginning of the gospel of Jesus Christ'). It alludes to the beginning of Genesis, '*o en arche*', 1.1 LXX ('In the beginning'). These verbal correspondences suggest that the creative power of God in Genesis is present at the end of the age bringing the new creation. Further allusions to the new creation are illustrated by the parable of the fig tree (13.28–29). This parable recalls the account of Jesus' curse upon a fig tree in chapter 11. Jesus is hungry and he notices leaves upon the tree but the tree has no fruit because it is not the right season (11.12–14). The account of the cursing of the fig tree (11.12–14, 20–25) surrounds the description of Jesus' action in the Temple. Just as the fig tree has failed to produce fruit, the Temple has failed to be a 'house of prayer for all nations' (11.17). The tree that withered from its roots symbolized the enormous destruction of the old age which bore no fruit. On the other hand, in chapter 13, the tenderness of the tree's branches is a sign that summer is near. The phrase *eygus to theios* (13.28) echoes Jesus' initial proclamation that the Kingdom of God is near (*engiken he basileia tou theou*, 1.15). The fig tree is expected to bear fruit in the messianic age (cf. Jer. 8.13; Isa. 28.3–4; Hos. 9.10, 16; Mic. 7.1).[7] The parable of the fig tree is therefore a sign of the imminence of the Kingdom of God.

The description of the return of the Son of Man also alludes to the new creation. The sun will be darkened and the moon will not give its light. This description looks forward to the darkness that falls over the earth at noon during the crucifixion (*skotos egeneto eph holen ten gen*, 15.33). Mark alludes to the darkness at noon in Amos 8.9, which represents mourning for an only son. As Dale C. Allison notes, darkness is an eschatological sign that corresponds to the tribulation at the end of the age.[8] In other apocalyptic texts the world returns to darkness before the new creation begins (cf. 4 Ezra 6.39; 7.30; LAB 60.2). Robert H. Gundry, moreover, proposes that light is implied at the death of Jesus because the centurion sees how Jesus died (15.39).[9] At the crucifixion Mark incorporates allusions to Genesis in order to show that Jesus' death overcomes evil and inaugurates the new creation. The end of the age is often described in terms of a new creation in prophetic texts (Isa. 65.17; 66.22) and in apocalyptic writings (1 Enoch 45.4; 4 Ezra 7.30; 2 Bar. 32.6). The term 'new creation' is also used by Paul (2 Cor. 5.17; Gal. 6.15). The creative power of God is invoked against the forces of evil to redeem human beings from the suffering of the present age.

To what extent, however, does Mark envisage a new heaven and earth? Mark does not give detailed descriptions of the Kingdom of God. The term *basileia* (kingdom) refers to the 'rule of God' rather than to Kingdom in the sense of 'place'. Jesus' prophecies end with the return of the Son of Man rather than with an account of life in the new age. Heaven and earth will pass away but Jesus' words remain (13.30–31). The term *logos* (word) is used of Jesus' proclamation in the Gospel in the parable of the sower (4.1–20), and of his teaching (8.32, 38). The word of Jesus also has the power to cast out demons (1.25; 5.8; 9.25) and to heal (2.11; 3.5; 10.52). Jesus' words may be identified with the word of God. In Genesis, God speaks and his word separates creation from chaos. In Mark's Gospel Jesus' words have the power to bring about the new creation. As Marcus points out, Jesus' words constitute the continuity between the old and the new age.[10] In chapter 13 Mark describes the dissolution of the boundary between heaven and earth (13.32). The description of the gathering of the elect is reminiscent of the gathering of the remnant at the end of the age (1 Enoch 57.11; 4 Ezra 13.32–50; 2 Bar. 78.1–7). In Mark the initial focus on the twelve is replaced by a mission to all nations, and the call to Israel is expanded to include the Gentiles (13.10).

The end-time prophecies describe horrific events that overcome human beings and lead to the devastation of the earth. Dyer notes that human beings may disregard ecological problems and await God's intervention to save the elect.[11] In Mark 13, Jesus gives an account of the events that take place in the lifetime of the last generation. Joel Marcus proposes that Mark's Gospel is written towards the end of the Jewish War.[12] Mark's community would therefore regard themselves as the last generation. Several events in Mark 13 also may be related to events that have occurred in recent years. There was an earthquake in Asia Minor in 61 CE, and volcanic eruptions took place in Laodicea and Pompeii in 63 CE. In Acts 12.28 Agabus prophesies a great famine throughout the world, which is described as occurring during the time of Claudius. In Mark 13 Jesus warns his disciples to flee to the mountains when they see the desolating sacrilege standing in the Temple. Marcus relates the reference to the desolating sacrilege in Mark's Gospel to the occupation of the Temple by Zealots during the Jewish War.[13] Eusebius records the flight of Christians in Jerusalem to Pella (*Ecclesiastical History*, 3.5.3). As Ched Myers points out, Mark's community are caught between the actions of the Roman oppressors and the rebels who take arms against the Romans.[14] The disciples must not take up arms, and are thus persecuted by both sides in the conflict.

In Mark 13, moreover, Jesus does not instruct the disciples to remain passive in the period before the parousia. He repeatedly warns his disciples to keep watch (*blepete*, 13.5, 9, 23, 33). The opening section is concerned with perception and the need for the disciples to understand the significance of the events they are witnessing. The disciples are instructed not to be led astray (13.5, 22). They must judge and discern the signs taking place around them. They must also preach the gospel to all nations (13.10), and stand firm in their trials. Jesus teaches his disciples the way of the cross. As Hooker observes, the disciples are handed over as Jesus has been handed over (9.31; 10.33) and as John the Baptist has been handed over (1.14).[15] The repeated use of the verb *paradidomi* (hand over) implies that God's purposes are prevailing through the arrests of John, Jesus and the disciples. The disciples' conflict is also a spiritual struggle. They are instructed not to worry about what they will say at their trials, since the Spirit will be given to them and will speak through them (13.11).

The Holy Spirit is the eschatological gift of the new age (Isa. 44.3; Ezek. 36.26–27; Joel 2.28–29). The Spirit descends upon Jesus at baptism (1.10), and Jesus carries out his mission of exorcism, healing and teaching in the power of the Holy Spirit. In chapter 13 this same power comes to the disciples bringing the disciples knowledge of what they should say to their accusers. The Holy Spirit corresponds to the creative power of God and is present at the beginning of creation hovering over the deep. It brings the disciples the ability to stand firm and bear witness to the Kingdom of God. In chapter 13, Mark depicts the new creation of the world, and also the new creation of humanity in the midst of the end-time struggles.

The Kingdom of God

Jesus' end-time discourse relates the events preceding the Kingdom of God. But what is the nature of the Kingdom of God? Throughout the Gospel Jesus' miracles are signs of the Kingdom of God breaking into the world. He casts out unclean spirits (1.21–28; 5.1–20; 9.14–29), and liberates human beings from the power of disease (1.29–31; 5.21–43; 7.31–37; 8.22–26; 10.46–52). Further signs of the Kingdom of God are seen in the account of the stilling of the storm (4.35–41) and Jesus' action of walking on water (6.45–52). Jesus' teaching of the Kingdom of God, moreover, is illustrated by the nature parables: the parable of the sower (4.1–20), the parable of the growing seed (4.26–29) and the parable of the mustard seed (4.30–32).

In each parable the new creation is depicted in terms of the processes of nature. The parable of the sower describes the seed that falls on four different types of earth. Some seeds fall on the path, some on rocky soil, some among thorns and some on good earth. In the first three examples, features of the natural environment prohibit the growth of the seeds. Birds eat the seed on the path, the sun scorches the seed on the rocky soil, and thorns choke the third group of seeds. The final group of seeds, however, encounters no obstacles, and it falls on good earth and produces a crop thirty-, sixty- and a hundredfold. In this parable the seeds that fall on the good earth (*ten gen ten kalen*, 4.8, 20) recall the goodness of creation in Genesis. In Genesis, the work of God is described at the end of each day as *kalon* (good, Gen. 1.4, 8, 10, 12, 18, 21, 25, 31 LXX). The term *kalon* indicates God's appreciation at the completion of creation, and the seed that falls on good earth foreshadows the abundance of the new creation.

The parable of the sower compares the actions of sowing and harvesting to the proclamation of the message of the Gospel, and the parable is given an allegorical interpretation. Satan takes the word away from the first group. The second group falls away on account of persecution or tribulation on account of the word, and the third group is distracted by the cares of the world, the deception of wealth and desires for other things. In contrast, the last group receives and accepts the word, and bears fruit. Mark depicts a correspondence between the natural world and human beings, since both are expected to bear fruit. The conditions of nature, however, are such that not all seeds and not all human beings will bear fruit. The parables also focus upon an abundant harvest, and human beings are instructed to observe nature and to harvest the crops at the correct time. In chapter 13 Jesus exhorts his disciples to 'keep watch', and they are warned against deception by false prophets. Jesus tells his disciples about the future events so that they will be prepared to act. The disciples are not left defenceless in their struggles because God intervenes in the power of the Holy Spirit at their trials.

The second parable describes a man who scatters seed unaware of its mysterious growth (4.26–29). He sleeps and rises until the seed has fully grown, and there follows the time of harvest. The parable relates three stages of growth. The seed first produces a blade and then an ear and finally a full grain. These three stages correspond to the seeds in the previous parable that bear fruit thirty-, sixty- and a hundredfold (4.8). The term 'a hundredfold' recalls Jesus' prophecy of the rewards to the disciples who will receive now in this age 'a hundredfold houses, family members, and lands with persecutions, and in the age to come eternal life' (10.30). The three stages emphasize that God works in history in discernible stages. Joel Marcus notes that the second parable alludes to the apocalyptic belief that a series of events must take place before the end. The parable indicates that God is working in history and will bring events to fruition.[16] As Charles Elliott, moreover, points out, this parable emphasizes that the Kingdom depends on both the power of God and decisive human action.[17]

The final parable describes the growth of a mustard seed (4.30–32). The mustard seed is the smallest of seeds but when it grows it becomes the largest of shrubs so that the birds of the air dwell in its branches. The parable shows that the Kingdom of God may have a very small beginning but will grow abundantly. In the parable of the sower the birds devour some of the seed (4.4). The mustard seed, however, becomes a large shrub that provides shelter for the birds (4.32). The final parable points to the emphasis on peace at the end of the age.

In Mark the parables of seeds have an eschatological focus in that they refer to the harvest at the end of the age, and they depict the future abundance of the Kingdom of God. These images are also connected to the Gospel's focus on bread and the feeding of human beings. The seed that is sown in the earth grows into plants that produce bread for human beings to eat. Following the parables of the seeds Mark narrates the feeding of the five thousand with five loaves (6.30–44) and the feeding of the four thousand with seven loaves (8.1–9). In each account everyone eats and is fully satisfied (6.42; 8.8). These passages, in turn, allude to the Last Supper in which Jesus identifies the bread with his body (14.22), and the wine as his 'blood of the covenant which is poured out for many' (14.24). Jesus prophesies that he will not drink again from the fruit of the vine until that day when he drinks it new in the Kingdom of God (14.25). The accounts foreshadow the abundance of the new creation in which human beings will celebrate the messianic feast (Isa. 25.6–8; 1 Enoch 62.12–14; 2 Bar. 29.5–8). In these parables Mark depicts the Kingdom of God in terms of the natural world through descriptions of a miraculous harvest and an abundant feast. These accounts emphasize the goodness of creation and the creative power of God working in the world.

Conclusion

Our analysis of Mark's Gospel has shown that Jesus prophesies the end of the world within a generation (9.1; 13.30). In Mark's apocalyptic world-view there is a separation between heaven and earth. The earth is ruled by evil forces, until Jesus, the Son of God, comes to redeem humanity and to inaugurate the new age. The end-time will be characterized by wars, earthquakes, famines and the persecution of the disciples, and these events reflect the tearing apart of the old age. These conflicts are not depicted as the judgement of God upon the earth and humanity. God acts to liberate the world, and the cosmic conflicts represent an intensification of the struggle between God and evil.

Mark does not denigrate the earth, since the new age is depicted in terms of the creation account in Genesis. The cosmic conflicts of the old age are paradoxically the 'beginning of the birth pangs' of the new age (13.8), echoing the opening verse of Genesis, 'in the beginning'. The Kingdom of God, moreover, is depicted in terms of the fruitfulness of the natural world. In chapter 4 Jesus likens the Kingdom to an abundant harvest and the miraculous growth of a mustard seed. In chapter 13 the sign of the new age is the flourishing leaves of the fig tree, a standard description of the messianic age (cf. Jer. 8.13; Isa. 28.3–4; Hos. 9.10, 16; Mic. 7.1). The accounts of the abundant harvest are also connected to Jesus' miracles of feeding the five thousand and the four thousand in which everyone eats and is satisfied (6.30–44; 8.1–9). These meals look forward to the messianic feast (Isa. 25.6–8; 1 Enoch 62.12–14; 2 Bar. 29.5–8).

Mark's apocalyptic world-view depicts the end-time in terms of a cosmic struggle between God and evil. How may we read Mark's Gospel today in light of a different understanding of the world? Mark's Gospel provides some insights and directions that may contribute to contemporary ecological struggles. Our discussion of Jesus' end-time teaching and his nature parables does emphasize the Earth Bible principles of the intrinsic value of the earth and the interconnectedness of all living things. Mark depicts the creative power of God working in the world, and the need for human discernment and decisive action. Mark 13 does not advocate that human beings should remain passive awaiting divine intervention. Jesus gives his life to inaugurate the new age, and his disciples are called to follow the way of the cross. Human beings are encouraged to participate in struggles within the world, seeking to discern the will of God. Unlike the Zealots, Mark does not propose violent opposition, but he does emphasize the need to stand firm. Throughout the Gospel, God's will works through the events that are taking place, and looks forward to a resolution. The paradoxical way of the cross promises the gift of the Holy Spirit at the point of human weakness. The visions of future abundance and the communal image of the messianic feast act as an encouragement to those caught in the midst of conflicts to stand by their convictions.

This essay has been completed shortly after the 2005 G8 Summit in Scotland. The issues of climate change and the imperative to reduce carbon-dioxide emissions have been placed on the agenda. Protests have occurred in Edinburgh and all over the world showing the concern of huge numbers of people about poverty in Africa. The richest and most powerful countries, however, have much to achieve in order to preserve the earth and establish social justice. My interest in Mark's Gospel developed through an awareness of the positive portrayal of many characters on the margins of society. Mark is critical of the religious and political authorities, and the twelve male disciples frequently misunderstand Jesus. On the other hand, individuals who are healed, such as the woman with the flow of blood, and the blind beggar, Bartimaeus, are praised on account of their faith (5.34; 10.52). Mark's Gospel offers hope that people who live outwith centres of power can make a difference. In the aftermath of the G8 Summit there is a need to keep up the momentum of protests, and Mark's Gospel emphasizes that death-dealing forces will be overcome through the paradoxical way of the cross. The final message is not one of a cataclysmic end to the world but of a fig tree whose branches begin to put forth their leaves.

Notes

1 N. C. Habel (ed.), *Readings from the Perspective of Earth*, Earth Bible 1 (Sheffield: Sheffield Academic Press, 2000).
2 K. D. Dyer, 'When is the End Not the End? The Fate of Earth in Biblical Eschatology (Mark 13)' in *The Earth Story in the New Testament*, Earth Bible 5, ed. N. C. Habel and V. Balabanski (Sheffield: Sheffield Academic Press, 2002), p. 44.
3 M. D. Hooker, *The Gospel According to St Mark*, Black's New Testament Commentaries (London: A&C Black, 1991), p. 299.
4 Hooker, *St Mark*, p. 308.
5 Hooker, *St Mark*, p. 315.
6 Dyer, 'When is the End', pp. 52–4.
7 W. R. Telford, *The Barren Temple and the Withered Tree*, JSNT Supp. Series 1. (Sheffield: JSOT Press, 1980), pp. 142–50.
8 D. C. Allison, *The End of the Ages Has Come* (Edinburgh: T&T Clark, 1987), pp. 26–50.
9 R. H. Gundry, *Mark: A Commentary on His Apology for the Cross* (Grand Rapids: Eerdmans, 1993), pp. 963–4.
10 J. Marcus, *Mark, Vol. 2*, Anchor Bible 27A (New York: Doubleday, forthcoming), p. 483.
11 Dyer, 'When is the End', pp. 45–6.
12 J. Marcus, 'The Jewish War and the *Sitz im Leben* of Mark', *JBL* 111 (1992), pp. 441–62.
13 Marcus, 'Jewish War', pp. 448–56.
14 C. Myers, *Binding the Strong Man: A Political Reading of Mark's Story of Jesus* (Maryknoll, NY: Orbis Books, 1988), p. 338.
15 Hooker, *St Mark*, pp. 309–10.
16 J. Marcus, *Mark 1—8*, Anchor Bible 27 (New York: Doubleday, 2000), p. 232.
17 C. Elliott, *Praying the Kingdom* (London: Darton, Longman & Todd, 1985), pp. 88–92.

15

Mark 13 in a different imperial context

CHED MYERS

'In those days if anyone says to you, "Look! Here is the great leader!" or "See! There he is!" – do not believe it. For false leaders and false prophets will appear and produce signs and wonders, to lead astray, if possible, even the elect. But be on your guard; I have explained all this to you beforehand.' (Mark 13.21–23)

Nearly two years after US President George W. Bush declared the second war with Iraq officially over, British and US soldiers remain mired in an increasingly violent and controversial occupation of that country. As of this writing, there have been almost six times as many US deaths in Iraq as there were during the 2003 invasion, while the Iraq body-count website (www.iraq-bodycount.net) estimates that as many as 11,200 civilians have been killed in Iraq to date. None of the original 'Coalition' rationales used to justify the invasion have been vindicated, and the Abu Ghraib prisoner torture scandal has undermined the waning public confidence in US/British policy. It seems a good time, therefore, to revisit the role of the churches in the public conversation around the Second Gulf War, what the gospel might have to say about the whole sordid affair, and how citizens might not get 'fooled again' in the future.

I was a visiting professor at Memphis Theological Seminary (Tennessee) in the spring of 2003, and learned quickly that most folks in the 'Bible belt' South didn't like to hear US policy criticized or a war effort questioned. In the days leading up to the invasion, as politicians fanned the flames of war fever, most local churches resorted to eleventh-hour ethical mumbling while scrambling to figure out a position that wouldn't be too controversial. But once hostilities began and the spiritual platitudes wilted, the majority of church leaders kept their heads down and concentrated on pastoral tasks: offering solace to a traumatized and confused citizenry; praying for those 'in harm's way'; and, eventually, burying the dead.[1]

I had a very different experience, however, working with several local African-American churches. While mostly conservative on cultural and theological issues, there is a strong strain of social progressivism in Black churches both 'high' (e.g. African Methodist Episcopal) and 'low' (e.g. Baptist or Holiness). And though Blacks still serve in the armed forces in disproportionate numbers (a phenomenon known as 'economic conscription'), African-Americans tend to be far more critical of US foreign policy than the mainstream White community (something the White peace movement still has not figured out). Indeed, African-Americans have a long history of being suspicious of any foreign military adventurism, particularly because of how it tends to compromise domestic social gains.[2]

This tendency was evident in Memphis, a poor city along the Mississippi River that is roughly half Black and half White. While White churches supported the Bush administration's Iraq policy by roughly a 75/25 margin, in Black churches it was the inverse, with about 75 per cent opposing the war. My critique of the war was warmly received by the majority of African-American congregants I spoke with, whereas I was not invited to preach in any White church until *after* Bush declared hostilities 'over'.

Rather than focusing my talks on the myriad of difficult political, moral and theological questions that US military policy was pressing upon people of faith, I determined instead to experiment with the power of one biblical text, to see how it might resonate among regular Christian folk in the midst of the public crisis of war. My text was Mark 13, the so-called 'Little Apocalypse', examined first in the context of its own historical moment of imperial crisis, and then re-contextualized into ours. Because Mark 13 represents Jesus' clearest teaching about war, I offered it as a singular and extraordinary resource for our lived moment.[3] This chapter summarizes my work with this text as a resource in the grass-roots struggle for hearts and minds in the contested time and space of wartime.[4]

Looking for guidance in the fog of war

Wartime is the worst time for Christians to try to search for their position on war. Once armed conflict becomes inevitable, it is too late to expect that there will be much substantive public discourse about the moral and political ramifications of military action. If Christians have not already clarified their convictions, it is not likely that many will be able or willing to swim against the heavy undertow of inflamed public opinion. Sadly, however, in the US context there are few congregations that practise as an ongoing part of their Christian life the discipline of engaged discernment around these issues. Consequently, when war breaks out (as it seems to on a regular basis now in the USA's global empire), one must invariably start from square one in most Catholic and Protestant congregations.

As part of the context-setting for my reading I offered three cautions. First, I warned that we Christians trivialize the reality of modern war if we talk about it as we would a joust, a duel, a musket volley or even trench warfare. We *must* think in terms of computer-guided cruise missiles, of artillery shells made of depleted uranium that poison soldiers and the environment, of the deliberate targeting of civilian infrastructure such as water plants and electrical grids and hospitals, and of the bulldozing of thousands of Iraqi soldiers into mass graves after an aerial 'turkey shoot'. (Interestingly, a National Security Strategy published by the White House in September 2003 defined terrorism as 'premeditated, politically motivated violence perpetrated against innocents'; this is, of course, a precise definition of modern warfare itself, which has in our time become hopelessly indiscriminate and disproportionate.)

Second, I acknowledged that the tradition of just-war casuistry was in fact more formative for Christian thinking about war than was Scripture, but noted its tendency to turn pressing issues of war into complete moral abstractions. I then offered some 'talking points' concerning the just-war framework as it specifically applied to the aims and methods of the Iraq invasion, looking both at the criteria for going to war (*jus ad bellum*) and the criteria for waging war (*jus in bello*). In fact, most leaders of mainstream Protestant denominations (as well as the US Catholic bishops) had already concluded before the invasion that it would *not* meet these criteria.

But such pronouncements only beg the question, 'How do churches that have made such a determination meaningfully resist participation and complicity in the war?' The just-war ethic assumes not only *co-operation* with the State (in its legitimate demands for self-defence), but also conscientious and collective *non-cooperation* in the event a war is deemed unjust. However, the credibility of this moral reasoning stands in direct proportion to the extent to which church communities have developed the competences needed for such resistance. The fact that churches have *not* done such preparation is precisely why just-war discourse has become so bankrupt – and why we might better turn to Scripture as a resource for discernment and practice.

Third, I cautioned against reverting to the myriad of simplistic biblical proof-texts traditionally used to justify military involvement. (I noted how the ubiquitous pop slogan 'What would Jesus do?' had mysteriously disappeared amid the public pressure to support the war effort, a failure of nerve that was parodied by the peace movement in a bumper sticker that read: 'Who would Jesus bomb?') None of the New Testament texts usually hauled out in these moments, including Romans 13, have anything to do with *war* as a political phenomenon in which states and other groups organize themselves ideologically, socially and technologically to conduct massive and systematic slaughter of real or perceived enemies. Mark 13, however, does, which is why it is the most appropriate (if widely ignored) text for guidance in the moment of war.

We then turned to examine the phenomenon of 'war fever', and the difficulty of trying to think on our feet theologically under its influence, which Mark 13 also specifically addresses. War fever has a strange, compelling and contradictory character. On the one hand, when war breaks out, *things are never clearer*. As the first sirens wail and bombs fall, we are confronted by our deepest fears of chaos and death. One need only think of the psychic jolt of Hitler's blitzkrieg of Poland, or of Pearl Harbor, or the Cuban missile crisis, or the Tet offensive, or the US invasions of Grenada or Panama, or September 11, 2001. Diplomatic talk is set aside and the real intentions of the nations are made painfully transparent. Life is thrown into sharp relief, suddenly fragile and vulnerable before the relentless assault of highly organized military and technological force. It shakes us to our core, and our true loyalties as citizens are unmasked. Are we thrilled or in agony? Are we reaching for the duct tape, the flag or the Scriptures?

The Bible knows about this dreaded liminality. The prophets wrote grimly about the advent of military invasion:

> See, waters are rising out of the north and shall become an overflowing torrent; they shall overflow the land and all that fills it, the city and those who live in it. People shall cry out, and all the inhabitants of the land shall wail. At the noise of the stamping of the hoofs of his stallions, at the clatter of his chariots, at the rumbling of their wheels, parents do not turn back for children, so feeble are their hands. (Jer. 47.2–4)

The crack of whip and rumble of wheel,

> galloping horse and bounding chariot!
> Horsemen charging,
> flashing sword and glittering spear,
> piles of dead,
> heaps of corpses,
> dead bodies without end –
> they stumble over the bodies! (Nahum 3.2–3)[5]

Such ancient accounts have been eclipsed and intensified by modern warfare, notably the terrorizing US/British 'shock and awe' bombing campaign in Iraq.

The biblical writers therefore saw the moment of war as *apocalyptic*, which means 'thrown open' or 'laid bare'. They understood that in war the lethal activity of the 'principalities and powers', so often concealed in human history, is exposed. The apocalyptic visionary and political prisoner John of Patmos, for example, envisioned the 'Four Horsemen' as different faces of the same scourge: imperial conquest, the sword of militarism, profiteering and death (Rev. 6.1–8). In the book of Revelation, *these* are the real forces at work when the elite decide upon war, and the ensuing public imperatives to sacrifice human life to 'the imperial Beast' become a severe test of the Church's loyalties and character.

On the other hand, when war fever descends, *things are never more muddled*. The revelation that 'war is hell' is quickly suppressed, and the conflict dressed up in far nobler garb by both sides – hence Aeschylus' famous dictum, 'In war, truth is the first casualty.' We discussed how sophisticated war propagandizing worked during both Iraq invasions of January 1991 and March 2003.

In both cases the corporate-owned press and the network news stepped in to 'rescue' the populace from the psychic vertigo of war's outbreak. Instantly the war became prime time, and it seemed as if the whole country was transfixed as television loyally 'mediated' the Pentagon's narrative of the unfolding high-tech blitzkriegs, presented like a video game. Ratings soared. These were classic cases of how war fever creates an almost irresistible and self-referential momentum, to which all but the most politically prepared and spiritually discerning citizens succumb. War brings unrelenting terror to those near the fire – Muslim women and Kurdish shepherds and Iraqi Christians. But for those watching from an insular distance, it engenders psycho-spiritual siege, manifested either as manic patriotism or as disorientation and depression.

In the moment of war, then, the Church must choose between apocalyptic lucidity and the fog of the dominant media. Unfortunately, the latter has tended to characterize the Church of the developing world historically. Yet as German Christians during the Third Reich discovered so painfully, how the Church responds in wartime is crucial to the future credibility of the faith. Similarly, as Martin Luther King reminded us during the Vietnam era:

> What more pathetically reveals the irrelevancy of the church in present-day world affairs than its witness regarding war? In a world gone mad with arms buildups, chauvinistic passions, and imperialistic exploitation, the church has either endorsed these activities or remained appallingly silent . . . The church must be reminded that it is not the master or the servant of the state, but rather the conscience of the state. It must be the guide and the critic of the state, and never its tool. If the church does not recapture its prophetic zeal, it will become an irrelevant social club without moral or spiritual authority.[6]

To be sure, extraordinary clarity and courage is demanded from Christians who would resist the idolatrous claims of strident patriotic wartime leaders, and who would publicly refuse to co-operate. But this is exactly the kind of discipleship called for in Mark 13.

'When you hear . . .': Mark 13 and war propaganda

The apocalypse of war was well known to the Gospel-writers. All three synoptic stories of Jesus were composed within a generation of the greatest historical cataclysm imaginable in their social world: the destruction of Jerusalem and the razing of the second Temple at the culmination of the Roman–Jewish war of 66–70 CE. Mark wrote during the darkest days of that conflict, and it fundamentally shaped his work. His story is structured around two fundamental 'moments': the inbreaking of the Kingdom of God (Mark 1.15) and the outbreak of war (Mark 13).

Each represented an existential crisis that challenged the audience with conflicting exigencies. The Kingdom, pregnant with the possibility of human redemption and transformation, demanded costly discipleship. The war, with its manic militarism, demanded an equally costly choosing of sides. While these two moments co-existed in the historical era of Mark's community, his Gospel warned against confusing them. Only one was the true *kairos* moment – the other only pretended to be.

To understand the truth of each moment, Mark argued, required 'eyes to see' and 'ears to hear'. Thus an overarching theme of his story is the struggle over these key senses, representing the 'faculties of critical perception' in ancient Jewish anthropology. The tragedy is that our perceptions fail us (Mark 4.12; 6.51–52; 8.17–21). The hope is that they can be healed by Jesus so we can properly discern the vocation of discipleship (7.31ff.; 8.22ff.; 10.46ff.). Accordingly, Mark's Jesus delivers two long parable-spinning 'sermons' to his disciples in the course of the gospel narrative. The first calls the reader to 'Listen!' (4.3, 9, 23, 33); the second, to 'Watch!' (13.5, 9, 23, 33). It is the latter that gives us insight into the struggle of Mark's community in the historical moment of war.

A Jewish insurgency had been brewing since the days of Herod the Great in reaction to decades of repression under Roman colonialism. In June of 66 CE, just two generations after the execution of Jesus, it reached a critical mass, and a coalition of dissident groups initiated open rebellion in Jerusalem by ceasing Temple sacrifices to the emperor. The uprising quickly spread to the nearby provinces, including Galilee. In November of 66, Cestus Gallus, Roman legate of Byria, marched on Jerusalem to destroy the rebels, but in fierce fighting was repelled. Stunned, the Romans retreated in disarray, sustaining severe losses as Jewish guerrillas pursued them to the coast. There was euphoria in Judaea: the homeland was liberated!

For some three years a provisional revolutionary government presided in Jerusalem, though constantly mired in internal power struggles. In 68, Vespasian, the greatest general of the time and soon to become emperor, began his campaign to pacify Palestine. He marched his heavily armed legions down through Galilee towards Judaea, and, encountering only scattered resistance, northern Palestine was soon recaptured. Vespasian left a scorched-earth trail of mercilessly plundered villages – and hillsides littered with crucified insurrectionists.

By June the Romans were set to lay siege to Jerusalem itself, but once again the unexpected occurred. The campaign was aborted as Vespasian was urgently summoned back to the imperial capital, which was locked in a fierce civil war. The Judaean rebels knew that sooner or later the siege would come, as indeed it did in the spring of 70 (after five months of 'economic sanctions' and pitched battle, General Titus sacked Jerusalem and burned the Temple to the ground). But during the autumn and winter of 69, the Jewish resistance had reason to believe that God had once again intervened on behalf of the holy city.

This may have been the precise moment of the composition of Mark 13. It does not take much historical imagination to appreciate the severe pressures being felt by Mark's community in re-occupied Galilee. On one hand, Roman counter-insurgency forces were rooting out those sympathetic to the subversives and demanding that locals renounce the nationalist regime – not unlike US/British forces in their post-war occupation of Iraq. Many Jewish leaders were persuaded to abandon the revolt as a lost cause, notably an officer named Josephus, whose later writings left us a detailed (if highly biased) account of the war. On the other hand, rebel recruiters covertly roamed the countryside, invoking the Maccabaean and Davidic glory traditions in order to draft faithful Jews into a holy war in defence of Zion.

As is always the case in the eye of the wartime hurricane, there was no neutrality and the stakes were high. Mark knew that only one voice could compete with the compelling but conflicting demands of collaborator and patriot – the living Word of Jesus of Nazareth. So to him the disciples in the story turn in a desperate plea for guidance: 'Tell us, when will these things take place, and what will be the sign of their accomplishment?' (Mark 13.4).

Mark also knew that the discursive tradition most appropriate for the moment his community was facing was the powerful resistance literature of apocalyptic. This late biblical and intertestamental tradition was forged during political/military upheaval. Daniel, for example, was written during the Maccabaean revolt; 1 Enoch during the breakdown of the Herodian dynasty; and Revelation during imperial pogroms under the emperor Domitian. Ancient apocalyptic symbolics used dualism and myth to excavate under the surface meanings being huckstered by the protagonists of war, in order to unmask the true character of historical events. But for modern readers, apocalyptic texts are difficult to interpret and therefore are easily ignored or exploited.

Jesus' sermon begins with a call for the 'overthrow' (Gk. *kataluthee*) of the very Temple-based system his disciples hold in awe (13.1f.). In Jesus' view, this institutional centre of the dominant political economy in Judaea functioned to oppress the poor. He has just made this clear in the preceding story in his condemnation (not commendation!) of the 'widow's mite' (12.38–44). The disciples respond with their anxious inquiry concerning the 'end of the age' (13.4). In apocalyptic discourse, the 'end' refers not to some absolute historical rupture, but to a fundamental transformation in the ordering of power in the world. The real theme of this discourse is not war, but what Walter Wink calls the 'Domination System' that perpetuates war.[7]

Mark carefully structures the first half of the sermon around a series of warning doublets:

'Watch out that no one deceives you' (v. 5) and
'Watch! I have told you all this beforehand' (v. 23);

'Many will come in my name, and will deceive many' (v. 6) and
'False leaders/prophets will deceive the elect' (v. 22);

'When you hear of wars and rumours of war' (v. 7) and
'When you see the abominating desolation' (v. 14);

'The one who endures will be liberated' (v. 13) and
'Unless the days were shortened no one would be liberated' (v. 20).

These refrains make it clear that deception is the central concern for discernment during wartime.

At this point in the study I offered an exercise in which we compared classic war propaganda with these exhortations. In modernity it has been the predictable pattern that some version of three archetypal arguments will be made by the dominant Powers to support a war effort.

It is claimed that the enemy's leader is a worse-than-normal bad guy, while *our* leader is portrayed as exhibiting grim determination, courage and sober initiative. The former is a madman, a devious tyrant, has no respect for life and is a threat to everything we hold dear. (One thinks of the cover picture of Saddam Hussein on *Time* magazine in 1991, slightly doctored to give an unmistakable hint of Hitler). Conversely, the latter must be supported in national solidarity – he might even be *Time*'s 'Man of the Year' (as were the two George Bushes in 1990 and 2000 respectively). Such exaggeration was clearly in effect in the intensely personal rivalry between George W. Bush and Saddam.

It is asserted that although war may be lamentable, it is absolutely necessary to solve the problem of the evil enemy, and no lesser response will do. The stakes are high: this is a 'war to save democracy' or 'the war to end all wars'; grand dramas like the US idea of Manifest Destiny or the domino theory are invoked. By successfully executing this war it is promised that history will be healed, that equilibrium and peace will be restored. There has not been a major modern war that was not marketed as the struggle for some form of a 'new world order'. In the case of the Second Gulf War it was sacred *jihad* on one side, and multiple promises on the other, from ending terrorism to bringing democracy to the region. All of these justifications are contemporary forms of the ancient 'myth of redemptive violence', in which the means are justified by the ends.[8]

To secure domestic support for the war, the enemy is inevitably blamed for one episode or characteristic that is so outrageous, so odious, that 'our side's' moral restraint must be lifted. The presentation of such a terrible violation means to trump whatever objections we might have to war. All reasonable and life-loving persons are called to support retaliation, because civilization itself hangs in the balance. Sometimes, the enemy gives a perfect excuse: Pearl Harbor, or 9/11. Sometimes, it is invented: the Gulf of Tonkin, or the story of Iraqis pulling babies off incubators in Kuwait in 1991 (later

proved to be a fabrication). In 2003 the focus was on (we now know) spur-
iously inflated claims about Iraq's threat of weapons of mass destruction.

It turns out that such arguments were common in antiquity as well – and
the first half of Mark 13 anticipates and rejects each one.

First, Jesus specifically warns disciples not to give credulity to the inflated
claims of the protagonists:

> 'Many will come in my name and say, "I am the one!" and will lead many
> astray.' (13.6)

> 'If anyone says to you at that time, "Look! Here is Messiah," don't believe it.
> For false leaders and prophets will appear and produce signs and wonders, to
> lead astray, if possible, even the elect. But be aware! I have told you all this
> beforehand!' (13.21–23)

The cult of personality during wartime is seen as nothing more than a tool
of duplicity.

Second, Mark's Jesus insists that war, though inevitable in the world
system, is emphatically *not* a sign of apocalyptic world transformation, *despite
its cataclysmic trappings*. He parodies the claims of those who would market
the conflict as an historic struggle: 'When you hear of war and rumours of
war, don't panic! This is not the *end* . . . but rather the *beginning* of labour!'
(13.7f.). War should never come as a surprise to Christians – we have been
forewarned (13.23). But Jesus does not fail to remind disciples that resisting
the demands of war leaders will result in systematic persecution (13.9–13).
He does, however, guarantee that the Holy Spirit will be our companion when
we are summoned before the authorities (13.11).

And Jesus anticipates the worst case scenario argument. In Mark's moment
this was the spectre of foreign armies occupying the Temple Mount, and
setting up their idols there – referred to in cryptic apocalyptic fashion as the
'abomination of desolation' (13.14; cf. Dan. 11.13; 12.11). This represented
the ultimate rationale for self-defence – equivalent to September 11, 2001 in
the American experience. Yet Jesus' astonishing counsel to his disciples is to
refuse the patriotic call to arms, and indeed to *flee* Judaea (13.14–20)! But
is this not shirking all civic responsibility, leaving to others the task of
'protecting the homeland'? Under such howls of protest, the Church has
historically withered. No wonder Jesus warned, 'You will be despised by all
sides because of my name' (13.13).

How can Jesus insist that disciples refuse to be driven into war's Faustian
bargain? That we must instead remain radically critical of both sides? Because
his deepest conviction is that *all military 'solutions' are by definition part of the
problem*, serving in the long run only to strengthen the very Domination System
they claim to be re-ordering. But to 'see' this takes profound apocalyptic insight.
Thus the second half of Jesus' sermon in Mark 13 is composed around a

repeated call to vigilance: disciples are to 'watch' for the true signs of trans-formation (13.23, 33, 37).

'When you see...': watching for the end of the world

Mark now turns to the high apocalyptic symbolism of the 'combat myth' (13.24–25).[9] In conservative Hellenistic thought, the 'Powers in the heavens' was a metaphor for the most fundamental structures of law and order upon which both the cosmos and society were built – they could or should not be shaken. Against this 'establishment' ideology Mark pitted the radical prophetic faith of the Isaian apocalypse:

> The windows of heaven are opened and the foundations of the earth tremble. The earth is utterly broken . . . . On that day Yahweh will punish the host of heaven in heaven, and on earth the kings of the earth. They will be gathered together like prisoners in a pit . . . Then the moon will be abashed, and the sun ashamed, for the Lord of Hosts will reign. (Isa. 24.18–23)

Apocalyptic faith looks for the demise of the Powers and their politics of domination, not their recycling by another name (see also Joel 2.10–11; Amos 8.9).

In an earlier era, the book of Daniel warned against taking up arms along-side Maccabaean insurgents, believing that true transformation could never be accomplished through partisan violence, but only through the courageous and costly non-violence of the 'wise' (Dan. 12). Jesus invokes this tradition and its portrayal of the 'Human One' (Dan. 7) in Mark 13.26f., and again as he stands trial before the Powers in the trial narrative (14.62). Ultimately, Mark portrays Jesus himself as the incarnation of the Human One 'coming in glory' as he hangs on the cross, the executed non-violent revolutionary (15.33ff.).[10]

Another Isaianic vision informs Mark's mysterious 'lesson of the fig tree' (13.28f.): 'All powers of the heavens will melt, and the heavens will roll up like a scroll, and all the stars fall as leaves from a vine, and as leaves fall from a fig tree' (Isa. 34.4). Mark is also here referring back to Jesus' earlier symbolic 'exorcism' of the Jerusalem Temple, an action that is bracketed by the equally symbolic 'cursing' of the *fig tree* (11.12–25). There is a tight rhetorical link between that story and this sermon:

> Rabbi, look! The fig tree you cursed has withered! (11.21)
> Look, teacher! What great stones and large buildings! (13.1)

The fig tree parable addresses the disciples' inquiry about 'signs of the end' in 13.4. They are to be 'seen' not in military heroics, which are merely symp-tomatic of the Domination System, but rather in faithful non-violent resis-tance that attacks the pathology at its roots, as demonstrated by Jesus' Temple protest.

Such practices bring the *kairos* near (13.29) – though exactly how and when the Powers will be overthrown is something we can neither control nor predict (13.32). In this way Mark's Jesus, like Gandhi, severs non-violent action from the tyranny of visible results. The sermon then concludes with a final parable about a vigilant doorkeeper (13.34f.). The call to 'Watch!' (Gk. *blepete*, v. 33) is now intensified with the imperative to 'Shake off sleep!' (Gk. *greegoreite*, vv. 35, 36). In order to remain alert to the unpredictable moment of the Kingdom's inbreaking, disciples must resist the sedation engendered by the predictable outbreak of war fever.

This struggle not to succumb to the coma promoted by imperial culture – particularly during wartime – will be dramatically enacted in Jesus' last moments with his disciples in Gethsemane (14.32ff.). There Jesus makes his choice to stay awake to the Kingdom – and takes the consequences. His friends sleep, and then bail out when the security forces come for him (14.43–52). Now we understand: Jesus' final parable portrayed the world as Gethsemane, in which disciples are called to 'historical insomnia'. Jesus' closing statement is directed to the Church in every age – especially to sophisticated moderns who would dismiss this sermon as the apocalyptic ranting of primitive Christians: 'What I say to you I say to all: Stay awake!' (13.37)

It is hard enough to be Black in the Deep South without also being anti-war. But many of the African-American congregants in Memphis who participated in these sessions took courage that there was indeed a gospel tradition of resistance they could draw on. Their own memory of the Civil Rights struggle made the call to non-violence both intelligible and credible (which set the stage for my invocation of the second text: King's historic declaration of resistance to the Vietnam War in 1967). As a result of our studies, some church members joined our public vigils against the war, and several ministers preached and wrote against the folly of Bush's Iraq policy. One evening at the largest Black church in Memphis an elderly woman grabbed my hand on the way out and looked at me hard, her eyes glistening: 'Been waitin' to hear that Word, brother. Been waitin' a mighty long time.'

It has been a long time indeed since our churches stood up to war, empire and its propaganda. And to be sure, in the spring of 2003 most US churches sleepwalked through another Gethsemane. But lamentably, there *will* be a next time. Will people of faith again credulously embrace the cynical promises of a better world hawked by the imperial architects of war? Will we languish, impotent? Or will we begin now to do what it takes to nurture political imagination, apocalyptic clarity and non-violent courage? Our choices, Dr King reminded us, are consequential: 'The chain reaction of evil – hate begetting hate, wars producing more wars – must be broken, or we shall be plunged into the dark abyss of annihilation.'[11]

Notes

1 This tendency was not untypical of churches throughout the USA. While there were notable exceptions to this pattern, for example among the peace churches (Mennonites, Brethren and Quakers) and the significant minority of peace and justice advocates who dwell on the fringes of mainstream Protestant denominations and Catholicism, these circles were unfortunately not well represented in Memphis!

2 Michael Simmons, a long-time peace organizer, summarizes these issues in an excellent interview found at <www.objector.org/articles/simmons.html>.

3 I also used a second text: Martin Luther King, Jr.'s 'Beyond Vietnam: A Time to Break the Silence' speech, given 4 April 1967 at Riverside Church in New York, exactly one year before King was gunned down in Memphis (in James M. Washington (ed.), *The Essential Writings and Speeches of Martin Luther King, Jr.* (San Francisco: Harper, 1986), pp. 231ff.). I presented this as one of the greatest public oratories in US history, which boldly reinterpreted the historical moment of the Indochina war from the prophetic perspective of the African-American Civil Rights movement. Its analysis of the interrelationship between the 'triple evils of racism, militarism and poverty', and its prescient take on the long-term implications of US foreign military intervention, still have stinging relevance even 35 years later. Unfortunately, to recount my treatment of this historic speech would take me too far beyond the scope and length allotted for this essay. The text and an audio excerpt can also be found at
<www.drmartinlutherkingjr.com/beyondvietnam.htm>.

4 These reflections concerning a more popular use of the text are, however, grounded in my detailed historical and exegetical work in C. Myers, *Binding the Strong Man: A Political Reading of Mark's Story of Jesus* (Maryknoll, NY: Orbis Books, 1988), ch. 11, as well as my political-ethical analysis in *Who Will Roll Away the Stone? Discipleship Queries for First World Christians* (Maryknoll, NY: Orbis Books, 1994), ch. 8.

5 See also: Isa. 5.26–30; 13.15–18; Jer. 50.41–43; 51.27–34; Ezek. 7.14–19; 21.14–16; 26.7–14; 32.9–15; and Nahum 2.

6 Martin Luther King, Jr., *Strength to Love*, in Washington, *The Essential Writings*, pp. 500f.

7 For a summary of Wink's work and further literature, see Walter Wink, *The Powers That Be: Theology for a New Millennium* (New York: Doubleday, 1999), especially ch. 2.

8 Wink, *The Powers*. For an online article summarizing Wink's description of the myth in antiquity and today, go to <www.biblesociety.org.uk/exploratory/articles/wink99.doc>.

9 One of the best monographs on the combat myth and its relevance for New Testament studies is Adela Yarbro Collins, *The Combat Myth in the Book of Revelation* (Wipf and Stock, 2001).

10 On this, see Myers, *Binding the Strong Man*, ch. 13, and *Who Will Roll Away the Stone?*, pp. 248ff.

11 King, *Strength to Love*.

16

Mark and the formation of community

CHRISTOPHER BURDON

For as long as I can remember, I have been familiar with the gospel stories, though initially with little awareness of the differences between one Gospel and another. Later, as a student of theology in the heyday of redaction criticism, I examined much more closely their distinctiveness and grew aware of the enigmas of Mark and of Mark's Jesus. Yet it was only when I was ordained deacon in the Church of England and had the weekly task of proclaiming or performing 'the gospel' (that is, the section appointed in the lectionary), and from time to time the task of interpreting it through preaching, only then that the sheer difficulty and excitement and challenge of those enigmas overwhelmed me. I had to take on my lips the words that 'will not pass away'. I had to relate them and their narrative setting to the humdrum and conventional British settings where they were uttered again.

Since then, I have been in positions of pastoral leadership in both parishes and educational courses – that is, with a place in structures of power but also a responsibility for the nurturing of human community. The kinds of community and power that Mark's Jesus endorses seem far in spirit from those I inhabit. It would, I suppose, be easier to let go of Mark's story, its hero and his words, if only they would let go of me. The reflections that follow are therefore very much 'work in progress' arising from that experience and study, from that attempt to use Mark as a vehicle of corporate wisdom and repentance.

It is not hard, and not particularly original, to sense the disparity between the life of the organized churches and the proclamation and world-view of Jesus as presented in the Gospels. The old quip is that Jesus proclaimed the coming of God's Kingdom but what actually came was the Church. Nor was it long before the Church modelled itself on imperial political structures. Many of those structures persist in worldwide and national communions today, making life comfortable for many – though rather uncomfortable for those groups and persons within them who attend seriously to the kind of life and proclamation that is modelled in the Gospels and to the kind of community that is presupposed or advocated in them.

I hesitate to use this word *community*, since it is open to such vague formulations in modern English: 'the international community', 'the gay community', and so on. But I am using it here to apply to *human groups that are sufficiently small to enable all members to know one another, at least by name, but that are not so exclusive or 'given' (as, for instance, is the traditional family) that people cannot enter or leave or belong simultaneously to other such communities.* Among communities there may be wide variety in structures, boundaries and rules, ranging from those of an enclosed monastery to a group of regulars at a pub. In scale and complexity such a community differs from an institution like a nation-state or an international Communion; yet for either to survive there must be some degree of shared story, mythology or ideology, and – although the forms may be very different – communities no less than institutions cannot be immune from power relations.

Mark's, like all the other canonical Gospels, came to birth within and has been preserved within specific human groups. In those communities, the gospel texts are used in liturgy, in proclamation, in instruction and in the definition of community itself. They may also (especially since the invention of printing) be used in private study and meditation, yet their function has been and remains principally a political one – 'political' in the broad sense of dealing with the structures of and the relationships within and between human groups. It is that political function that I wish to explore, in the light of my own experience of participating in learning and worshipping communities and of studying and teaching the Gospel of Mark.

What kind of community?

So long as Mark's Gospel is read canonically and liturgically it will be at work in the politics of community, whether or not the hearing communities are aware of such work going on. It may also be at work among other communities and readers, who are not hearing it in the liturgy or doing 'Bible study', nor adhering to the Christian creed or canon of Scripture, yet for whom the words of Mark and of Jesus may provide a goad to the formation or reformation of community. Tracing this 'work' of the individual Gospels in the centuries since their writing – articulating their *Wirkungsgeschichte* – is difficult, owing to the deep-rooted custom in the Church of reading the Gospels synoptically. It is particularly difficult in the case of Mark, who was at an early stage misidentified as the 'abbreviator' of Matthew and began to creep out of the latter's shadow only towards the end of the nineteenth century. But in the past hundred years Mark has come into his own. Greater scholarly attention has been accorded him since his widespread identification as writer of the first Gospel and then since the advent of redaction criticism and the realization that evangelists were also theologians. Meanwhile, within most western churches, changes in methods of adult catechesis and the adoption of the Common Lectionary (where Mark presides over 'Year B', albeit with some Johannine infiltration) have exposed the text to greater scrutiny and allowed it in turn to scrutinize the Church's life. And well beyond the normal orbit of the churches, the Gospel's brevity and its strong but profoundly enigmatic story have opened Mark up to the world of public reading and performance. Unless all this attention to and use of the Gospel is limited to the worlds of entertainment, of historical curiosity and of individual devotion, then Mark's *Wirkung* in the current Christian and post-Christian worlds must be widespread and lively.

Yet identifying and evaluating that work remains difficult. Take the experience of hearing Mark performed, whether in the liturgy or in the theatre. This Gospel is very easy to listen to, for it tells a fast-moving story. But it is simultaneously very hard to listen to, for its teaching and dialogues range from the infuriatingly cryptic to the hyperbolically direct (which may be another way of saying that we the hearers or readers see but do not perceive and hear but do not understand). Is the listening then to remain at the level of an aesthetic conundrum, or perhaps a utopian imagining? How easily can Mark's narrative and rhetorical situations be paralleled in current communities? How easily can its theological or ethical thrust be translated into praxis?

These difficulties in listening, imagining and translating relate to the further *historical* difficulty of identifying the community, or at least the kind of community, from which the Gospel sprang and for which it was written. Despite the growing sophistication of historical, sociological, socio-literary and socio-rhetorical methods in biblical studies, 'Mark's community' remains for many as opaque or esoteric as his story. Detailed and plausible constructions have been made of 'the Johannine community', 'the Matthean community' and to a lesser extent 'the Lucan community', while Paul's letters are in varying degrees revelatory of the world of their readers.[1] At the same time, it is not hard to identify today styles of Christian community which reflect or consciously model themselves on those that seem to underlie such New Testament writings. You do not have to look far to find, say, the didactic 'Matthean' church practising its righteousness, or the eager and expanding 'Lucan' church, the introverted 'Johannine' church or the ordered submissive church that heeds the Pastoral Letters. But where is, where was, 'the Marcan community'?

On the historical question, interpreting the runes of Mark's text has led to conflicting pictures, as can be seen from the thorough but diverse investigations undertaken by Howard Clark Kee, Ched Myers and Richard Horsley. Kee argues that 'Mark was produced by an apocalyptic community', perhaps in southern Syria, counter-cultural and sectarian in its outlook yet 'at once esoteric and evangelistic'.[2] Myers posits a Galilean community more politically engaged than this while nevertheless 'non-aligned', committed to a 'radical discipleship' that subverts conventional political and religious structures.[3] More recently, Horsley, while also proposing a Galilean provenance, sees neither 'discipleship' nor Christology as crucial to Mark and depicts not so much a community, let alone a new religion, as a campaign: 'Mark portrays a mission focused on villages as whole communities . . . [the readers, like the twelve, being] envoys commissioned to expand Jesus' programme of renewal in village communities.'[4]

There are strong arguments from the text for each of these pictures, yet none of them entirely convinces me; moreover, parallels to them do not abound today. Rather than undertake further historical or sociological investigation, I wish to consider some of the sayings and narrative features from Mark that have led to such reconstructions and to see how they are or could be active in the politics of different communities – small learning groups, activist organizations, local parishes and alternative religious communities. The most prominent features of 'Mark's community' for such an exercise – or, more accurately, the most prominent features of the Gospel's ideology – are the apparent absence of leadership, the nature of power, the redrawing of boundaries and the call to repentance.

The absent Messiah and the pathology of leadership

Unlike Matthew's, Mark's Gospel has no place for the 'Emmanuel' who will be with his Church to the end of the age, present wherever disciples gather in his name (Matt. 1.23; 18.20; 28.20). Here, rather, the people are 'like sheep with no shepherd' (Mark 6.34). The shepherd or leader or Messiah does indeed come to them, with power, truth and authority, yet he is struck and the sheep scattered (14.27), and at the mysterious end he is still not with them but rather goes ahead into Galilee (*proagei*, 16.7; cf. 14.28; 10.32). And as that same shepherd–leader–Messiah addresses Mark's readers *via* the fictional audience on the Mount of Olives, they are to ignore future claims to messiahship, which will be false ones even if they display impressive signs and wonders (13.5, 21–22). The 'looking' – enjoined on the community in the repeated use of *blepete* and *grēgoreite* – is not a search for a 'leader' but an alert waiting and observation in the leader's absence (13.23, 32–37). There is no mystical or sacramental or ecclesial presence of the Messiah, only the subversive memory of his words that will not pass away (13.31). But for Mark's ideal reader that is enough – however frustrating it may be for us, as no doubt it was for Matthew, that Mark preserved so few of those imperishable words.

The natural political consequence for a community with an absent leader is that another should be appointed or appoint himself in the leader's place, attempting to continue or perhaps supplant the leader's work (as explored quizzically in *Measure for Measure*). There are indeed in Mark clear indications of men, and occasionally women, who are closer to Jesus than others – the twelve who are appointed with authority (3.14; 6.7), 'those around him' (4.10; 6.30) and within their number the privileged three or four (5.37; 9.2; 13.3; 14.33) and the particularly prominent Simon Peter (1.36; 8.29; 14.54; 16.7).

Yet it is precisely this most obvious candidate for vice-regal authority who is rebuked with the greatest severity (8.33) and who later publicly denies the leader, while it is another of the leading twelve who hands him over to his enemies. Jesus' own family are left outside, with 'those around him' declared to be his new family (3.31–35; cf. 10.29–30). These are declared now the 'insiders', given the secret of the rule of God (4.11); yet they in turn are later revealed as the outsiders, their hearts hardened, their eyes unseeing and ears unhearing (6.52; 8.18; cf. 10.31).

The potential leaders' hopes and aspirations are burst again after each of the passion predictions. In rebuke of Peter's own denial of the Messiah's suffering comes the call to take up the cross and lose life (8.34–38). In response to the argument about who is the greatest, Jesus puts a child at the centre and announces that the one who wants to be first must be last of all and servant of all, *pantōn eschatos kai pantōn diakonos* (9.33–36). Instead of the leadership and honour to which James and John aspire, come the call to share in the cup and baptism and the further (ironic?) proclamation that, in contrast to the power, hierarchy and honour cultivated by the nations and their rulers, 'it is not so among you': rather, again, the 'first' must be servant of you . . . slave of all, *humōn diakonos . . . pantōn doulos* (10.37–44). There are, in other words, no 'first' at all, other than the one who, baptized in water, in spirit and in death, has now gone ahead into Galilee (1.8–10; 10.38; 16.7). Mark's Gospel unveils a pathology of leadership according to which all the fashionable courses in 'church leadership' can only be deemed heretical.

If this Marcan process of reversal is to be at work today, say, in small learning communities, there will be a subversion of the political dynamic of such groups which has been common in both ancient and modern times. The group's desire to have an expert leader, coupled with the leader's desire to assert his or her authority or knowledge over the group, will be thwarted by the insistence on the diaconal role of the one who is 'first' and by the fragility of any position as 'insider'. Both customary political dynamic and customary educational method are undermined by this abolition of the leader – or more accurately, perhaps, by the displacement of the leader to a realm of absence so that only his memory and his words remain accessible, and even they are in parables and riddles.

With regard to educational method, for instance, Mark can inspire a rejuvenation of the Socratic style, in which the process of learning is thrown back to the group, and a corresponding abandonment of the catechetical style, in which an instructor conveys knowledge. While the latter may be appropriate for children, *technē*, it is not the way of learning wisdom, *sophia*. So in the absence of the leader – though probably with the assistance of a 'facilitator' – the group breaks the traditional conjunction of 'wisdom and instruction' (*hokmah wumusar*, e.g. Prov. 1.2).[5] The attention, the 'waiting', is focused not on the leader as source of knowledge but on the elusive wisdom which goes before the group, which is sought but cannot be possessed, or on the text or parable which is trusted as the way towards such wisdom. Educational method is thus inseparable from political dynamic. The facilitator or *diakonos* may have a crucial role in the community's learning process and search of wisdom; but he or she sits in the circle with the other members, like them committed to the knowledge or goal that is not yet possessed, like them subject to marginalization and reversal.

Powerless power

A second feature of Mark's Gospel which has led to reconstructions of its original context is its ambiguous approach to power. This is a Gospel about power, about the conflict between Satan and Holy Spirit. Its hero is first introduced as 'the more powerful one', *ho ischuroteros* (1.7). Yet it ends with the execution of that hero at the hands of religious and military power. The vocabulary of political power and kingdom, *basileia* is, rather obliquely, attached to Jesus, who is and is not 'son of David' (10.48; 11.10; cf. 14.62); yet the only royal homage that is paid to him is done in mockery (15.16–19). Again, when two disciples ask to sit at his right and left 'in his glory', Jesus diverts their request but does not deny that such seats exist (10.40); however, 'those for whom it has been prepared' prove to be neither the disciples nor heavenly courtiers but two bandits (15.27). The authority and uniqueness of Jesus is magnified: he is the one who calls and appoints those with him, *hous ēthelen* and dispenses supernatural power, *exousia* (1.16–20; 2.14; 3.13–15), the one whose teaching is 'with authority', whose words are obeyed by wind and sea and will never pass away (1.27; 4.41; 13.31). But in the second half of the Gospel that spiritual power is no longer physically demonstrated and is, as it were, transposed into the future return of the Son of Man, so that the continuing conflict between Spirit and Satan takes place in his absence but in the active presence of the waiting community.

For this community, the full power of the Kingdom of God, *basileia tou theou*, lies in the future, not in present experience, and the extravagant gifts promised to them come 'with persecutions' (10.29–30). Yet the charismatic power and *exousia* previously displayed by Jesus are handed over also to them, for with sufficient faith and prayer they will be able to exorcize demons and even move mountains (9.29; 11.22–24). Remarkably, however, and in contrast to the usual pattern of charismatic movements, such power is to be exercised within a strictly egalitarian community where the first is last. This unlikely combination of charismatic authority and egalitarian living is expressed in the stark juxtaposition of the command to mutual forgiveness immediately after the promise of the miracles that may be wrought by prayer (11.25). Equally, the community that is called actively to harness the power of the rule of God, to move mountains and expel demons, is called also to endure tribulation and simply to await the intervention coming 'in clouds' (13.24–37). The community is to develop a politics which is both active and contemplative, both charismatic and mutually submissive.

Such a politics, seeking to act powerfully in the world yet refusing the internal structures of power, is hard to practise. There are nevertheless instances of it in those groups committed to radical change which are aware that the *basileia* they seek is incompatible with inherited patterns of management and accountability. The most prominent instance in recent British history is that of the Greenham Common women, who combined a vision for global change (the end of nuclear weapons) with a specific practical goal (prevention of cruise missiles entering the base) and expressed both in an experimental praxis (equality, common life, ritual, mutual education). Much of the inspiration of this praxis was from secular feminism, and I know of no evidence that the women drew intentionally from Mark's Gospel – though the Christian and post-Christian Quaker tradition had a significant influence. Yet, both in the apparent failure of their immediate objective and in the effect they had on the politics of other activist communities such as the miners' wives' groups of 1984, those women displayed the same remarkable symbiosis of active and contemplative, of charismatic and egalitarian, that I have identified in Mark's theology of power.

Such groups, perhaps like 'the Marcan community' and like Jesus himself, are constantly liable to failure and dispersal. Their refusal of mere activism and the consequent tension between impatient protest against the status quo and patient building of and waiting on the new reality mean that they are open to manipulation, to dissension, to loss of heart, to compromise of their hopes and aims, and indeed to persecution. As it happens, all of these possibilities are specifically addressed in Mark 13 (cf. especially 13.9–13), where the simple solution of the crisis by a new messianic leader is also summarily dismissed (13.21–22). The call is not, however, for passivity but for watchfulness and endurance and for adherence to the words of the original vision (13.13, 23, 31, 33–37). So it may be that this authoritative charge, delivered on the Mount of Olives in a very specific setting, whether historical or fictional, and calling on an alien apocalyptic world-view, is nevertheless one that can be generative of a practical politics for radical action and contemplation today.

Boundaries crossed, abolished and redrawn

The power that Jesus demonstrates in Mark's Gospel and that he in some sense transmits to his followers is expressed most dramatically and explicitly in exorcism. As well as the four exorcisms recounted in some detail (1.21–28; 5.1–20; 7.24–30; 9.14–29), there are accounts of multiple exorcisms (1.34; 3.11f.) and strongly exorcistic overtones to the calming of the sea (4.35–41) and the healing of the deaf-mute (7.31–37). The opposition to Jesus from scribes, Pharisees and others in authority is the main engine of Mark's plot, and it is strongly hinted that this too is actually a cosmic fight between Satan and the Holy Spirit (3.22–30) or a theological one between human tradition and the word of God (7.13). Myers reads the two principal exorcisms – in the synagogue in chapter 1 and by the lake in chapter 5 – as the inaugurations of 'campaigns' against the powers centred in Temple and empire respectively.[6] The disciples within the story are conscripted into these campaigns and given authority over demons which they successfully employ (3.15; 6.7, 13). It can also be assumed both from the rhetoric of the story and from the 'longer ending' of Mark and other parts of the synoptic tradition that these powers continue in Jesus' absence (e.g. Mark 16.17–18).

The verb consistently used for exorcism is *ekballō* ('throw out' or 'expel'), which occurs in this sense no fewer than 11 times in the Gospel. Expulsion is an authoritative action that clears the person, the land and the community from impurity and danger and restores the sacred boundaries: as elsewhere, exorcism appears to be a means of preserving sanctity for the elect. Yet that supernatural drawing or restoration of boundaries is undermined in several ways in the Gospel. Significantly, at the first use of *ekballō*, Jesus himself is not the subject but the object: the stronger one who baptizes with Spirit is himself ejected by the Spirit into the desert (1.7, 8, 12), so that the later verbal echoes in the exorcism accounts bear the suggestion that it is from beyond the boundary of civilization and sacred land that this authority is exercised. Then at least two of the exorcisms – those of the demoniac and of the Syrophoenician woman's daughter – are pointedly aimed at restoring purity for those who are and remain outside the holy community of Israel, so that the healings can be seen as both restorative and subversive (cf. especially 7.26). Nor do Jesus and his companions in the new community of God's *basileia* hold any monopoly of exorcistic power, as Jesus' rebuke of John's own rebuke of the 'unauthorized exorcist' makes clear (9.38–40). 'Whoever is not against us is for us', proclaims the supreme exorcist, suggesting a superfluity of spiritual power overflowing and questioning the boundaries of communities sacred and profane. Similarly, the attempt to exclude children from contact with the Holy One is rebuked (10.13–16). Most scandalously, Jesus' praxis of open table fellowship declares a redrawing or even abolition of customary ritual and moral boundaries (2.13–17).[7] This Jesus confirms in the subsequent dispute about purity with Pharisees and scribes, in which all foods are made clean and defilement comes not from without but from within (7.1–23). So a political irony is constructed by the Gospel. The call to join Jesus' campaign or belong to his community is a highly demanding one, a call to share his cross, his cup and his baptism (8.34–36; 10.38). Yet the *basileia* is open to all except those who exclude themselves (10.17–22). The community is both distinctive and promiscuous, the members 'having salt' among themselves and simultaneously being 'at peace with one another' (9.50).

The modern Church still claims through a variety of doctrines and symbols to be in succession to the community of disciples and apostles founded by Jesus. If, however, Mark is taken as an authoritative interpreter of the shape of that community, it may be hard to see the continuity being enacted with great faithfulness today, or indeed at earlier stages of church history. Local churches and larger denominations tend to be either 'distinctive' or 'promiscuous' but rarely both. Thus there are many parish or local church communities that maintain a strong sense of distinctive witness and teaching, whether grounded on biblical authority or on church tradition. Faith and/or baptism confers membership of a community with very precise boundaries, admission to the table remaining subject to moral, ritual or disciplinary tests. To those members has been given the mystery of the Kingdom of God, and outside the bounds of their group or like-minded ones are those who see but do not perceive, who hear but do not understand, among whom reliable truth cannot be found. So there is no room for an 'unauthorized exorcist'. Awareness of the costliness of the calling and of the risk of persecution serves to strengthen the community's stance over against the world and other religions and philosophies. The politics of such a community – which internally may show strong signs of hierarchy and submission – is dictated above all by its maintenance of boundaries and its exclusion of 'sinners' unless they repent.

Other local parish and church communities, on the other hand, particularly those rooted in historically national or established churches, will often demonstrate clearly and even proudly the promiscuity of Marcan praxis with comparative disregard for distinctiveness. Baptism and creed are probably in the background, and there may still be some distinction between those who are 'members' and those who are not. But what boundaries there are are fluid, for the church's openness is seen as key to its integrity, and truth or righteousness can be found among 'gentiles' perhaps as surely as within the church community. So any form of exorcism and any test of doctrinal, moral or ritual fitness for participation are shunned: the table is open, and harsh words from the tradition about conditions of life within or waiting upon the Kingdom are played down. That 'Kingdom' now is not an apocalyptic gift for the elect, the *eklektoi*; it is liberal and democratic.

These two pictures are perhaps caricatures, but within them are recognizable, clear features both of contemporary church communities and of Marcan ideology. In them the two paradoxical strands of that ideology are held firmly apart. Yet there *are* instances of Christian communities whose politics reflect the tense symbiosis of distinctiveness and promiscuity that is found in Mark – in some cases, by deliberate reflection on that Gospel and by action in pursuance of its perceived slant. They may be found in or attached to traditional religious communities living under vows and in 'alternative' or radical Christian movements, but also among larger 'mainstream' churches. They may continue within conventional family and domestic structures or may create their own. Either way, the distinctiveness of the community's theology and praxis over against that of the dominant world order is celebrated without embarrassment. This may be represented in the thoroughness of the critique, even exorcism, that is conducted against political, economic, military and cultural power structures, or in the seriousness with which vows of baptism or of religion are taken, or again in the conscious construction of 'cells of resistance'.[8] Something equivalent to the battle between Satan and Spirit is recognized. But if that apartness were to be at the cost of excluding the 'tax-gatherers and sinners', then it would betray its own political critique. So, without minimizing 'the cost of discipleship', the boundaries are loosely drawn, and the community and its table remain open to all. Whether the community is large or small, successful or outwardly failing, is a matter of indifference. What counts, as in Mark 13, is that it endures to the end, 'looking' and 'watching' not just the signs in the heavens but the ordinary reality, truths and needs around its open boundaries.

Provisionality in politics and liturgy

Mark's story opens with a man *kērussōn baptisma metanoias* – literally, 'proclaiming immersion in change of mind' (1.4). Repentance, the turning around of a person's and a people's world-view and lifestyle, is there at the beginning, and so the Gospel continues, with the call to the same immersion in parable, argument and exorcism. The ultimate but still not final immersion, both for Jesus and his followers, is that of death (10.39).

Despite the apocalyptic proclamation of both John and Jesus, and despite the subsequent development of Christian baptism, this Marcan repentance is not once-for-all, nor is it the entry into personal salvation. The people are transformed by the *baptisma metanoias* into a community subject to further *metanoia*, where the security of ritual boundaries is broken, where insiders become outsiders and outsiders insiders. And – since this is a missionary community – that continuing transformation is a transformation both of the community itself and of the world it inhabits. The future shape of the world, code-named *basileia tou theou*, is not provided as blueprint but given as *mustērion*, as 'mystery', in parable. So the aims and structures deemed essential for political effectiveness are left infuriatingly indistinct. Repentance is a way of living for individual and community that provisionalizes all aims and institutions and thus engenders a politics of provisionality, the uncomfortable home of an *ecclesia semper reformanda* – a church always in need of being reformed. That is not to say that the 'Marcan community' in the first or the twenty-first century lacks any structure or ritual or power relations, for no human organization can exist without these. But the continuing call to repentance does mean that all of these are subject to testing and reformation within a community with no leader, where boundaries are transgressed and where power is exercised in waiting and in looking.

To put some flesh on this provisional politics of repentance, let me end by pointing to two sections of Mark's story which epitomize persistent elements of first-century and twenty-first-century churches alike. These are Eucharist and mission – the liturgy of the altar and the liturgy of the world.

After Jesus through the sign of the fig tree and through his teaching on the Mount of Olives has prophesied the Temple's destruction, and after his anointing at Bethany 'for burial', the story returns to Jerusalem for Passover. Here the *naos*, the holy of holies, of the Temple is symbolically replaced by the Body of Jesus, which from now on becomes the moving sanctuary of God's action in the world. The Body is not what was buried by Joseph of Arimathea: that was *ptōma*, not *sōma*. It is identified rather in the upper room with the broken bread and with the companions of Jesus. By their physical consumption of the bread these men become, as it were, complicit with Roman and Temple authorities in the execution of Jesus, but simultaneously complicit with Jesus in his cup and his baptism of death, the ultimate *metanoia* and dispersal.[9] For in Mark's imagination neither the cross nor the resurrection constitutes the permanent replacement of the now defunct Temple sanctuary. There is no holy place, only a eucharistic community that gathers, remembers, eats and drinks and scatters – or even flees (14.50). It is bound through ritual, memory and praxis to the absent Leader, but in a sense the Body is formed only at the table: for the rest of the time it is dispersed and provisional, subject to continuing repentance.[10]

Coupled therefore with this liturgy of the shifting altar is the liturgy of the world, what is normally called 'mission'. That too is founded on repentance: after Jesus has instructed his disciples and sent them out in pairs, Mark writes, *kai exelthontes ekēruxan hina metanoōsin*, 'and they went out proclaiming that people should repent' (6.12). But there is no evidence that this *metanoia* is a 'conversion' that transfers the person or community into a new institution or guarantees salvation. Neither these apostles nor the one who sends them are actually making disciples or giving instructions, in the sense of the command at the end of Matthew's Gospel (Matt. 28.19–20). They are simply exorcizing and healing and announcing God's rule, so enabling a change of mind and a liberation from Temple and empire in some who see and hear what is happening. Having visited one village, the missionaries proceed to the next, dependent for their resources not on their sender but on their receiver (6.8–10).

Proclaiming a gospel of repentance and living by a politics of repentance, the Marcan eucharistic community will find no permanent boundary to contain it nor power structure to sustain it, no comforting evidence that they the insiders are bringing either salvation or judgement to the outsiders. Taking Mark's Gospel seriously involves a purging of the institutional ecclesiology, missiology and sacramental theology that have been erected over the centuries. I have argued that there are diverse instances of this purging occurring practically in the contemporary world. Jesus, according to Mark, is the one who goes ahead and so cannot be contained in sanctuary or political structure. But wherever people gather, remember, eat, drink, scatter and proclaim the *basileia tou theou*, there is gospel being enacted.

Notes

1 For instance, Raymond Brown, *The Community of the Beloved Disciple* (London: Geoffrey Chapman, 1979); J. A. Overman, *Matthew's Gospel and Formative Judaism* (Minneapolis: Fortress Press, 1990); D. C. Sim, *The Gospel of Matthew and Christian Judaism* (Edinburgh: T&T Clark, 1998); Philip Esler, *Community and Gospel in Luke–Acts* (Cambridge: Cambridge University Press, 1987).

2 H. C. Kee, *Community of the New Age* (London: SCM Press, 1977), pp. 176, 162. See esp. ch. 6.

3 Ched Myers, *Binding the Strong Man: A Political Reading of Mark's Story of Jesus* (Maryknoll, NY: Orbis Books, 1988). See esp. pp. 85–7, 434–4.

4 Richard Horsley, *Hearing the Whole Story: The Politics of Plot in Mark's Gospel* (Louisville, KY: Westminster John Knox Press, 2001), p. 90. See also pp. 177–83.

5 Perhaps what is happening is that, in a new kind of *musar*, the force of the Hebrew root *yms* is altered from that of disciplining by a parent or teacher to refer instead to a process of mutual discipline in search of *hokmah*.

6 Myers, *Binding the Strong Man*, pp. 137–43, 190–4. Cf. Christopher Burdon, 'To the Other Side: Construction of Evil and Fear of Liberation in Mark 5.1–20', *JSNT* 27.2 (2004), pp. 149–67.

7 Cf. Walter Wink, *Engaging the Powers: Discernment and Resistance in a World of Domination* (Minneapolis: Fortress Press, 1992), pp. 115–16.

8 Cf. Myers, *Binding the Strong Man*, pp. 434–4.

9 Cf. John Fenton, 'Eating People' in *More About Mark* (London: SPCK, 2001), pp. 97–113.

10 Cf. Christopher Burdon, *Stumbling on God: Faith and Vision through Mark's Gospel* (London: SPCK, 1990), pp. 55–64.

17

Mark among the soaps

IAN WALLIS

Houghton-le-Spring is a township of approximately eleven thousand people within the City of Sunderland in the North-East of England. Although its roots are in agriculture, mining was responsible for rapid expansion in the nineteenth and twentieth centuries. Since the closure of Houghton Colliery in 1982, local employment has been provided by the Council, small businesses and larger operations based in surrounding industrial estates. According to the 2001 Census, the community is almost exclusively white (99 per cent) with 83 per cent of members describing their religion as Christian. Employment runs at 51 per cent of the resident population aged 16–74 with another 11.6 per cent classified as permanently sick or disabled. Over 40 per cent possess no formal qualifications.

People watch a lot of TV in Houghton. There are few front rooms unanimated by the animated screen. It's not so much a source of entertainment as a household companion. A reassuring 'presence' rescuing from isolation while affording relatively safe and restricted access to a world beyond the front door. Yet, interestingly, the programmes most in demand tend to focus on what's happening behind someone else's front door. 'S/he liked the soaps' is a regularly rehearsed line during pre-funeral visits (which need to be scheduled carefully!), while the Christian names of the newly baptized chronicle the rise and fall of those enjoying the limelight in TV's 'takes' on living.

Why it is that so many of us spend so much of our lives watching how other people spend theirs is a profoundly intriguing question. One answer, I suppose, is because it's easier and less risky than living our own. It can be more interesting too. A form of existential surrogacy in which we are able to experience intimacy, excitement and scandal through another – the 'kicks' without the 'consequences'. But such vicariousness may also conceal a lack of confidence and motivation; a reticence to take control and inhabit 'real time' where we are exposed to the scrutiny of others and held responsible for our choices. Much safer to inhabit a sort of virtual world.

Soap operas and the like, though, are only some of the manifestations of living by proxy. Watching how other people live their lives is closely allied to allowing other people to take control of ours. We all, knowingly or otherwise, find ourselves enmeshed within a complex and organizing web of strategies for social conformity and protocols for facilitating societal existence. Language, currency, education, employment, welfare and government are but some of the syntax enabling us to survive, even to flourish, in relation to others. Most of these conventions are regulated by authorities which, although staffed by individuals discharging their duties through democratic mandate, develop in the popular consciousness a gestalt of their own which can be both oppressive and disempowering.

In Houghton, the 'system', in its many guises, pervades. No person with a name decided to route the A690 dual carriageway through the town centre or to coerce the workforce into dependency through wholesale pit closure or to subject our young people to suffer unsuitable school curricula. These are manifestations of a faceless, parent-like god who watches over us, determining our fate, while engendering an almost pathological suspicion and adolescent desire to kick against the goads. One obvious expression of this is the way in which the f-word is used in public by all ages – this ubiquitous obscenity constitutes a monosyllabic protest against the oppressive forces policing the conforming grammars of community.

Interestingly, the erosion of standards is no one's fault either. No one drops litter or pushes drugs or acts antisocially or burgles houses or mugs residents. At least none of us. Nor is it anyone's fault when someone is overweight or addicted to nicotine or alcohol, or unable to retrain. Even children are increasingly abandoned to the system by parents who've lost touch with their instincts as well as those broader networks of relatedness which in previous generations would have nurtured them in the parenting art. All this is symptomatic of a morally disabling climate, increasingly inhabited by the ethically challenged who, whenever called to account, enter a plea of diminished responsibility.

This climate, though, is not omnipresent. There are pockets of entrepreneurial self-determination. Heavy investment in regional regeneration continues to facilitate business opportunities of all scales, causing our commuter belt to expand a couple of notches while converting a few locals to middle-class aspirations. Yet these government-led rescue strategies fail to touch many of working age who either have given up hope of paid employment or have been drawn into alternative economies operating alongside their 'legitimate' counterparts. Significantly, though, for all the cash injections to improve infrastructure and opportunity, crime continues to be one of the few career choices in Houghton to support a well-resourced apprenticeship scheme, syndicated by local dynasties capable of providing aspiring teenagers with their quickest route to a BMW.

One of the problems with outside assistance is that 'solutions' are rarely owned by their supposed beneficiaries, who tend to view them with suspicion, treat them with contempt or are simply left untouched. The 'system' interfering again! Upgrading housing stock is a good case in point. It is a conspicuous 'value-added' initiative, easily quantifiable for government statistics, to improve quality of life. And sometimes it does, but not often. Why? Because changing the front door doesn't alter what goes on behind it. The feel-good factor soon wears off as residents are left looking out of their prisons through recently installed double glazing.

The 'New Me' course, run by a voluntary organization with an established presence on one of our housing estates, is a notable exception. Probably because it is a 'bottom-up' initiative which grew out of local, grass-roots consultation. The focus here is self-empowerment through building confidence and raising horizons – residents being encouraged to help themselves. It has proved remarkably successful, at least for those able to muster the wherewithal to give it a go – who, through coming to see themselves differently, have been liberated to view the world and its opportunities in a new light.

But the pervading world-view remains 'watching and being watched', the lingua franca of Houghton (perhaps, of many places!). The politics of passivity in which 'victims', bound by forces beyond their control, are reduced to spectators in their own lives. And from this outlook, St Michael's church is viewed in variegated light. From one perspective, the church is allied to the system, perhaps a benevolent manifestation, where important life business can be transacted on behalf of others. Hatch, match and despatch – rites of passage – remain vital touchstones. Is it superstition? Is it the remaining vestiges of a passing era's conventions? Or does it speak of a need to be associated at key points in one's otherwise unremarkable and unpredictable life with something bigger that is able to remember us and confer significance. Something permanent and reliable, capable of affording a telephone land line with a number that doesn't change.

The Church also provides an alternative viewing platform, giving access to what is perhaps the longest running soap of them all – a drama of epic scale and seemingly limitless potential which has been screened for two millennia and has embarked on a third. Cue Mark's Gospel or, more accurately, the access it affords to its main character. The distinction is revealing. We recently purchased a new set of pew Bibles, readily paid for by the occupants of the pews who are happy for them to remain on the shelves. The issue is not principally one of literacy, but of dependency and orality. Taking responsibility for reading the Scriptures is no small undertaking and, for some, it is overwhelming. And in any case, watching words is not a natural modus operandi for a community formed around the mouth, where speaking, like food, is consumption – supply and demand, public performances with audience participation. No point speaking if no one is listening, no point listening if no one is speaking. In the battle for air time meanings only matter if they improve ratings.

This is why Mark is pre-eminent among Jesus' agents. Fast moving, vivid in characterization, stylistically economical, graphic and eventful, free from introspection, raw and uncut, suited for serialization. The second evangelist is the people's choice. But they don't want to read it. Nor do they want their Jesus packaged up in some period drama or historical documentary. It's got to be a soap – the new sacrament of the present moment in which Jesus has not only to appear, but be fascinatingly as well as energizingly evident. An imperative that presents a searching challenge for the Church's programme-makers. The viewing public needs more – more than remembrance and promise, more than a bag of beliefs and a rule of conduct, more than Bible study and catechesis. They need encounter – a real-time Jesus accessible within human experience. And if his body can't be exhumed and reinvigorated then we must explore ways of embodying his presence within ours.

Here Mark is a genius. He (or she) offers us an invitation (Mark 1.17) – not to school to learn about Jesus, not to church to sing his praises, but into human experience. Mark invites us into Jesus' company. It is a risky and inno-vative strategy in which Jesus' reputation hangs in the balance. He remains no one until he becomes some one, for us. And who he becomes emerges from the time we are willing to invest. For Mark, destinations emerge from journeys undertaken. From this perspective, there can be no absolutes, only a stream of provisional confessions chronicling progress: Son of God and Son of Man, insane and malevolent, healer and heretic, teacher and guide, story-telling charismatic, purveyor of wisdom, disturber of orthodoxies, courting death for his convictions, crucified insurrectionist (. . . and what was that scantily clad 'follower' doing in the garden, Mark 14.51f.?). The tomb is empty. There are rumours of resurrection awaiting confirmation through fresh embodiments of his presence within the lives of his followers – 'But go, tell his disciples and Peter that he is going ahead of you to Galilee; there you will see him, just as he told you' (Mark 16.7). And we all know what hap-pens in Galilee (cf. Mark 1.14ff.)!

How then does Mark help us to discover Jesus in our Galilees? The sim-ple answer, I think, is by helping us to experience life in the light of his. Whatever else Mark's Jesus has to offer it is companionship – to eat bread together in the company of whoever finds a place around Jesus' alternative altar, constituting an alternative community . . . 'Why does he eat with tax collectors and sinners?' (Mark 2.16) . . . 'Who are my mother and my broth-ers?' (Mark 3.33) . . . 'I will never again drink of the fruit of the vine until that day when I drink it new in the kingdom of God' (Mark 14.25). 'Follow me', on Jesus' lips, is nothing less than the offer of companionship in pursuit of a particular vision conveyed by these final words. And although the fulfilment of that vision remains in abeyance, its anticipation is the vocation of the present. To this end, 'Follow me' implies a particular kind of compan-ionship in which Jesus takes the lead. Further, when he goes on to say, 'I will make you fishers of men' (Mark 1.17), it is clear we are being encouraged to join him as apprentices rather than passengers. Which, in turn, begs the ques-tion of the substance of our novitiate – of what it is that Jesus exemplified personally and is able to engender in his followers. Mark seeds the answer in our minds at the outset: 'The time is fulfilled, and the kingdom of God has come near; repent, and believe in the good news' (Mark 1.15). Kingdom living, the artistry of faith, inhabiting a world impregnated with divine substance.

It is Jesus' embodiment of human being that Mark offers us in his Gospel. Our task is to make it live today in such a way that it not only attracts an audience but invites emulation. The temptation at this juncture is to package Jesus up in some way to aid access, availability and distribution. The Alpha Course phenomenon is an obvious case in point – appealing across denominations, it is rapidly becoming one. Alpha is incontrovertibly popular, but so also is the Atkins Diet and a host of other 'off-the-shelf' solutions to life's problems. Rapid weight loss can be exhilarating and, in a strange sort of way, compulsive. So also can be attending a well-run Alpha. But keeping weight off, like living our lives as authentically as Jesus lived his, is a 24/7 vocation requiring a fundamental change of self-perception and re-ordering of existence. Perhaps, Alpha and Atkins are able to deliver this; but, if so, why do so many participants end up becoming dependants?

At St Michael's, we've grown suspicious of miraculous panaceas. For one thing, panaceas tend to diminish by reducing our humanity to its lowest common denominator. Before Mark's Jesus attempts to save the species from the consequences of sin (cf. Mark 10.45), he draws close to persons in their particularity – Bartimaeus (Mark 10.46–52), Jairus (Mark 5.22), Legion (Mark 5.1–20) and the small army of anonymous witnesses who testify to encountering Jesus at their point of need, for whom Jesus is significant precisely because of his impact and ability to help. This is the substance of their confession – a common, yet personal, experience, rather than any shared conviction about Jesus' identity or purpose. An observation no one claiming to minister in his name can afford to overlook (cf. Mark 9.37–39) and one which continues to spawn new initiatives here in St Michael's, including supporting asylum-seekers and young families, helping to establish a credit union, providing financial assistance, offering advocacy, and increasing access to learning, skills and training.

And for all its promise, the language of miracle needs to be used with care. It can readily dis-empower by communicating a sense of being at the mercy of forces beyond our control, reinforcing victim status – our greatest oppressor in Houghton at this time. Significantly, one of the themes implicit throughout Mark's Gospel surfaces in the twice-repeated, 'Your faith has saved you' (Mark 5.34; 10.52) – although, I suspect 'Your faith has brought you to life' conveys Jesus' meaning more adequately. A saying that no more proffers a cult of the self than confirms us in our powerlessness; rather, it seeds within our consciousness the tantalizingly intriguing prospect that in Jesus' company we discover the faith to save ourselves.

But how are such encounters possible today? How does Jesus continue to make friends and influence people? In the light of the previous paragraphs any way forward must be provisional which is itself significant. Interestingly, no soap opera would survive if it simply replayed the same episode over and over again. But nor would it last long without familiar story lines and continuity between instalments. Sameness and strangeness, monotony and incongruity, are equally able to sound the death knell when it comes to securing the viewing public's allegiance. There must be connection, across the series and through the screen. The key is to portray the familiar in an unfamiliar or intriguing light. To draw on the archetypal themes of human experience and to clothe them with context and characterization. In this way, programme-makers in effect present us with ourselves, as, in our company, actors rehearse life as we know it or wish we could. There is, I suspect, a pronounced narcissistic dimension to all this which, as we suggested earlier, can foster a kind of living by proxy, but it needn't. Sometimes, in the business of people-watching, mirrors become windows – when, within our own reflection, we encounter something or someone as yet undiscovered.

We must, then, shun the desire to serve up Jesus pre-prepared, packaged and ready for immediate consumption. Equally, there is little to be gained by presenting him as some sort of freak of nature or alien from outer space. We are not unfamiliar with 'virgin births' in Houghton, where vulnerable girls find themselves at the mercy of 'forces beyond their control' exercised by predatory males excusing their behaviour on the same grounds; but they are rarely a source of deliverance. And official visitors who arrive with their 'saving solutions' to our 'intractable problems' tend to be received as the latest manifestation of autocratic manipulation. We need a Jesus who has got something to do with us. Someone with a past we can relate to and who faces an uncertain future with a faith that won't stretch our humanity beyond where we are able to reach in his company. Once again, Mark scores. Unlike Matthew, Luke and John who make Jesus appear from a puff of smoke, Mark's Jesus emerges from the crowd of undifferentiated humanity who, like football supporters en route to the stadium, are heading for the Jordan in search of something to make a difference.

He's also not afraid to die. This matters in a way that those of us with a career, mortgage and pension, who intend to preserve this pleasurable life for as long as is feasibly possible, struggle to appreciate. By contrast, when you don't possess much, flirting with death promises to make you wealthy – rich in adrenaline rushes, rich in the produce of lawless living, rich in the experiences of life without limits. Dying young is still commonplace in Houghton. Not just the early deaths caused by unhealthy lifestyles, work-related disorders and the alarmingly high incidence of cancer. But because of a new brand of martyr: the dispossessed victims of a democratic society from which they feel excluded and who, having nothing to lose, choose to demonstrate their despair through desecrating that which others hold most precious – life itself. And for every martyr there are untold numbers who share their conviction even if they lack their courage. For them, Jesus' crucifixion demands attention, not because it belongs within some divine rescue initiative, but because it bears witness to a hitherto alien prospect, namely that there are things worth dying for precisely because they are worth living for.

By now it will have become apparent that the way we approach Mark's Gospel in St Michael's is rather unusual. It's not so much about the exegesis of a text to unlock its meaning as excavating the imprint on our humanity left by a particular person in order to discover whether there is anything to be gained by placing our lives next to his and attempting to follow in his tracks. What we're after, then, is nothing less than Jesus' take on being human, his characterization of personhood, the habitus of faith he embodied, that once identified we may attempt to inhabit it also. This is an heuristic enterprise through which Jesus not only becomes visible but is also reconstituted within the faith of his followers. It is a high-risk strategy which requires us to take ourselves rather more seriously than most of us would wish to do; to be 'larger than life' and through doing so to expose ourselves to the inevitability of failure and to the even more daunting prospect of success. In Mark, the disciples regularly get it wrong and make a lot of mistakes along the way (e.g. Mark 4.13, 35–41; 8.31—9.1; 9.14–29; 10.13–16, 35–45). They desert him and deny him, but through this painful process of disillusionment and reorientation the life embodied in Jesus begins to form in them also. Their experience is surely emblematic of all serious Christian discipleship and, as such, challenges us to embrace the inevitable growing pains of faith with equal seriousness and tenacity as we allow Jesus to scrutinize our motivations, reset our aspirations and catalyse our human being.

Unlike Matthew and Luke, Mark doesn't give the Baptizer much air time. He's the warm-up act for Jesus (Mark 1.1–14) before finding himself served up as a hate offering within the unfolding sexual intrigues of Herod's court (Mark 6.17–28). Interestingly, though, Jesus is twice likened to him (Mark 6.14–16; 8.28). But they are not the same! This is Mark's point. Jesus doesn't carry on where John left off. His approach is fundamentally different. No more locusts and hair shirts. No more fasting and demonstrations of mourning or remorse. The captivity is ended and the business of lamenting God's absence is over: 'The time is fulfilled, and the kingdom of God has come near; repent, and believe in the good news' (Mark 1.15).

There is more than a whiff of revolution in these words. In effect, Jesus is refocusing the locus of divine activity as well as re-imagining what divine presence means. Whatever the word 'God' in its various forms conveys or signifies awaits discovery within the fabric of our humanity. As a consequence, there is little to be gained by waiting for some distant saviour figure to secure on our behalf what is already among us and can only be accomplished through our agency. Nor is Jesus any less radical in his understanding of repentance. Judging from the rest of the Gospel, it has precious little to do with admitting culpability, saying sorry and making amends – the approach reinforced by most of our liturgies. It is far more radical than that. Repentance is like mobile phones, satellite TV and low-cost air travel all rolled into one. It's about recognizing that the prison door is ajar and accepting faith's invitation to venture forth.

According to Mark's Jesus, repentance grows out of forgiveness. When a finger even more gratuitous than the divine digit of those early Lottery adverts points in our direction and says not 'It could be you', but 'Follow me'. No deposits or medicals required. No risk assessment at all, at least, none on the part of the inviter. The gift is absolutely free, but like landing the Lottery Jackpot it will change your life. Here, though, the similarities cease because while we think we know why we want to be rich, few of us have much idea what Jesus has to offer, at least at the outset. So why bother? Why respond to Jesus' invitation to break out of the past in order to share his company. The answer can only be, as it was from the outset, because he fascinates us. We see in him something we lack. We see in him the person we long to be. Not that we want to be Jesus, really, any more than we really want to be the icons of our dreams. But we do want to discover what makes him tick – what life-force animates his humanity – and through doing so to allow something of his presence to infuse our living also.

Like falling in love, this is irrational or at least supra-rational. Encountering Jesus is not an exact science and can never be reduced to one – a point programmatic approaches to evangelism can easily overlook. Persuading 'inquirers' into Christian allegiance by presenting Jesus as Lord, Messiah, Son of God, etc. is like wooing a prospective partner with your qualifications or pedigree. They may bite, but for the wrong reasons. True enough, there are plenty of titles pregnant with theological meaning filling the airwaves of Mark's Gospel, but Jesus makes little of any of them, with one possible exception. 'Son of Man', if an epithet at all, is hardly the most elevated of appellations. In truth, it sounds more like a non-title, a refusal to be stereotyped by the pervading profiles of godly heroes or saviours from above. By referring to himself in these terms (e.g. Mark 2.10, 28), Jesus places himself firmly in the 'home team' where his genius emerges as it rubs off on those around him. Son of Man is the means of reference of one who shuns exclusivity in order to pursue a way of being human that is open to all.

Here, again, the second evangelist is unrivalled, mediating repeatedly that extraordinary quality of encounter between Jesus and those who, drawn into his company, find themselves in the presence of an energizing mystery: 'What is this? A new teaching – with authority! He commands even the unclean spirits, and they obey him' . . . 'Who then is this, that even the wind and the sea obey him?' . . . 'Where did this man get all this? What is this wisdom that has been given to him? What deeds of power are being done by his hands!' . . . 'He has done everything well; he even makes the deaf to hear and the mute to speak' (Mark 1.27; 4.41; 6.2; 7.37). Nor should we overlook how Mark's Jesus also uses the same inclusive Son of Man terminology with reference to the costliness of pursuing the way of faith, as well as to the means of its consummation. If the human spirit is able to find forgiveness within its depths (Mark 2.10), then suffering for another's sake (Mark 10.45) or even becoming the agent of your own salvation (Mark 8.38) are no longer off limits – for, in Jesus' company, faith redefines the possible and lays down the contours of authentic, kingdom living (cf. Mark 9.22; 10.27; 11.22–24).

Forgiveness as encountering the energizing mystery of the Son of Man is what we're about at St Michael's. Put like that, it sounds rather pretentious and undeliverable. That's part of its appeal, it's a real soap – a living experiment in which a random and often unlikely cast find themselves energized into life and catalysed into community by the story of the lively dead man. In a sense, there is nothing else on offer at St Michael's than the common life we share. There isn't God and the common life. There isn't a body of belief separate from our bodies that can be communicated in abstraction and posted on a website. There is just your life and my life lived in the company of his life, where Jesus never seems to be more present than we are able to be present – for ourselves, as well as for those around us.

This last comment needs unpacking. In the earliest manuscripts, Mark's Gospel takes the form of an indigestible string of letters without break or punctuation. Even in its more familiar oven-ready form, translated into our vernacular and dissected into bite-size portions of words, verses and chapters, it remains latent and inert. Until, that is, we consume it, trustingly. Then its nutritional value is released, building us up into the stature of the one in whose company we find ourselves. Or, from a different tack and following Jesus' precedent and command, eucharistic hospitality is the constituting resource of our community. Wafers on a paten, wine in a chalice – at best, a morsel for those who have already eaten. Until, gathering at his beckoning, shoulder to shoulder, hands outstretched, a curiously catholic cross-section of appetites, experience and ailments, we encounter something altogether more satisfying – a taste of wholesome integrity, as we participate within a living memory capable of containing our biographies and reconciling them with one another, replenishing sacred hunger seasoned with joyous anticipation.

Subtle and ill-defined. It sounds liberal, woolly and wishy-washy. Not full-strength Christianity. Perhaps, not Christianity at all. But, as Mark reminds us, in Jesus' company, faith-filled kingdom living isn't accessed through the mediation of the Temple, the ministrations of priestly professionals or attention to the Scriptures. Nor is it delivered by a God 'out there'. Jesus' altar is an open table, his teaching is wisdom distilled from experience, his authority is the vocation he embodies so totally and the emancipating confidence he engenders in others to do likewise. Of course, there is more too it – there are consequences and end-time scenarios beyond human orchestration, reminding us that we are not ultimately the masters of our destinies (cf. Mark 8.38—9.1; 10.23–30; 13.20). Yet, in Jesus' company, this 'remainder' neither empties the present of significance nor paralyses us from embracing God's future, now. On the contrary, it beckons us on by adding impetus and urgency to the business of the day – 'Truly I tell you, there is no one who has left house or brothers or sisters or mother or father or children or fields, for my sake and for the sake of the good news, who will not receive a hundredfold now in this age . . . and in the age to come eternal life' (Mark 10.29–30).

This is subversive stuff. It makes salvation just too immanent and accessible. It invests the present with potential. It encourages us to start believing that things can change, not only out there is somebody's else's existence, but in ours. But, there again, as Mark reminds us from the outset, in Jesus' company God's Kingdom is in danger of becoming a reality (Mark 1.15)! Yes, we can share the Baptist's preoccupation with sin and unworthiness. We can pursue the decent, upright way with the Pharisees or the ritualized establishment life of the Sadducees. We can even attempt to eke out Christendom through conflict with those zealous freedom-fighters. Or we can follow Jesus into a world where God awaits us and into a way of being present for ourselves and for one another that is nothing short of transforming.

Here our role in the Church is to get people moving – out of the armchair and on to the stage. Into the living soap where we are no longer content to watch other people living their lives or manipulating ours. Instead, together, in Jesus' company, we start to explore what it means to take responsibility for our own lives – in the light of his and within a world where faith is the art of the possible. When you've been paralysed or blinded or impotent for longer than you can remember this is no small task. After all, powerlessness, like ignorance, can be comfortable and we all possess at least a schizophrenic acquaintance with the identity of the patient. Here, we have found the key to be playfulness. In truth, Jesus' summons to follow is, in effect, an invitation to play. Not in any trivial sense or even by assuming the guise of another. Rather, discovering what it means to play ourselves in a different light, his light. Within the relatively safe environment of a church community and taking Mark's Gospel as our script, enabling Jesus to become visible as we attempt to act out our lives through faith as fully and wholeheartedly as he performed his.

It is, I think, for this reason that there are no resurrection narratives in Mark, no final act, only the promise that Jesus will be found wherever his faith is practised, his vision embraced and his ministry continued. For this is the substance of the risen life. Glorious karaoke!

Afterword

Future directions?

JOHN VINCENT

The perspectives of contemporary personal and political interests which we have brought to the Gospel of Mark, and the tentative conclusions, or at least applications in terms of attitudes, disciplines and policies provoked in us by them, might suggest some new directions for Mark's future among us. I reflect on three areas: gospel studies, contemporary discipleship, and theology.

Gospel studies

The notion of Mark as a 'Gospel of action' is a familiar enough one in New Testament circles. Many readers and commentators have observed how Mark proceeds quickly from one action story to another, hardly ever staying to comment on them, often introducing each story with a peremptory 'and' or 'then' or 'immediately'. It is as if one action has scarcely had time to develop its effects before another action suddenly takes place. The Gospel itself appears as a fast-changing tableau of dramatic incidents involving the central character, Jesus, each incident itself invariably originating in some new character or situation confronting Jesus with a new situation of need, or opportunity or conflict or confusion.

In terms of authorial intention, or redaction criticism, we might begin to ask: why does Mark rarely have a moral, educational or theological 'conclusion' to his pericopes? Why do the individual narratives end so inconclusively? Did Mark have secret codes, trajectories, preoccupations, prejudices, which invite the reader in, without telling the reader exactly where they will lead, or even what precisely they mean?

Again, the recent emphasis on Mark as 'story' and as 'narrative'[1] inevitably invites the question, 'What provokes the story, the narrative?' One only tells a story when one wishes to pass on a description of something striking that has happened. We add: story and narrative need to be projected further to ask, 'What action made the story and narrative possible or necessary?' And what similar actions today would produce comparable stories and narratives? Narrative presupposes practice, action, events, happenings.

Also, the more recent emphases on 'outworkings' and 'reception' need to lead in the same direction. The history of a story's impact or effects or outworkings – *Wirkungsgeschichte* – inevitably places a new concentration on the action and practice behind the story. What impact, effect or outworking is already visible in the story itself, linked to the action described in it? What impact, effect or outworking in Mark's perception, or in the experiences of the first readers, can be deduced from such recorded action? Similarly, the history of a story's use or 'afterlife' or reception by others then and through history – *Rezeptionsgeschichte* – inevitably raises questions of action and practice. What actions and practices of particular people at particular times provided 'sites' where a specific story got to be 'received' as something significant? What actions were legitimized or threatened by this story?

Our collection is a contemporary 'outworking' of varied strains in Mark, a practical reprise of some of the Gospel's 'workings'. It is also a contemporary 'reception' by various disciples and scholars of these workings, within our own time and experience and experimental practice. Whether and how the wider academy can work with these remains to be seen.

Contemporary discipleship

Morna Hooker comments that 'It is for each individual reader of the gospel to decide the extent to which Mark's interpretation rings true', and, 'Inevitably, we read it in the light of our own presuppositions.'[2] Our 'presupposition' as students of Mark and contemporary disciples is that we might find something useful in this narrative. The consequence is that it has an ever-widening future, which we can here only glimpse, as pieces of Mark's action seem to 'reconstitute themselves' in people's discipleship and vocation, politics and communities.

There seem to be several areas which might be future directions for Mark-faithful or Mark-coherent discipleship and community-political practice.

In Geoffrey Harris, Christopher Burdon and Ian Wallis, as in John Riches and Susan Miller, there is a strong sense of alternative communities being created in reflection of Jesus' nascent kingdom community. In Christine Joynes, Ched Myers, Susan Miller and Christopher Burdon, contemporary politics evoke gospel confrontations. Susan Miller's Mark 'offers hope that people outwith centres of power can make a difference'. Christopher Burdon says, 'wherever people gather, remember, eat, drink, scatter, proclaim the *basileia tou theou*, there is gospel being enacted' – and elements of new politics and new community being embodied. Can Mark inspire new alternatives for communities?

There are glimpses of Christian communities always under reformation, back to God's word (Zwingli!). So we have Mary Cotes' South Wales chapel opening to the homeless, Andrew Parker settling with the dispossessed, David Blatherwick welcoming ministerial straitjackets, John Fenton seeing hope for the affluent in the call to fasting, Susan Miller hailing a new created world of humanity in mutual sharing. So we ask, what other stimuli from this often outrageous document will draw us on?

Yet also through these constraining disciplines there are practices of self-realization and discovery and significance – Ian Wallis's people rollicking into a Jesus-style church life, the groups of John Riches and Susan Miller domesticating Jesus and discovering him different, Leslie Francis's witnesses expanding through identification with discipleship partners, Christine Joynes's suffering John Baptist giving strength for empowerment, Christopher Burdon's picture of Jesus' community giving support to alternative and marginalized groups, John Vincent's 'Losing life – gaining life' constituting a significant political vocation and method, Ched Myers' 'Watch' giving a counter-hegemonic vocation against all Powers. The question for the future must be, 'Can Christians follow these radical, anti-hegemonic, counter-cultural hints into relevant new attitudes?'

There is also what I can only call the vulnerability and sense of inadequacy to which followers of Mark's Jesus seem to be reduced. David Blatherwick and Andrew Parker echo Mary Cotes's comment that such following 'is actually quite a painful business'. Disciples know both the acceptance and joys of Galilee and the tragedies and failures of Jerusalem. Discipleship is inevitably 'drawn to the centre', but it must always be, in Marcan terms, an odd kind of flowering, a new world still cruciform – as Susan Miller, Ian Wallis and Ched Myers observe explicitly, but as, I guess, we all experience. And we all stand under the question, 'Do you not yet understand?'

Beyond that, it is always back to Galilee (14.28; 16.7). It is the Jesus of Galilee who gets condemned in the Great City. In Galilee, disciples are called to be co-workers, co-celebrators, co-embodiments of Kingdom, and the seeds of new realities constantly reappearing. That's where it starts, that's where it ends, that's why it gets crucified, and that's what keeps it going, and keeps us going with it. If others outside might be with it (9.40), in what specifics, where, how and with whom are we not against it?

Theology

It might seem odd to bring in 'theology' in the final paragraphs!

Yet it cannot be without significance that some of the great theological preoccupations of Marcan studies over the last half century here receive not merely no reference whatsoever, but even appear as less important than they once appeared. The favourite preoccupations of Marcan studies in the decades before the 1980s seem to have disappeared from view. One may name the question of Jesus as Messiah, the meaning of Son of Man, the presumed Paulinisms, the perspective of salvation history, the issues of Jewish or Gentile bias, or theologies of God, providence or even the Kingdom of God as an organized concept.

Of course, all these matters could have been in our minds, or at the back of our minds, as we wrote. But we did not write them. Is it that the theology is a presupposition, behind the discipleship and the community? Or is it that the discipleship and community life themselves are constituting theologies, only partially worked out then, and hardly yet seen by ourselves?

In fact, there have been shifts into the directions of both discipleship and politics which have not been visible in Britain, but which have been more prominent elsewhere. Ched Myers' concerns in both directions have been followed by others, both in terms of discipleship[3] and in terms of politics.[4] British Marcan students, meantime, on the showing of our book, have been following their own journeys, working and living with the text, and especially specific parts of it. As a consequence, they have discovered different ways of doing discipleship and politics. At least now here there are the beginnings of *British* contextual readings to join the contemporary pantheon of social and cultural interpretations.

These new routes are essentially theological in themselves, we must insist. But the theology now does not derive from our contemporary theological presuppositions, problems and issues. Rather, the theology has to be tentatively approached on the back of our practice and experience, both personal and political. The so-called 'great questions of theology' will doubtless look rather different as a result.

Notes

1 David Rhoads, Joanna Dewey and Donald Michie, *Mark as Story: An Introduction to the Narrative of a Gospel* (Philadelphia: Fortress Press, 1982; rev. edn, 1999), p. 142.
2 Morna D. Hooker, *The Gospel According to St Mark* (London: A&C Black, 1991), p. 26.
3 Cf. especially Ched Myers, 'Mark's Gospel: Invitation to Discipleship' in *The New Testament: Introducing the Way of Discipleship*, ed. Wes Howard-Brook and Sharon H. Ringe (Maryknoll, NY: Orbis Books, 2002), pp. 40–61.
4 Cf. especially Richard A. Horsley, *Jesus and Empire: The Kingdom of God and the New World Disorder* (Minneapolis: Fortress Press, 2003).

Bibliography

Books particularly related to the approaches of this volume

Burdon, Christopher, *Stumbling on God: Faith and Vision through Mark's Gospel*. London: SPCK, 1990.

Fenton, John, *More About Mark*. London: SPCK, 2001.

Francis, Leslie J., *Personality Type and Scripture: Exploring Mark's Gospel*. London: Mowbray, 1997.

Horsley, Richard A., *Hearing the Whole Story: The Politics of Plot in Mark's Gospel*. Louisville, KY: Westminster John Knox Press, 2001.

Joynes, Christine M., *Mark's Gospel through the Centuries*. Oxford: Blackwell, forthcoming.

Miller, Susan, *Women in Mark's Gospel*. London/New York: T&T Clark International, 2004.

Myers, Ched, *Binding the Strong Man: A Political Reading of Mark's Story of Jesus*. Maryknoll, NY: Orbis Books, 1988.

Myers, Ched, *Who Will Roll Away the Stone? Discipleship Queries for First World Christians*. Maryknoll, NY: Orbis Books, 1994.

Rowland, Chris, and Vincent, John, eds, *Bible and Practice* (British Liberation Theology series, Vol. 4). Sheffield: Urban Theology Unit, 2001.

Segovia, Fernando E., and Tolbert, Mary Ann, eds., *Reading from this Place: Social Location and Biblical Interpretation*. Vol. 1. *in the United States*. Vol. 2. *in Global Perspective*. Minneapolis, MN: Fortress Press, 1995.

Vincent, John, *Radical Jesus: The Way of Jesus, Then and Now*, 2nd edn. Sheffield: Ashram Press, 2004.

Vincent, John, *Outworkings: Gospel Practice and Interpretation*. Sheffield: Urban Theology Unit, 2005.

Vincent, John, *Mark: Gospel of Practice: Discipleship and Community, Then and Now*. Forthcoming.

Wallis, Ian, *Holy Saturday Faith: Rediscovering the Legacy of Jesus*. London: SPCK, 2000.

Index of Marcan passages

Only passages treated in some detail are indicated

Index of biblical and ancient texts

Index of authors

Index of subjects

Abu Ghraib 164
academic Bible study 4, 6, 23, 31, 33, 123f.
action-reflection 4ff., 22, 31, 124
acts, of Jesus and ourselves 6, 12, 15, 24, 29, 30, 184, 192, 194, 197, 204
actualizing scripture 4f., 12, 196
African-American churches 164f., 174
allegory 17, 48f., 160
Alpha Course 192
ambiguity of texts 28, 32, 34ff.
analogy 6, 34, 165, 170, 172–5
apocalyptic 155–9, 161ff., 164f., 167, 185
arguing with Jesus 112f., 115, 123
asceticism 67
Ashram Community 76
asylum-seekers 123, 125, 192

Black Christians 10, 174
British contextual readings viii, 3, 10f., 204

call 39, 40, 41, 53, 66, 83, 93, 104, 106f., 110, 165f., 195
Christology 72f., 134, 203
churches, contemporary 22, 55, 56, 58, 89f., 94, 109, 111, 112–16, 118, 124f., 140, 164ff., 168, 174, 176f., 184f., 187, 190, 192, 202
class *see* social location
colonial/post-colonial readings 10, 169

community viii, 31, 42, 56, 76, 89, 139–42, 176–87, 188, 191, 202
congregation as context 11, 15, 42f., 89f., 182
congregational/community readings 7, 9, 22, 41, 42, 107
context, social/cultural 5, 10–13, 27, 32, 34, 40, 76, 98, 107, 121, 151, 165
contexts, debate between 11, 34ff., 116, 118, 122f., 151
contextual Bible study groups 109, 121–4
conversation/dialogue 34, 110, 114, 120f., 123, 125, 190
correspondence of relationship 6, 11f., 15
Corrymeela 140ff.
cosmic struggle 157–63, 172–5
creative fidelity 12, 25

disciples, contemporary viii, 11, 45, 181ff., 191
discipleship: alongside the poor and marginalized 39, 49–51, 69, 79–92, 111, 193; denial of Jesus 65f., 70, 89, 93, 159, 172, 174, 182f., 194, 203; following Jesus viii, 30, 57, 59f., 69f., 71, 74, 83f., 107, 131f., 169, 182, 191, 203; in mission 107, 131f., 181f., 182; radical 64, 75, 91, 92–6, 131ff., 169, 183, 203; of women 79–97

ecology 41, 155f., 161f.
effect of texts *see* impact

embodiment 4, 28, 30, 36, 74, 191, 197, 203
emotional, feeling response 104ff., 111, 114, 119, 123
empire, imperialism 41, 164–75, 204
empowerment, political 41, 190
endogenous analysis 32
ethnicity *see* race
Eucharist *see* Lord's Supper
exegesis 4f., 17, 24f., 31, 36
experience and scripture vii, 4, 12, 34, 45, 120
expert/facilitator, role of 23, 33, 69, 114, 121, 123f., 180f.

faith 40, 56, 80f., 115, 129f., 133, 192, 196
faiths, different 141, 114, 120f., 123
family 53, 87, 105, 112, 129, 137, 155, 192, 196
fasting 62–7
feminist readings viii, 3, 10, 28, 40, 94f., 98, 115
filling in gaps in texts 26, 27ff.
forgiveness 133, 138, 195f.
form criticism 13

G8 Summit 162f.
gaining life 51, 68–78
Galilee 136, 169
Galilee, return to 84, 96, 179, 191, 203
gender 5, 10, 11, 84f., 94, 98, 115
Gentiles, mission to 114, 134f., 139, 182–5, 203
geographical movement 135ff.

209